THE

JOTTINGS OF A THAMES ESTUARY DITCH-CRAWLER

NICK ARDLEY

Best Wishes

Nick Ardley

AMBERLEY

To Alan, Laurie, Shirley and all who crafted Finesse yachts

Front Cover: Ditch-crawling at sunset in Kirton Creek, Suffolk (top); a still evening, South Deep, The Swale, Kent (bottom).
Back Cover: The *Three Sisters* rests with swans in attendance, Kirton Creek, Suffolk.

First published 2011

Amberley Publishing
The Hill, Stroud
Gloucestershire, GL5 4EP

www.amberley-books.com

British Library Cataloguing in Publication Data.
A catalogue record for this book is available from the British Library.

ISBN 978 1 4456 0100 7

Typeset in 10pt on 12pt Sabon.
Typesetting and Origination by Amberley Publishing.
Printed in the UK.

Contents

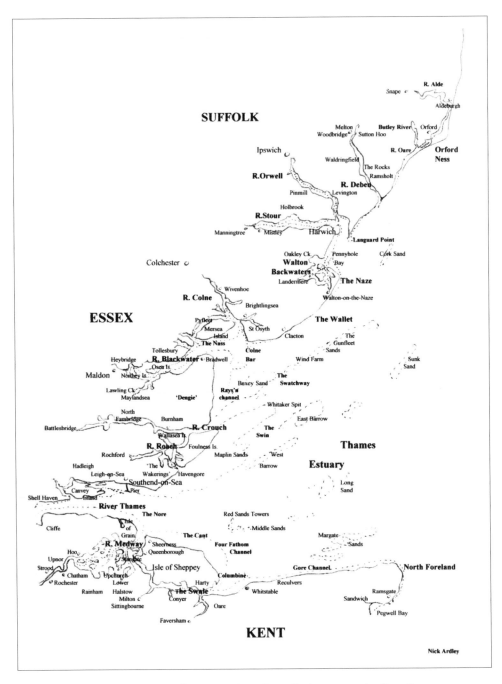

The skipper's Thames estuary sailing grounds, universally known as the East Coast.

PREFACE
Author's Notes

Sailing, boat owning and living on a Thames spritsail barge had coursed through the veins of the skipper's family since the early 1930s, and it had instilled in him a profound love for salt, marsh and mud.

In this volume we find the skipper looking at how it used to be in the early days of Corinthian sailing: all around the Thames estuary there are passages that those sailors used. Many have long since disappeared, other than in name or memory. There were industries with their waterside paraphernalia cluttering and polluting the land edges. Most of that industry, not so distant in historic terms, has completely disappeared and often only marginal evidence of our forbears' endeavours exists. The skipper looks too at the history of his own boat, an estuary classic.

Throughout the last century after man's most damaging era, the Victorian period, the boundaries of the Thames estuary's rivers and creeks have remained largely unaltered, except post-1953, when many creeks were dammed. The century too saw a fundamental withdrawal of coastal industry that left our world far cleaner, accentuating its beauty. The vastness of England's Thames estuary and its myriad of rivers, in that respect, make it unique: the softness of the land edges around North Kent, Essex and Suffolk made it a suitable environment for man's sculpting, but in places man has had to let go hard-won areas and those edges are softening again. This is a process that we have little power to prevent.

During the 1960s through to the 1980s there was a massive growth of glass-reinforced plastic craft, some good, some not so good. There were many wooden vessels: traditional, old and new, and of plywood construction too. It was a world of much simpler sailing, a time when clubs would arrange meets up a muddy creek and go ashore, braving a slippery, slivery sea wall to enjoy an evening's barbeque. The type of sailing pursued had not been far removed from that experienced by an owner's parents or grandparents.

It was into that world during a short cruise in 1979 that the skipper introduced his mate, on a friend's Peter Duck-class ketch. Their first yacht was then sought out and found. She was a twenty-three-foot plywood vessel dating from 1953. After a few years of gentle sailing, and the odd frightening experience, the mate was baptised. In that time she grew to love the creeks and rivers of the Thames estuary, so they moved up to a twenty-four-foot clinker sloop. That boat was completed in 1984, and since then she has continued to serve for nigh on thirty years. Familiar to perfection, she fits the skipper and the mate like a glove. Her story and that of her sisters is fondly told.

Since the 1980s, boats have changed. They have become highly technical, shiny and pristine. They have space-age navigation consoles and people are often seen sailing along gazing intently at the plethora of dials and screens arrayed before them. It seems that simple sailing and the pleasure of watching bird life or looking at remnants of man's past largely eludes them. Below, those vessels are draped in the fripperies of a home dwelling. Comfortable, for sure, but creek mud, bad enough on deck, had better stay out there … or else.

In the skipper's view, during the passage from the far humbler cruiser of yesteryear to today's expensive toys driven by marketing men intent on seducing a husband's wife, sailing had become sterilised. Mud, that natural compound in which an anchor is generally set, rarely touches the decks of craft that seemingly zip from one marina to another, ignoring the wonderful possibilities of secluded anchorages between. Strangely too, although modern boats have progressed to such peaks of conjugal domesticity and homeliness, seeing women afloat other than for that obligatory summer's week, maybe, is not as common as some would like us to think. It is that, more than anything else, which the skipper feels to be the greatest sadness.

Yet, out there, there remain kindred spirits, both men and women, who continue to love the top ends of Britain's estuarial rivers and creeks, seeking out solitude, to be at one with the environment that surrounds: it is that environment that actually allows for the enjoyment of ditch-crawling. For all those who know of this, and those that have it all before them, this is for you.

Bon voyage.

Nick Ardley

Acknowledgements

There are many sailors and non-sailors who have kindly and keenly helped me where a need arose during my writing of *Jottings*. If you are not specifically mentioned, I apologise: doubtless you rest between the pages. The many include the following people: Alan and Shirley Platt, of Finesse yachts fame; John Webb, boat builder; Patricia O'Driscoll, barge historian; Professor Richard-Hugh Perks, historian and author; Vic Hardingham, long-time Finesse owner; John Lewin, from Lower Halstow's dock; Guy Hannaford, from UK Hydrographic Office; Geoff Gransden, current owner of the *Edith May*; John Langrick, Dauntless Association; Wendy Eagling, of the Royal Corinthian Yacht Club, Burnham-on-Crouch; Janet Harber, editor of *East Coast Rivers*; Alice Everard, great niece of Sir Norman Angell, and husband George, who has, sadly, passed away; Barry Pearce, barge historian; Mike Gunnill, journalist, from Upchurch; Richard Walsh, marine historian and publisher (Chaffcutter Publishing); Helen Bowley, from *Yachting World* magazine (IPC Media); Peter Waghorn, Leigh-on-Sea sail maker; Bob Clark; Gus Lewis, of the Royal Yachting Association; Margaret Mellard, daughter of Stanley King, the proprietor of Kings of Burnham-on-Crouch; Peter Pearson, current chair of Burnham-on-Crouch museum; the many publishers' staff who kindly responded to cries of help; my publisher Campbell McCutcheon and my editor Louis Archard; Alexander Ardley, my son, for his studious copying of old pictures for illustrations; my mother for her lovely artwork, capturing that moment; and finally, I need to add Christobel, my wife, the mate, the wielder of 'the red pen' to all my initial drafts. To you all, I owe a great debt of gratitude indeed.

Foreword by Dick Durham

This is a book written by a delightfully eccentric chronicler of delta ghosts. Nick Ardley is a yachtsman who cherishes the past: his own, spent growing up aboard a sailing barge, and that of the lost world of the Thames Estuary.

May Flower, the barge of Mr Ardley's childhood, was moored in Kent, about which some long dead PR man dreamed up the phrase 'The Garden of England' because its orchards once provided London's fruit. But as the author re-visits his salad days he discovers that a better metaphor might have been 'The Builders Merchant of England' because the mud of its marshy borders produced the bricks and mortar from which the capital was constructed. Or perhaps 'The Landfill Site of England' as much of Victorian London's rubbish lies interred in its pastures, too.

Essex, the next county of Mr Ardley's cruise, has not escaped this fate either: it's a place where muck away has produced mountains today, and, as he notes, a huge tract of marshland is destined to become the dump site for London's Cross-Rail excavations, dressed up as a 'wet-land' for wading birds.

Suffolk, the third county of the author's ditch-crawling escapades, pretends to be slightly more upmarket, and could be described as the 'Aspiration of England' as Londoners choose Southwold and Walberswick over Frinton or Margate in which to buy damp Labradors and settle.

This whole watery world is the author's playground, the indeterminate no man's land where plough meets sail, where grass meets marsh, and where mud merges with topsoil. Offshore, from a boat's deck, it appears as a smear on the horizon, a smudge where land and sea merge yet remain undefined.

Mr Ardley and his wife Christobel's mission is to photograph, sketch and research the rotting hulks of abandoned sailing barges; the meandering creeks buried under developer's concrete and the wasteland of industries now obsolete along this ancient coastline.

These little voyages of lament for a world which has long gone are almost predetermined by the boat they sail. The symbiotically named *Whimbrel* looks like a giant wooden dinghy with a lid on top, and that's just what she is ... a toy for a Peter Pan sailor. Her shoal draught and comfy cabin are purposely designed to explore the very ditches of the book's title, even in some cases the land drains. She's not a boat in which to stray on the wrong side of the Thames Estuary's guardian shoals and into the threatening North Sea.

Between their modest voyages of re-discovery, the pair ruminate and ponder in *Whimbrel's* cabin, sustained with cups of hot chocolate, over the books previously written about the area. In so doing Mr Ardley uncannily affects a transformation which resonates with characters from one of his favourite authors, Arthur Ransome.

Already writing in the third person, calling himself 'skipper' and his wife 'mate', his adventures appear to dip from fiction into non-fiction and back. Like the coastline they are investigating, the narrative is suitably blurred.

'Clip on ...' the mate had said, quickly, with some earnestness too.

'I am.' He'd smiled, too.

'Too right you are ...'

'Excellent ship's safety officer, I love you' The skipper had thought, as he'd gone forward, while the mate eased the main sheet to feather the sail.

The pair have, to all intents and purposes, metamorphosed into Roger and Titty from Ransome's *We Didn't Mean To Go To Sea.*

It's a novel device for these charming local historians to use and an effective one, to boot.

We readers can only hope that Mr Skipper and Mrs Mate do mean to go to sea for many more chapters yet.

Dick Durham

How It All Began …

The mate had turned to the skipper and asked, inquisitively, 'I wonder what happened to our People's Boat …'

That boat, *Blue Tail*, had been the skipper and mate's first yacht, of course. The mate had always referred to the dear little ship as 'her'. It was not purely because boats had generally been referred to as 'her' or 'she', although even Lloyds of London no longer used the term for ships – it mattered not: tradition was a stronger bond. It had been apt because the mate's earnings had essentially made the possibility a reality many years beforehand.

They were in some place or other, swinging to their anchor, up one of the many creeks that indent the greater estuary of the Thames. It had probably been round the back of the Swale, or off the River Medway, tucked up in Stangate Creek: they were the places the mate had first learnt about sailing … The skipper, though, had merely said, 'I don't know …' He'd paused, for he had remembered where the boat had gone after they'd sold her, but that had been nearly thirty years before. The boat had sailed off to the east coast's premier racing river, the Crouch.

It had been their first boat and she'd had a special place in both their hearts for that singular reason. For the mate it had been the boat upon which she had been properly baptised into sailing. It was a process that had started several seasons before with a trial trip on a motor boat pottering up to Letchlade from Didcot and back along the upper Thames. That had been followed by a long weekend on a friend's yacht over on the River Medway. Both trips had cemented the idea of owning their own little vessel. The skipper, of course, had had a salty upbringing and his feet were well and truly pickled in brine. The mate, however, had only previously had a trip on the River Leam; a ferry voyage across to the Isle of Wight; and been rowed round the Serpentine, during their courtship days …

'She was a People's Boat,' the mate had commented, 'but what was that?'

'Yes,' the skipper had said, answering her first statement. Then, thinking of the second, had added, 'She came out of a competition for a simple little boat cheap enough to get people afloat during the decade of austerity that ran on after the Second World War.'

'Oh, right.'

'Do you remember her going …?' the mate had said, her lips puckering slightly, before smiling and running a hand gently down the slope of their Finesse 24's cockpit sides … stroking her lovingly.

'Oh yes,' the skipper had replied, grinning at having seen his mate's sensuous actions, and thought, 'She's got feelings for boats too!'

The mate had sat smiling, seemingly miles away, and whatever her thoughts were, the skipper hadn't been party to them.

Realising that the mate wasn't going to speak, the skipper had said, 'The chap that bought her said he'd not be able to get out of the creek we were moored in … Tewkes wasn't it?' He'd grinned at his rhetorical question before continuing, 'I went out with them – there were three hulking great brutes that'd normally raced from one of Burnham's Royal clubs.' The skipper and mate had then belonged to a lovely little club, the Tewkes Creek Boat Club. Sadly the club had folded many years before, but the old dinghy compound had soon been occupied by a Sea Cadet group, keeping the creek alive.

As was likely to happen, the skipper's thoughts had quickly drifted off on a tangent. It was an interesting one though … not unconnected: many creek and marshland areas had similar places.

Tewkes was a little creek whose main function at that time, and since, had been as a drain for one of Canvey Island's many drainage dykes. The creek had once run deep into the island from Hadleigh Ray. The Ray had then run closer to Canvey Island, but had since transferred its main run to the north of an island of marsh known as Marks Marsh. Tewkes Creek's inner passage had since been closed off by a sea wall but it had long formed a drain from the island's renowned and lengthy banana-shaped lake, which itself had once been the inner end of Oyster, or Smallgains, Creek. The island's drains were a complicated web and many now ran in pipes terminating at pumping stations.

At a point close to the present drain into Tewkes Creek there was, the skipper knew, a section of high ground which had a firm shingly top to it covered in sea couch and the such, grasses found in that intertidal zone at the top of the tide line. This had been known as the Bay Way and would have been a point of export and import of goods. Further inland up the semi-tidal remnant of the creek, by an old inner wall near to a walkway known as Central Wall Path (the path had later given its name to a road),

Blue Tail, shortly after purchase in May 1980, lying off Chalkwell, South Essex. The simplicity of her hard chine hull shape can be seen.

there had been a wharf. It had sat close to a place marked on an old Admiralty chart of 1836 as Oyster Church Wick, and was probably a farm. The skipper had found, however, that on a later Ordnance Survey map of *c.* 1890, the place had become known as Knights Wick, also a farm, and strangely some distance from the present 'town' centre and shopping arcade that had been given that name. Knights Wick farm's location had then been immediately east of a drain that ran north into Tewkes Creek. The drain had existed then, and had remained in use, and was one of the drains from the island's lake. Both the wharf and the Bay Way had been marked on the 1836 chart; therefore, 'the Bay Way had continued in its importance,' the skipper had concluded, as it had existed sixty years later, '... but for how much longer?' and chuckling the skipper had thought, '... there was an old metal ship's lifeboat mouldering in a nearby gulley when *Blue Tail* had enjoyed the creek's protective mud and marsh embrace ...' There was now little sign of that vessel.

The Tewkes Creek wharf appeared to have been in use long before later wharves along Oyster (Smallgains) Creek, although a farm wharf existed just inside the present dam. Barges had, however, long used an inlet at Thorney Bay. There was also a wharf near the Point on the Thames shore and the hard: the island's crossing to South Benfleet. The Tewkes wharf had had the name Tootse [?] Dock and was thought to have last been used by F. W. Hester for shipping in coal for an electricity plant for an abortive rail system on the island.

Realising that the mate had been gazing at him, the skipper had murmured, 'Ah well ...' and sighed deeply ... remembering much besides. And after a more recent visit to the area he'd seen that silting, like everywhere else, had increased markedly in that little backwater.

'That's right,' the mate had murmured slowly in response to the skipper's comment about where their old boat had gone (it had seemed an age too since their last exchange) and added, 'I watched from the sea wall ...' The skipper had clearly remembered that when he'd got back ashore in the dinghy, which had been needed for their next boat, the mate had shown visible signs of a few tears: her face had been streaked with their salty stains. Her eyes had been puffed too!

'*Blue Tail* was built by George Holmes,' the skipper had said. 'The class was designed with self build in mind ... there was a craze for that during the 1950s and 60s ... then it was home completion when plastic came along.' The mate had known about home completion – 'sail away' was the name that the marketing men had dreamt up – they themselves had toyed with a Steadfast 24. It had even gone as far as a trial sail on Southampton Water, an interesting experience. But a more tempting and infinitely more suited craft had beckoned them all along: that type of lady had long infatuated the skipper – but that was another story.

'Where was she built?' the mate had asked, awkwardly for the skipper: he hadn't known then and the subject had lapsed into stasis for many months. It had been no use searching out old George: sadly, he'd drifted into that other world many seasons beforehand.

It was a year or so later when the skipper had finally stumbled upon information about their old boat. He'd discovered that George had built his boat in the back yard of a shoe shop that used to sit along Leigh Broadway, above Leigh-on-Sea's steep hillside in South Essex. The shop, Freeman Hardy Willis, had been double-fronted – two opened-out Victorian terraces – and provided plenty of space in the yard behind. The provider of the information, a fellow sailor and Leigh-on-Sea artist, had said, chuckling, '... can't see that sort of thing happening today ... lots of people built their own boats then ...' The skipper had been visiting while researching another matter and the chap had proved to be a wealth for local information.

It transpired that People's Boats were built to varying stages, from bare hull to completion, by a yard up Conyer Creek, off the Swale, in Kent. The yard was thought to be Jarman's old yard on the site of the old Co-op and Mercer brick wharves and barge yard. That area was now all part of Swale Marina at the head of that muddy ditch. The conversation with the artist had set the skipper thinking and after seeing the chap, he'd said to the mate, 'Perhaps I should find out more about those craft ...' He'd interrupted her reading at the time and she'd cast one of those wifely looks, of the type that all men know of, as she'd lifted her head, in half-interest, from her novel. So, smirking, he'd added, '... People's Boats ...'

Looking across at the skipper, the mate, while frowning lightly, had merely nodded. Though the frown had barely disguised her thoughts of, '... now what are you on ...'

'*Blue Tail* ...' he'd stuttered, 'I'll find out more about her ... well the class anyway.' Again she'd nodded, ever so lightly, and looked across at the skipper and said nothing. Her thoughts were bottled.

The skipper and mate's People's Boat, *Blue Tail*, had come out of a design competition sponsored by *Yachting World* magazine – that the skipper knew, but little else of her history. She'd been constructed of plywood. She'd had slab-like sides and hard angled chines. A 'V' bottom ran into her keel. She'd been like many other craft of that era – but the skipper hadn't realised the importance of his particular boat's design. Her draft had been around two feet four inches, with a fair depth to her long keel configuration below the garboard, which housed a centre plate. The keel was marginally cut away towards the bow too. The transom was sexily raked. She'd been twenty-three feet in length, with a beam of around seven feet. Their boat had been rigged as a simple sloop with varnished pine spars. The boat had still possessed two Egyptian cotton sails, a Genoa and what was termed a bob-a-link spinnaker while they'd had her (it was stamped on the sail's head, a semicircular wood plate). The sails were so soft that when they were dropped to the deck they curled in sensual rippling folds. Their ship had been built in 1953, they'd been told, and she'd had PB4 on her mainsail. When purchased, the boat had had a propeller shaft but no engine. After a season this was remedied with the fitting of a Vire petrol engine. The boat had had a centre plate, but it had been long rusted into its keel!

There were other boats seen about the rivers then, but none in more recent travels. The skipper had remembered one he'd looked at out of the water at Bradwell Marina some years before. It had had a deep keel, with a draft of around four feet, at least. Other than that she'd looked exactly like the boat they'd owned.

The skipper had indeed got on with it and researched their old boat. He'd started with a call to a contact at *Yachting Monthly* ... it had run on, to a delightfully helpful lady at *Yachting World*; 'I've found someone to help me ...' he'd hollered out to the mate: he'd been invited to research that magazine's archived back issues.

'The magazine's offices were very grand ...' the skipper had bubbled at the mate after his visit ... 'nothing like my college holes I go to ... or your school, for that matter. It was all glass ... steel, open, airy and nice ... what a place ...'

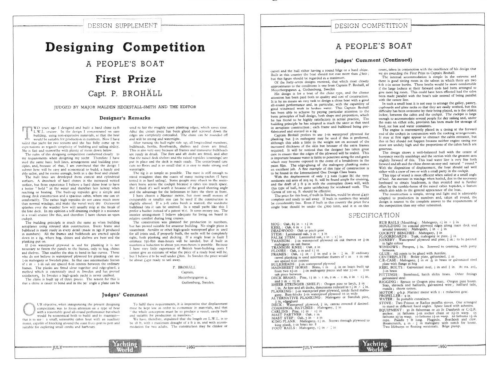

Above left Remarks by designer Captain P. Brohall, and judges' comments on the winning design from *Yachting World*, July 1950. By permission of *Yachting World* magazine.

Above right Judges' remarks on Captain P. Brohall's winning design continued, from *Yachting World*, July 1950. By permission of *Yachting World* magazine.

'Did you get anywhere ... was it useful ... what did you find?'

'Oh yes, I hit the jackpot ... jumped straight into the right year ... Had a good gander through – it's amazing to see those old magazines.' He'd paused. 'They're better than today's in many respects ...'

It transpired, as the skipper read, that *Yachting World* had been running design competitions since 1944, when it had become apparent that the war in Europe was entering its final phase. Their rationale was to give fresh young designers the opportunity to produce modern post-war yacht designs for differing sizes and types of craft. There followed, for some years, a line of competitions. Initially, due to paper controls, the magazine was limited to internal distribution in Britain. As controls were relaxed the magazine, again, went Empire-wide and ultimately worldwide. Entrants, too, became international in flavour, adding designs for craft that operated in similar but different waters. Things were beginning to be spiced up in the British yachting world.

'A food simile ...' the skipper had thought, '... was the creation of Coronation Chicken ... that tasty concoction of chicken, mayonnaise and sultanas, spiced with Madras curry powder ...' It had been created, of course, for Elizabeth II's coronation ...

In the skipper's view, the most important of *Yachting World*'s competitions was for a 'People's Boat', which began in January 1950 with a challenge. A prize of £30 was offered for the best judged entry too. The design was aimed at something easily sailed; it should have good performance and be sea kindly; have room for two people to cruise in comfort; be able to take more people on day sailing trips; be of no more than twenty-three feet length overall and have a shallow draft for creeping into creeks; and most importantly, cost no more than £600 ready for the water. Another point was for the possibility of self build, for the amateur to build at home.

The winning design was won by Captain P. Brohall, from Gothenburg, Sweden. The results of the completion appeared in the magazine's July 1950 issue. The competition was judged by a panel of just two, the magazine's editor and Major Malden Heckstall-Smith, who presumably had had knowledge of such matters. 'Whoever the Major was, they were right ... our boat never let us down ...' the skipper had chuckled, but he'd also remembered a couple of self-inflicted hair-raising moments.

Yachting World's stated editorial policy, following the publication of the People's Boat drawings, was to pursue their competitions, but that a fresh direction was needed. None was intimated at the time. Dabbling through the back issues of the 1950s, the skipper found that the magazine wandered along a path that dwelt on little mignons of creek sailing ('Little gems ...' thought the skipper) mixed with articles about big yachts. As time progressed, the magazine had indeed changed direction and became infatuated with the high end of the market, leaving the bottom of the creek to new publications like *Practical Boat Owner*. Since then, in the skipper's view, even the good old yachtsmen's friend, *Yachting Monthly*, seemed to lose its way in the heady world of £100,000 yachts ... as starter packs. But in those rarefied earlier days, *Yachting Monthly* had still been under the careful tutelage of Maurice Griffiths, a strong proponent of shoal draft craft. The craze for yachting on a small income had largely become something magazines would rather '... us ditch-crawlers didn't do ... we're all supposed to be buying something big, fancy and shiny ...' the skipper muttered, '... but not me ...' All the same, the skipper had continued to enjoy articles of varying types over his years and had had one or another of the country's yachting magazines to hand for more years than he'd care to enumerate. So, all in all, their job had and continued to be done!

'However, back to the competition,' the skipper had thought.

In the June 1950 issue of *Yachting World*, in the judges' competition report, they were particularly enamoured with the quality of the designs that had been selected as their top batch. They were from both sides of the Atlantic. The main point against one was that the designer hadn't knowledge of British (or European) building techniques or cost overheads. They said, '... for it is doubtful whether this beautiful little cruiser could be built within the £600 limit ...' and later as '... an American ... must naturally have found it difficult to estimate cost of labour and materials'. That was after praising his concentration on low cost!

The skipper had remarked, to himself, of course, 'Err ... they were a little pompous ... I think!'

By May 1951, Moyles Marine Products of Hampton, near Kingston upon Thames, were advertising the sale of iron ballast keels for the People's Boat. In that issue too was a single-page feature on a prototype vessel that had been built in France in Brevands, Manche. The magazine had accepted an invitation to go over and sail the boat. One of the judges had gone and he was suitably impressed.

On his return to the bosom of his mate, the skipper had burbled excitedly about something that had tickled him immensely. It was akin to a very funny bit in the film *Notting Hill*, where the lead character, played by Hugh Grant, suddenly became a

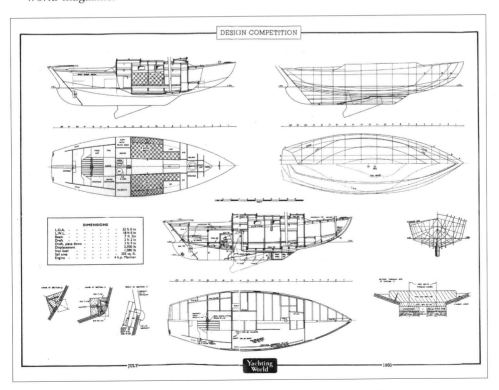

Right Sail plan of Brohall's People's Boat from *Yachting World*, July 1950. By permission of *Yachting World* magazine.

Below Designer's hull details from *Yachting World*, July 1950. By permission of *Yachting World* magazine.

feature writer for the *Horse & Hound* magazine at a film event ... 'I turned a corner ... looking for the gents ... and stumbled into the domain of the *Horse & Hound* ... I envisaged the toot of a hunting horn and a host of horsy gals surging towards me!' At which point he'd been in hysterical fits.

The mate had enthused about the information the skipper had found, but not his thoughts of horsy gals ... She'd then sat poring over an artist's impression of the boat, pointing out little differences and bubbling with excitement. But, she'd been quick to say, 'I wouldn't swap our present boat though ...'

'There was a rash of plywood boats after that,' the skipper had said, 'Dear old Maurice Griffiths, magazine editor, author, sailor and designer, turned his hand to a range of craft. The Eventide was one ... others followed in her path, getting bigger as they went and being given different class names. All had hard chines and most had a three-keel configuration.' Pausing, the skipper had added, 'Conyer Marine used to make the larger designs in steel – they were a Spears–Hundy–Griffiths joint approach, though – that was at the old White's barge yard ... It was run by the Spears family.'

'I remember you talking about those boats when we've been out ... and I remember the yard,' the mate chuckled, cutting in quickly: she was about to be left on the beach.

The skipper had not been put off and he'd added, 'There were Canvey Island's Prout family ... deeply into early ply boats ...' Pausing, he'd thought about Geoffrey Prout, and later his sons Roland and Francis, their connections to his own club, the Island Yacht Club's early years. And too of Prout's folding ply and canvas boats, canoes, tenders and little sailing dinghies. The company had been started in the aftermath of the Second World War and traded on the island until about 2000. Roland had died in 1997 and Francis in February 2011. The family deservedly sit proudly at the table of British greats in the field of small craft design and innovation. Canvey Island had had a large family of boat builders ... then finally he added, '... there was the Silhouette class – later built in glass fibre – and a rash of others, like the Yachting Monthly Senior ...' That last had been designed by an M. S. Gibbs, probably under the auspices of *Yachting Monthly* magazine. 'Then there were all the dinghy classes ... Cadets ... Hornets ... Fireballs ... Mirror ... GP14s ... Enterprise ... Miracle ... and a host more.'

'Alright!' the mate had exclaimed firmly, calling a halt to the skipper's flow ... And he'd wandered away to put a kettle on.

One day, during the research of their old boat, the skipper had chuckled and the mate, sitting next to him, had looked up and asked, 'What's up now then ...?'

'I was just remembering when we worked out our communication signs ... when one of us is forward and the other aft ... coming up to a mooring for instance ... with usually loads of watchers and listeners around ... on our People's Boat.'

'Oh yes ...'

'Hmm, I don't suppose you remember our arrival in Tewkes Creek all those years ago when ...?'

'Too right I do ...' the mate had said forcefully, butting in indignantly, colouring as she'd done so. In those days, in Tewkes Creek, the craft were moored fore and aft along the tidal stream. Coming in on the flood one day, the skipper had wanted to leave the boat the usual way round, bow up the creek. Their pre-berthing discussions weren't as developed as later on. The mate was supposed to catch the bow mooring buoy as the skipper got hold of the aft one ... The skipper had been exhorting the

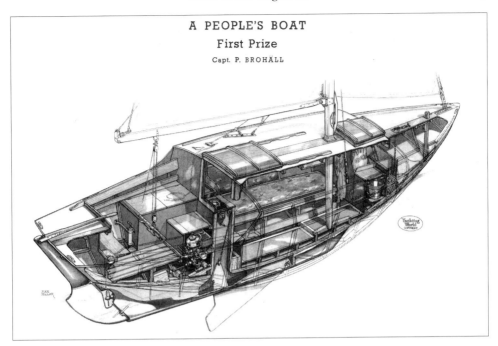

A PEOPLE'S BOAT
First Prize
Capt. P. BROHÄLL

Artist's impression of the little boat's layout from *Yachting World*, July 1950. By permission of *Yachting World* magazine.

mate to hook her end … louder than he'd thought … suddenly the mate had turned. She had held the boat hook firmly upright as it had thudded down on the deck and smartly saluted while shouting, 'YES SIR!' It was loud, audible and it had reduced the skipper to a cringing cretin trying to hide in an open cockpit … there had been an audience on another boat … watching and laughing at the goings on.

While they were having a spot of reminiscing, the mate had decided to add her pennyworth too. 'There's one you should remember …' she'd said, '… that time you frightened me … I very nearly gave up sailing too …' The skipper hadn't ever needed reminding of that incident. It lived within him. They had departed from their mooring and were on the way down past Southend Pier when the mate had said, 'Where's the compass?' The skipper had looked at the mate and she'd looked back at him … 'It's usually out when we go …' She'd gone below to collect it from where it should have been … It hadn't been there.

'Oh damn …' the skipper had suddenly said, angrily, 'it's at home …' A long pregnant silence had followed.

'We'd better go back for it … I'll get a taxi …' the mate had said, imploring, 'It won't take long … Queenborough tonight and sail up the coast tomorrow …' A sensible string of suggestions they'd been, too. The skipper hadn't listened!

Yes, they could have gone over to Queenborough and bought a new compass even … But no, the skipper had decided. 'It's okay,' he'd said, firmly. The mate hadn't been happy and quite rightly too. The skipper had been more Bligh than Christian in those days … He had, however, learnt from his mistakes, especially where it affected the mate: he'd not wanted to end up running a bachelor boat, like so many men experienced.

All had gone well until the skipper made his third mistake of the day. He'd insisted in sailing down the Swin. An admirable thing when time or wind is on one's side, but not as the afternoon starts to give way to early evening ... especially without a compass. Their charts were up to date, corrected ... Visual sight of land had gone ... dusk had fallen ... dim lights flashed around them ... a mist had come down ... they were lost somewhere near the South Buxey ...

That night was horrendous. It had been spent anchored in the shallows along the edge of the Buxey Sands. Not a good place at the best of times, but the skipper had thought they'd sufficient water. They'd gone aground too ... He'd walked the anchor to the edge ... So close, yet so far ... They'd had soup, with the mate doing wonders with their cooker propped up level. It had been quiet at first, but as the tide had run its ebb and turned, the wind had freshened appreciably. Soon, the noise of the fresh flood creeping inexorably towards the boat had awoken them from a fitful sleep. Not that much sleep had been possible with the *Yachting World* People's Boat resting on her bilge. The first slaps under the bottom boards told the skipper that it wasn't going to be a gentle lifting. It hadn't been either. The dinghy had gone ballistic. It broke the yacht's outboard bracket ... before the skipper had had time to get his act together. He should have moored the tender down wind and tide ... hauled it aboard ... or something ... The mate had sung songs ... she was frightened, beyond anything else she'd ever known, but somehow, with much trepidation, she'd kept her skipper's chin up through a shameful time.

Finally, as dawn had come up over the horizon and they'd swung to their anchor, the skipper had sorted out their position – well, sort of. It was while setting the sails that the mate had called out, 'Look there's a fishing boat going in ...' and they'd followed at a distance, the skipper feeling extremely chastened, indeed.

The skipper had been humbled. He had been terribly wrong, very wrong indeed: it could so easily have ended so differently ...

Chuckling at that memory, the mate had said, 'And that wasn't all was it ...?' On the way through Burnham's anchorage, the skipper had decided to anchor along the shore adjacent to a line of house barges. The holding hadn't been good and the anchor had dragged! Finally, they'd fetched up in a tangle with a trot of dinghies. That little bother had been eventually solved by taking the strain on the trot mooring and their anchor had been freed. It had been an inauspicious start to their first coastal cruise beyond the Medway and Swale areas ...

For the rest of that season they had sailed without an engine. When the wind had faded on coastal passage up the Wallet, they had lashed the dinghy alongside and with their outboard running had gone nicely across Penny Hole Bay ... The breeze had returned by the time they reached the outer Walton channel. It led to another episode that the mate had always remembered, for all the good reasons other than having to do it ...

'Yes,' the mate had added: there was more. 'We had to tack up through the moorings ... anchored in the Twizzle I seem to remember.' (One could do that then ...) She'd then chuckled, 'You assured me that when leaving the next day it would be easy ... it wasn't because we had to tack out!'

'No,' the skipper had said grinning. 'The wind had gone right round ... good practice though.' Chuckling, the skipper had added, 'I did the same this year when I was on my own ... after the Jolly Boys ... went all the way up to the Walton & Frinton

IN July, 1950, issue of *Yachting World* we published the plans of a little yacht, winner of first prize in our designing competition for "A People's Boat," a small centreboard cruiser of 18ft L.W.L. having accommodation for two adults and suitable for coastal cruising. The design came from the board of Captain P. Bröhall, Egilsgatan 11A, Uppsala, Sweden, who was up against stiff international competition.

This clever single chine boat is of plywood construction on built-up frames and she fulfilled both the letter and the spirit of the competition, for it is difficult to imagine a more simple, commodious and attractive little auxiliary sloop.

Letters have been coming ever since from all over the world asking for plans and more information about this boat. She was

A PEOPLE'S BOAT

TRIALS OF PROTOTYPE

obviously what many people had been waiting for. We therefore bought the world copyright of the design from Captain Bröhall, and intend at a date which will be announced later in *Yachting World* to publish the plans so that they will be available to readers.

The first boat, *Radiance*, was built in France in the yard of M. L. F. Gancel, Brevands, Manche, and we accepted his invitation to go over to Cherbourg to sail her. It was mid-March and on the day of our arrival it was blowing a gale. With two reefs in the mainsail and a small jib we found that *Radiance*, carrying little appreciable helm, got to windward in no uncertain manner and on all points of sailing handled perfectly. With her full sail area she showed the same high qualities and proved herself a good seaboat, dry, and, considering her shallow draft, stiff and well able to take care of her crew.

The amount of accommodation is surprising. The cockpit is roomy and the horse which runs across the middle seemed, in practice, no detriment but rather an advantage to the helmsman.

As one of the judges of the competition we were most interested to see our high opinion of the boat, which was of necessity based entirely on the plans submitted, so amply fulfilled, and we have great confidence in her future as an attractive little auxiliary cruiser at a reasonable cost.

The photographs beginning with the top right hand one and working round anti-clockwise show :—Radiance beating to windward under reduced canvas—A pretty hull. Weight of crew does not put stern down unduly—Travelling fast on a reach—Under full canvas—In choppy water—Roomy cabin. Note floor unobstructed by plate case

240

The prototype was sailing by March 1951 at Cherbourg, France, and was reviewed by one of the judges in *Yachting World*, May 1951. By permission of *Yachting World* magazine.

Blue Tail, People's Boat No. 4, sails serenely into the Medway with her two cotton headsails at work, early July 1981.

Yacht Club, turning off their clubhouse.' Laughing, the skipper had told the mate of the crowd of spectators that had appeared on the club's veranda ... 'I gave them a cheery wave, tacked the boat right round and ran back out ... it was exhilarating.'

'I loved that boat ...' the mate had suddenly said. 'Even though she had no head room ... no proper loo ... she taught me how to handle a boat ... that boats have characters ... souls even.' Then she'd said, 'I remember so many drifty sorts of days,' as her voice had faltered. Then laughing as a wee tear drop, like a bead of pearl barley, drifted down a cheek, she'd added, 'Do you remember that "seal surf" trip down the coast and then the day when you photographed the boat from the dinghy ... well you did it a lot ... still do ...' Both trips had been different, one on the back of an east north-easterly which had carried them furiously across the outer Thames reaches, surfing from one crest to another. The other had been a long lazy affair that had ended with a gentle sea breeze wafting them through the last few miles ...

Well, all of that had been long ago. The skipper had nodded. He smiled gently, thinking of their People's Boat and what it had done for them both. Then reaching across, he'd ruffled his mate's hair, kissed her gently and given her a hug. He was a lucky man ... a lucky man indeed ... to have met a land lubber who'd taken to being nurtured in among the creeks and ditches around the Thames estuary ... a place she'd developed a deep love for ...

The Finesse Story

The skipper had slowed. As soon as he'd been sure of his cycle's footing, he'd glanced backwards with one eye to check on the whereabouts of his mate: he'd heard a muted 'Wait for me' as he emerged into dappled sunlight from a wood. His eyes had lit up …

Grinning widely, the skipper had then whispered to their son, then a mere babe and tightly wrapped in a baby sling strapped across his father's chest, 'It's alright little man … your Mum's right behind us …' The babe's little eyes had been feverishly looking around. Feeding time – perhaps? His dad wouldn't have been any use there! During that quick glance, he'd spied the mate, as she too had emerged from the semi-darkness of the woodland to leave behind the heavily rutted and shaded lane that they'd been cycling along.

The skipper had then come to a stop on the firmer, but roughly metalled surface of a proper road; well, it was a lane really. It was lined with overhanging hedges, wispy, with trailing fronds. There he'd awaited his mate. The sun, nearing the midway point on its path across their hemisphere, left dappled patches of light all around as it had filtered through the leaves and tree branches. Reflecting on the flickering light patterns, the skipper had chuckled at what he'd seen moments earlier. The young lad was oblivious of his father's thoughts and had gurgled too, as the skipper had chuckled, 'That's my boy.'

'What was that?' the mate had asked as she'd drawn up alongside them.

Chuckling again, he'd said, 'Nothing …' but his grin said more …

'Hmm!' she'd intoned, but thought, '… something's tickled his fancy …' and her penetrating look towards the skipper spoke volumes.

Inwardly the skipper's heart had fluttered: emerging from the woods, his eyes had widened as he'd seen that the skirts of the mate's frock, thick with frothy lace, had billowed in tremulous folds … the first beam of dappled sunshine had lit and heightened the colour of an expanse of exposed thighs … like gold … The skipper had quickly reflected too that the floaty folds of the mate's skirts, and their movement, were reminiscent of the way a breeze lifted, rippled and played with the Egyptian cotton Genoa of their present yacht, as it was dropped onto the foredeck. 'Should I tell her …' he'd thought, mouthing, 'Mmmm … best keep it to myself …' Much later, he'd told the mate and they'd both laughed about it … It was years later, but her embarrassment was clear!

They were on their way to a boatyard. The yard, they'd heard, lay in some woodland. 'It's off a rough track beyond Hadleigh Great Wood …' they'd been told, '… if you go through the wood … on the right …' Reaching a stony lane, lightly potholed and leaf-covered, they searched its depths for the elusive yard.

'Come on,' the mate had said, 'Mrs Platt said it was right down the lane ... past the triangle ...' They'd soon found a turning on their right ...

The skipper had set off again, bouncing the babe as he cycled after the mate across the stony surface. Ahead, the mate had stopped. Catching her up, and before she'd been able to speak, the skipper had exclaimed, 'Look!' pointing into the shadow of all the surrounding trees, 'Boats!' And in front of them was a yacht, a beautiful wooden creation. She'd sat on a trailer ready for delivery to a new owner. Another vessel, unseen, sat under an old tarpaulin near a stack of timber – 'Awaiting work, perhaps ...' the skipper had mused as he'd alighted from his bike to leave it propped against a fence. The mate had followed suit.

The skipper had purred. He took an instant pleasure in the pleasing line of the boat's deck, the cocky pick-up to her ends and the proud rake of her stem. The air was thick with the heady odours of wood and freshly applied paint. One of the boat's cabin sides twinkled in the bright sunshine. Varnished golden iroko dazzled ... Her sides glistened and gleamed. She was glorious. The skipper walked round the craft; he looked; he stroked; he ran his hands to and fro, feeling, with pleasure, her curves ... her buttock lines ... her runs aft ... to her gently raked transom. Finally, he'd stood back and gazed again at the sweetness of her sheer. It was ecstasy. He was smitten.

The mate had followed in his path. She'd whispered quietly, '... he's in love ...' and exclaimed softly, 'Wow! So am I!' They were thoughts for her alone: the boat looked, at first sight, what she'd envisaged when discussing the imminent (they thought then) departure of their first little boat. Both had looked at the Finesse's fine shape when sailing and had been gently and teasingly smitten from a distance for too long. But seeing one, closely, it was real. The mate was in raptures of delight ... but had thought, being ever the practical one in that world, 'But ... what's she like inside ...?'

Recovering themselves, the skipper and mate had taken a step back and with deep breaths had looked at one another. Their looks had said, 'This is it.' They'd turned towards the yard. Through the branches of the leaf-covered trees, they saw other craft were chocked up – perhaps early arrivals for winter lay-up? In front of them, to one side of a house (then the builders' house, it transpired), was a shed. It was the building shed, the doors were ajar, and a vessel sat within. The sounds of tools working wood and rich peppery scents emanated. 'We'd better go to the office,' the mate had said. They made their way to a hut. Across its doorway it had a sign. It said, 'Finesse Yachts'. Knocking, they shuffled in.

'I'm Mrs Platt, can I help you?' a bright and cheerful lady with a friendly voice asked as she'd looked up from her desk, scattered with correspondence.

'We've come to look at your boats,' they'd both chimed ... looking at one another ... 'Err ... Mr and Mrs –.'

The lady had smiled broadly. 'Been watching you ...' she'd said as she reached out and tickled the babe's cheek. A few questions had followed. Finally she'd said, 'Alan's in the shed ... go on in ...' She must have known that a yacht had been sold.

Some hours later, the skipper and mate had slowly cycled away. They were not just in love with the boats. They were bewitched, besotted even. They'd run through many details; obtained current prices; extras lists; and most importantly, build times: the skipper worked away at sea and he'd wanted to be able to programme their new 'baby' around his work and leave patterns, for a launch early after a homecoming ... an old boat had to be sold first though ...

It was to be another year before they were able to return to the boatyard to place their order. Their *Yachting World* People's Boat had been sold a few days earlier. The mate, with tears running down her cheeks, had watched from the sea wall that ran alongside the little creek, Tewkes, where the boat's mooring had been, while the skipper had piloted the new owner clear of the muddy and marsh-fringed ditch: when the deal had been struck the new owner had said, 'I don't think I'll be able to get her out of here ... Could you be on hand old boy when I come for her ... I've only ever raced on the Crouch ...' The skipper hadn't wanted that last job. But it had been done!

For that intervening period of barely a year, and it had included time away deep-sea, the skipper had still had a boat. She was a Mirror dinghy, sail number 959, hailing from around 1963. The dinghy had belonged to the skipper's father. It had been the skipper's and his siblings' plaything when youngsters. The mate 'enjoyed' a few light-weather sails with the skipper: she wasn't enamoured with that type of sailing. The skipper, though, had roamed the creeks and marshland waterways, creeping in and out of the saltings, enjoying himself. He'd always returned home beaming broadly. It was a return to his childhood, when he'd lived on a spritsail barge, among the Kent marshes. It was a brief and enjoyable interlude ...

Before the end of the skipper's leave they'd moved their dinghies to a new club they'd joined. The club sat up Smallgains Creek, on Canvey Island. It had had a set of dinghy racks set above the marshes along the edge of the creek, up near a concrete slipway. The dinghy had lasted only a few more years. It had been used, though. It was also towed astern of the new clinker yacht, up the coast, in use as their tender too ... Then, finally, it had been consigned to a bonfire around 1990. That creek had since been their new and present boat's home for around thirty years ...

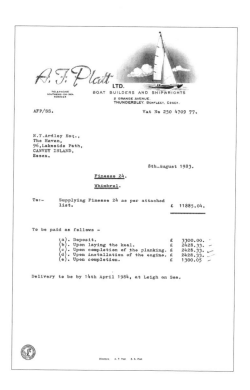

The stage payment plan for the skipper's Finesse 24, *Whimbrel*, sail number 64, from A. F. Platt Ltd, in August 1983.

The new boat was given a hull number upon the signing of the papers in 1983. She was to be number 64 in the fleet of the Finesse 24s; her name too had been decided upon, when quietly leafing through a bird book, mulling the boat over in the confines of their back garden. It was *Whimbrel*, a northern curlew. It was the bird's call that had sealed it! Knowing that the skipper was going to be away at sea, Mrs Platt had impressed on the mate that she was to call the office from Hadleigh when visiting the yard. (The skipper and mate hadn't a car then ... priorities first ...?) Mrs Platt, bless her, had dutifully picked the mate and babe up (with pushchair) for every visit until the boat was completed. That act of kindness had never been forgotten. It was all part of the Finesse ethos.

Early in the build, the mate had received a call from the yard to say that the keel was laid and, '... could you come up and sign for our payment?' (They'd put a decent deposit down and had taken out a loan for the rest ... ultimately it had been quickly cleared.) The mate had to witness work done and sign for a series of stage payments. Photographs were taken; unfortunately they weren't of a very high calibre ... the skipper had later found upon receiving them in some far-flung place around the globe. Digital cameras were still in the future – never mind the coming explosion in home PCs – but he'd blessed his mate all the same!

When the mate had seen the keel, she'd exclaimed in a letter, 'There was just a funny-shaped chunk of metal and a piece of wood bolted to it ...! It's cost ...!!!' But, week by week, as the boat had grown, she'd enthused as their 'new baby' became a living entity, her heart was being lovingly cocooned within peppery iroko planking and danta ribs. All she awaited was her soul. The mate watched it all happen with awe and excitement. By the end of the boat's build, the wee babe, the human one, had grown too. Enough to climb a ladder in front of his mother, watched approvingly by the yard's staff, as they'd both boarded, long before the skipper ... afloat on his ship on that far-flung ocean. The skipper had one last exciting letter before his appointment on his much larger ship drew to a close. It had said, 'She's finished ...' The skipper had been agog at his mate's words. A certain jealousy had crept into his thoughts too.

Finally, in early spring of the following year, the skipper had arrived home. It was 1984 and a year of internal strife within our green and generally well-watered land; Arthur Scargill, the motivational mine union leader, had coerced groups of coal miners to take on the government. It was a political battle to prop up a spent coal industry. The skipper had always supported just causes, but not that one! It was a dire time: the country was almost on its knees. Life went on, though. Within a day the skipper was up at the yard. He'd cycled. The boat was completed, apart from a few little jobs. With her varnished cabin sides and creamy painted hull as if gold, her blue boot top over a brown bottom, she'd looked startlingly resplendent. A real lady: perfectly fitted for the estuary for which she'd been designed. Within two weeks, the skipper and mate's pride and joy had been launched from a local slipway. Her life then began in earnest and she'd gained her soul.

There followed many season-filled years when the skipper and mate had wended their way in and out of a myriad of salt-marsh-fringed creeks, ditch-crawling, mudlarking, exploring the past, but most of all enjoying their little clinker yacht. In their early days they'd always had their son aboard as 'ship's boy' and he'd continued to sail when grown up, enjoying a few days with the skipper. From time to time too,

Above left Whimbrel takes to the water, Saturday 14 April 1984.

Above right The skipper and mate, when a little younger, anoint their ship with champagne.

the skipper and mate had visited the little clinker yacht's builders, perhaps for a piece of wood, once for a new centre plate, and strangely the builders had never forgotten that yacht's first owners. They'd had a surreal meeting in an eating parlour prior to a theatre visit … recognition over the heads of a hoard of noisy, happy diners. It was the same for many owners, the skipper had thought: each was bonded in some way. People only bought a Finesse yacht after much forethought – all had a love for the little wooden ships. And in the case of the twenty-four-footer, sail number 64, the bond had endured as the partnership approached a fourth decade.

Over the years, the skipper had seen that there had been much protracted discussion about the lineage of the Finesse class of yachts. It had done the rounds of a nautical website too. Locally, there was tension when the subject was raised among older people in the business or attached to it. The history of the class was mixed up, unknown publicly, and 'needed to be told', the skipper had remarked to his mate. That was the overriding criteria that the skipper had when he'd set out to investigate Alan Platt, the builder, and Laurie Harbottell (pronounced Har bot-tell), the designer of the Finesse 21 – the forerunner of the longer and much more capacious Finesse 24.

The skipper had sought out the boat builder to elicit his story – the Finesse story – in so many ways the nub of the design. The man, the builder of the class, Alan Platt, had started life living along the top of Hadleigh Downs, in a row of houses in Sea View Terrace. His father had then worked for the Salvation Army in their market garden branch. Alan had been born in 1935, into a world that was greatly different to the high-tech throwaway age of the twenty-first century. 'As I grew up, the Salvation Army provided most of the clubs that us kids could go to,' Alan had said.

'Alan didn't say if the family were Salvationists,' the skipper had said to the mate later, when talking about his first day with Alan, 'though he joined the Salvation Army band as a youngster.' Alan hadn't had a connection to the Salvation Army for many, many years though, and had left the band by the time he was around eighteen years of age, he'd related to the skipper. The mate had had an animated expression of only mild surprise ...

Of his start in life, working, Alan had said, 'Old Frank Parsons of Sea Craft was a bandsman too. We both played the trombone ... when I got to school leaving age he offered me a job ... that was in 1951.' Sea Craft had operated as a boatyard near to the Smack Inn down in the old town of Leigh-on-Sea for decades at that time. 'The business was started by Frank's father,' he added. 'It's not the same firm, with the same name, that's down on the old timber wharf ... used to be where the Boatyard Restaurant is now.' The skipper had nodded: he'd known that. The firm had been adept at producing one-off craft, such as bawleys, fishing boats, dinghies and yachts. 'Frank always built most of the boats that Gilson of Southend needed in those days ...' Sixty years later the Gilson family still fish the waters of the Thames estuary, but the boats are vastly different now. Alan added, 'I was signed up for a six-year apprenticeship. The first year was to see if I was likely to be any good ... if you weren't then you got the heave ... I was taken on. The yard had plenty of work just after the Second World War. We built some yachts from Maurice Griffiths' designs while I was there.' That had been Alan's first connection to Griffiths, the revered Magician of the Swatchways.

Alan had grown up with a love for messing around and working with wood; he found the feel of it and what could be done with it as something quite wonderful. It was a tactile and therapeutic thing ... 'I loved being creative,' he said, playing with his hands as if caressing a small piece of wood gently with a spokeshave. It was that strong interest which had led Frank Parsons to offer him an apprenticeship. 'I hadn't any great interest in boats, or sailing for that matter ... then,' he'd said. 'It was the wood ... and what I could do with it.' The skipper had watched and smiled as Alan's face creased in a broad grin. 'It was a huge stroke of luck really,' he added, '... one of life's chances. I grabbed it!'

As the skipper had looked on, Alan said, 'We used to take the yard's dinghies, work boats really, out on the water from the yard.' Chuckling, he'd added, 'When the tide was in during our lunch breaks getting out, messing around and nearly sinking the things in our jollity and exuberance ... was a relief for us young chaps.' Pausing, Alan had then said, 'The lads left ashore would throw chunks of timber – to splash us as we rowed past – some of it was big stuff. There were boatyards all along that shore then.'

The skipper had grimaced: now such polluting of the waterway was utterly verboten!

Returning to more serious matters, Alan had said, 'I remember one of the big jobs we did while I was at Sea Craft.' Alan had paused briefly. He'd then chuckled, 'Well there were many of them ...' Moving swiftly on, he'd said, 'Some of it was big work too. Spritsail barges would be brought in to have engine beds and a propulsion plant fitted. We fitted timbers to the inner and outer hull faces and bored the hull for the stern tubes.' He added, 'It was bread and butter work for the yard.' The skipper had then found himself in the world of Old Leigh and some of its boatyard history.

Many spritsail barges had their trading lives extended to compete with the growing numbers of Dutch motor coasters that had flooded the British waters within a decade of the war. The barges Alan had worked on were berthed at Theobalds Wharf, further up the creek from Seacraft. Above Sea Craft's yard was Sea King's shed. Sea King was owned and operated by Reg Patten and later with his son Keith, then finally under Keith and his wife. The shed was on the same site as Sea Craft. Beyond that had been the wharves of Leigh Timber, the later name of Theobalds wharf, and the gas works. Coal was brought in to one end of that wharf too. And beyond again were the cockle sheds. After the sheds, there was a short stretch of hard foreshore which led to the larger building enterprise of Johnson & Jago built on the site of old oyster pits. There, many fine, much-needed Motor Torpedo Boats slid down their slipway during the Second World War. Another yard sat further up the creek. It lay beyond the saltings and a collection of houseboats that inhabited the creek edge then and was reached via a lane across the marshy ground – since reclaimed. The yard, Alan had thought, sat on the ground that had later become the headquarters of the Leigh Motor Boat Club, a thriving self-help club with its own lay-up facility. In Alan's day the proprietor, Leslie Warland, had had a couple of old barges, 'retired spritsail barges,' Alan had said, '... open at one end and used as dry docks ...' Similar scenes had become a common sight at various yards around the East Coast, and beyond for that matter. The dock craft tended to be old steel lighters, motor coasters or even redundant flat-topped pipe or crane barges. All had the facility to be sunk and refloated – the important criteria. They were used for repairs or bottom refurbishments, or for complete rebuild operations. Warland's yard, the skipper knew, was across the creek on Leigh Marsh, at the eastern end of Two Tree Island, though.

Towards the end of his apprenticeship Alan married his sweetheart, Shirley, and from that union (it was more than a marriage) a partnership was born. It was a partnership that ultimately produced a host of small, fabulous, pretty and capable yachts. Alan had known all through his apprenticeship that a shadow loomed: it affected most men then. He had been called up to do his National Service in 1957. He was twenty-one, or a little over. He'd started some months late: the system allowed people to complete their apprenticeships prior to their compulsory two-year stint in Britain's forces. 'I had a two-week break,' Alan had said, laughing, 'to get myself together and report to some place ... Malvern ... that was it. I very quickly found I'd been enrolled in the army.' Grinning, he added, 'It began with a short introduction to square bashing and getting used to many painful shouts from frustrated sergeants! Then I was assigned. I loved it though ... really ... it added immensely to my boat knowledge.'

Alan had served with the Royal Engineer Transportation Group, now part of the Royal Corp of Transport. The group was responsible for anything from railways, boats, tugs, landing craft and a large coastal ship requisitioned from Germany. 'Oh, and bridges,' he'd added, chuckling. 'It was fun!' Alan had been based at Southampton – well, to be precise, Marchwood, across the water and upstream of the village of Hythe. It was a place that the skipper had known well too from when he'd been an engineer officer with the Royal Fleet Auxiliary ... the very people he'd been working for when his own boat had been built by Alan. Marchwood was not the place that

Alan remembered, though, but the little shipyard of Husbands still operated from its location, virtually surrounded by the military establishment. 'It was down a country lane. The barracks were across the road from the port ... we got a train down to the water ...' He'd grinned broadly. Alan had by then grown to love the water.

Alan had trained as a marine engineer. It was another stroke of luck: later it gave him the knowledge base when he set up his enterprise, Finesse Yachts. It negated the need for 'expert' help. It added to the training received from Frank Parsons and his workforce too. Alan said that he had spent most of his time in and around the military port, never going abroad. 'I found myself working on the tugs, later becoming a chief engineer ... we'd sometimes lose a barge,' he said. 'It wasn't yachting type of work either ... we went out in all weathers ... if a barge was needed around at Portsmouth ... we jolly well towed it.' He chuckled as he remembered broken tow ropes and having to get a line attached in a busy shipping route ... the barge dancing and slewing around ... and crewmen who'd rather have been elsewhere, jumping the gaps ...

Late in 1959, and by then twenty-three years of age, Alan was discharged from the army to return to civilian life. The house in the wood up its leafy lane, which was later to include the yard, had been acquired before Alan had gone off to complete his National Service. It, and his sweetheart, always provided welcome relief when he was on service leave, and surrounded by ancient woodland, that little patch had remained their home. It was the place where they'd raised their family. A daughter continued to live next door to their delightful bungalow, the original boatshed, soothingly clad in wood and utterly at harmony with its subliminal leafy surroundings.

Initially Alan had returned to his old place of work, to his old tutor, for a job. Firms were supposed to keep places open for National Service returnees but, 'Old Parsons hadn't enough work to keep another in pay ...' said Alan, reflectively. 'There were no hard feelings ... everyone was struggling.' He added, '... people ... youngsters today wouldn't understand any of that.' Alan was quite stoical. 'I just had to go looking elsewhere. A year was spent as a freelance boat worker, wherever I could find work. Many yards in those days did not like what we today refer to as "contractors or sub-contractors." It was hard. It was no laughing matter,' he'd ended grimly.

Then Alan had laughed as the skipper glibly said, '... they became the much maligned white van brigade ...' Now, of course, most yards have accepted that outside contractors need to access their yards to work on an owner's vessel.

'In my day, managers or owners of yards would get angry ... They often charged a percentage ...' Alan had said. The skipper was aware that now they at least had to report their presence. It was a fact of life, let alone common decency, and for obvious health and safety reasons. Alan said, 'Even between the yards there was little contact: they were all in competition ... we never socialised.'

'Then,' Alan had continued, 'I got a job with Tepco, a little firm building dinghies in Leigh-on-Sea. The building shed was above a garage in Woodfield Road and it was quite a way from the water ... above the Ridgeway and station at Chalkwell ... I worked there for about a year.' Alan had then talked about Tepco. It had been run by two sons of a Mr Grisley, Ken and James. Alan had thought that the father owned the premises, but the garage was run by a chap called Doug Clements. 'It was there that I worked with Colin Knapp, who had been building dinghies and boats for some years.' Alan had chuckled and added, 'I already knew him ...'

Colin Knapp had had a yard based at a hut on Victoria Wharf, down on Leigh-on-Sea's waterfront. 'His first boat was a twenty-five-foot yacht,' Alan had said, adding, 'He built several others ... Colin had first worked for Johnson & Jago's and then he'd "gone fishing" ... he had a boat called *Cornucopia*. He wasn't at Tepco very long.' Neither, as it had turned out, was Alan.

It was also at Tepco that Alan had first met Laurie Harbottell, who, just a few years later, drew up the hull lines of the Finesse 21. 'Laurie was around fifty then ...' Alan had murmured. 'We used to both smoke like chimneys ... each having a smoke alternately from each others' packets ...'

There was another young craftsman, John Webb, who came to work at Tepco too during that period. Of that bunch, John and Laurie remained close friends until Laurie's death years later, John had told the skipper while yarning together one day.

Alan said, 'Laurie designed one of the Tepco dinghies, the dinghy, of around eight feet, was soon much sought after by yachtsmen.' At that the skipper had chuckled: in those days it was still de rigueur to tow a safe, practical, and substantial dinghy ... small enough not to cause too greater drag on the mother ship's progress ... as the skipper himself had continued to do so. In that respect, it must be said that the skipper was one of the few who had stuck to that tradition: for those moments of enchantment and enjoyment, it had been priceless.

Laurie had also redesigned the Tepco eleven-foot dinghy. 'It used to ship too much water ... and it wouldn't hold three people in safety ...' the skipper had been told by a local sail-maker, who'd been part of the boat-building world locally too. And he had built his own clinker vessel that seemed, to the skipper, to sit halfway between a Folk Boat and a Finesse 24.

Alan had said of the eleven-foot Tepco dinghy, 'The boat had insufficient shear, and rise to the stem ...'

Within that year, Alan had decided, with Shirley, to take the plunge, '... and strike out on my own ...' Alan had said, hesitantly, before adding, 'But I was lucky though ... Shirley had been trained as an accountant. It stood me in good stead.' During a later talk, Alan had added more. His first boat had been a Heron dinghy; also he'd advertised in *Yachts & Yachting* magazine, Essex-based and now a specialist in the dinghy sailing world, for over a year before orders really started coming in. 'Our first shed was a little ramshackled ... prospective owners had to have great faith in me ...' and he'd laughed at the memory.

It was bold and brave decision. Down on the waterfront at Leigh was the yard of Sea King, and up Benfleet Creek, by the bridge onto Canvey Island, was Dauntless; both were then building little clinker sloops and cutters. The Dauntless boats had a very dinghy-like shape to their hulls, with a shallow keel, and were often internally ballasted too. The superstructure was simple but effective. They made relatively inexpensive river craft, capable of crossing and traversing the estuary. The sailing vessels ranged between around nineteen feet, up to a larger twenty-three-footer by the time the yard stopped building wooden boats by the end of 1973 (Dauntless Association records show that the last of the clinker sailing boats was built then). Dauntless had also built a range of motor boats up to twenty-four feet in a cruiser and day-fishing version. It seemed that the company could do anything to fit in with a prospective owner and some 2,000 craft left the yard. Sea King built a similar vessel, but their hulls had been deeper in the

A. F. Platt

TELEPHONE
SOUTHEND-ON-SEA
525593

BOAT BUILDERS AND SHIPWRIGHTS

2 GRANGE AVENUE
THUNDERSLEY ESSEX

AFP/SS.

V.A.Hardingham Esq.,
12,Hazeldene Gardens,
HILLINGDON,
Mddx.

Started enquiries

1st.April 1962.

FINESSE 21' SLOOP.

To be built for the sum of...................£740.10.0. + 120 - 6 - 4

= 860 - 16 - 4
724 10 - x

Extras included in above price.
Terylene Mainsail & Jib.
Simpson Lawrence or South Western Marine Toilet.

136 - 6 - 4

To be paidas follows:-

(a) Deposit..£ 74.10.0.   1 April
(b) Upon laying the keel..........................£200. 0.0.   7 aug
(c) Upon completion of the planking...............£200. 0.0.   18 June
(d) Upon installation of the engine or upon stepping
    of the mast whichever is the earlier.........£170. 0.0.   2-0 Sept
(e) Upon completion after acceptance..............£ 96. 0.0.

Any additional extras will be quoted for separately before
commencement of additional work.

Delivery afloat at Leigh or Ex.Works.

Above Finesse 21
No. 1 in 1961. Note
the sheer line: it was
far flatter than later
boats. Courtesy of Vic
Hardingham.

Left Stage payments
for Finesse 21 No. 2,
Dolphin. Courtesy of Vic
Hardingham.

water and were built with a ballast keel. Those little ships had a jaunty rake to their stems; however, their transoms still had what the skipper would call a dinghy shape, with no tuck, where there was a sharp butt to the keel as the planks worked up from her garboards. The cabins also, generally, had a concave line that was opposite to their shallow sheer lines. Dauntless had, however, continued as a building yard. They had fitted out Nelson-class motor launches for police, harbour and workboat uses. Those were forty-foot craft. Alan had also mentioned that he had been competing with another Leigh-on-Sea boat builder, Russell Marine, who built their Alacrity and Vivacity class GRP (Fibreglass) boats during the 1960s and early 1970s.

'Before I really got going,' Alan had said, '… It was after I'd left Tepco … I built a boat in Hadleigh with a chap who lived there …' Alan's eyes had sparkled as he'd added, 'She was a Buchanan design and was called *Pied Piper.*' He'd paused, and then said, '… around 1961, I believe she's still about …'

From the start, Alan's boats had a 'typically spritsail barge-shaped transom' with a sweet flattened-wine-glass flow, similar to the cross section of the Babycham glass that was in vogue during the middle of the twentieth century. All his boats were characterised by a luscious sheer, 'Sexy-looking even …' the skipper had oft remarked to his mate. A group of Finesse 21s and Finesse 24s in particular will show different curves, or fall of their sheer lines. The cockiness of some bows and the kick-up of transoms varied just a little too. The skipper had often said to anyone interested, '… they're all different … just look closely … and run your eyes slowly over them …' Most had thought him mad, for many years!

Of the other yards along that southern shore of the Thames estuary, Alan said, 'Contrary to anything people say, I never worked for either Dauntless or Sea King, or Johnson & Jago for that matter.'

The stem, keel and transom of an early Finesse 21 set up on blocks in Alan's shed. Courtesy of A. F. Platt.

At first, Alan had started out building dinghies, building small 'one-offs' and fitting out the newfangled glass-fibre hulls coming onto the market. 'We had much glass fibre work with Snapdragon's up here, fitting them out,' Alan had said, 'They came from Wakefield & Walsh, down on the island [Canvey Island] ... they later became Thames Structural Plastics.' Alan had been quite correct too.

Alan had chuckled when the skipper had said, 'There are still many of those boats pottering around ... there's a few in my club.' The hull and superstructures were often fitted out by people in their gardens ... It was a cheap way into the sailing, or cruising scene. The bits came as a rough kit. Alan had approved of the robustness of the hulls and their ability to take the ground along the Southend shores.

'I'd built the Buchanan design and did a couple of Griffiths' Storm-class designs for people too. It all kept us going ...' Alan said, smiling. 'There was a twenty-three-foot motor boat, built for a Mr Suckling. It later went to a Mr Redman and sank at some stage. We had her back and fitted a new three-cylinder Yanmar into her.' Chuckling, he'd added, 'She was what we called the Stormalong Class – but there was only one boat though,' and looking towards the ceiling, as if for inspiration, or the ghost of a memory within the rafters of his home, he'd added, 'There was a John Leather boat too. She was a Blue Peter design and was carvel built.' He'd chuckled: the skipper suspected it was because many had never considered Alan as such an all-round boat builder ...

'Later on,' Alan had added, 'there was another one-off boat ... she was a Finesse 21, finished open. The owner, a joiner from down the coast at Shoeburyness, fitted her out himself ... with a doghouse and short foredeck ... when I saw her later.' That was during the mid-1960s, though. The skipper had then pulled a wry-looking grin before he'd told Alan of the open gaff cutter, *Arab*, that he'd come across in his research.

One of the Maurice Griffiths designs built by Alan during the 1960s. She is a Storm class. Note the similarity of the vessel's hull shape to that of a Finesse 24 seen in a later illustration on page 54. Courtesy of A. F. Platt.

The boat had been based near Pembroke in Wales and very pretty she looked too. The owner hadn't any information on when the boat had been converted. Her sail number was 30, which dated her to the mid-1960s. It was possible that she'd been converted after a deterioration of her decks and cabin structure.

Times had been pretty hard during the decade after the Second World War; the country was broke – as it had again been made at the time of writing – from political folly and greed ... Then, as the 1960s dawned, people were beginning to have a little left over at the end of a month. As savings were built up, a use for the money was easily found: holidays, abroad for many; caravans; and of course, boating. The Norfolk Broads enjoyed several decades of boom, with the area's boat builders enjoying good times. An upsurge in river, estuary and coastal cruiser sailing was about to begin, with people wanting their own craft. The skipper and Alan had chuckled over all of that: now moorings and marinas were clogged with thousands of underused and very expensive craft ...

Moving on, Alan had said, '... so around 1960, or early 1961, I asked Laurie Harbottell to design me a boat of around twenty-one foot. I planned to design the top and layout myself ... which I did.'

The skipper had nodded, in the knowledge that Laurie Harbottell had not generally designed cruisers, though he had an extensive and interesting career with boat building and designing ... but more of that later.

Alan had continued, 'The first boat came out of the shed soon after ... it's difficult to remember ...' Alan had paused as he'd spoke, as if trying to remember the person. He'd then talked about brand connections that customers had built up with him and one in particular stood out. He was Vic Hardingham, whom the skipper later met up with, not far from the water, at Shotley Gate, in Suffolk. The Hardingham family eventually had a long history with the Finesse class of yachts, but the skipper would get onto that in time.

The skipper had also been told by John Webb that the plans for the Finesse 21 had a usage fee for each boat. It had been settled at two guineas and remained unaltered to the end. Alan had added to that, 'Five boats were built alongside each other at the peak of our orders ... it was good deal in the 1960s ...'

The first boats hadn't been fitted with a ballast keel. The ballast had been arranged internally, like the Dauntless craft built locally. The change to external ballasting came early in the class's history. The basic boat had been priced at around £625, all ready for launching. As with all boats, extras are not a new thing and many essentials had to be added by owners at the build stage, thus upping the 'basic' price paid by a customer – it could be construed as 'easy money'!

By 1965 Alan and his team had built twenty-one Finesse 21s and by 1972, when the larger twenty-four-foot boat was also on the go, the class had risen to sixty boats. One of the last, or the last, to be built had been *Drifter*, No. 73, in 1985. The three points indicate a clear sense of the ordering trend of those boats.

Alan's eyes had lit up as he'd reminisced about the Finesse 21. 'I think she was the prettiest boat I built, especially when I redrew the lines of her cabin top to mimic the later twenty-fours which had the stepped coach roof from the beginning. She was a nice compact design and sailed well ... yes.' All the time he had been rubbing his hands, the skipper had noticed, as if handling a small piece of wood.

ARAB, Finesse 21 sail number 30, converted to a day boat. Note her sweet sheer. The boat is currently based in Pembrokeshire, Wales. Courtesy of Dave Walters.

ARAB taking part in the Milford Haven regatta in 2010. Courtesy of Roger Paice, photographer, Pembrokeshire, Wales.

The skipper had said, 'I agree … mostly … but being a twenty-four-foot owner, the smaller boat can't do what mine does though – especially in rougher conditions …' He'd known that many Finesse 21 owners had done extensive passages and added, 'Yes, both have excellent qualities. The big plus for me is that the larger boat has so much more internal volume … incredible room inside … all in that extra three feet. But yes, the twenty-one is a delightful, cocky little cruiser …'

Alan had listened quietly before nodding his head slowly, as if waiting … When the skipper had stopped, Alan had smiled knowingly and said, 'That's why we didn't build so many twenty-ones after the twenty-four came along.' Pausing, he'd added, 'People wanted the extra space … for a little more money … they got it. It was important to the sailing wife especially … with perhaps two youngsters … to look after, feed and entertain.'

'Marketing …' the skipper had said while chuckling. Alan had joined him!

Alan had then continued, 'The Finesse 24 … when people wanted a bigger boat … built from wood, I drafted out a longer design.'

'She's obviously twinned with her smaller sister,' the skipper had quickly remarked. Alan had nodded his head gently as a ghost of a smile wrapped his face.

It was then that the skipper had quickly recollected his earlier discussions with John Webb, a boat builder he'd met at the old Dauntless yard. John had been coming to the end of the build of a very fine vessel indeed. The boat was a gaff ketch and she was a thing of beauty of around fifty feet (sixteen metres). The skipper had chuckled inwardly as he'd also remembered shouting at his mate one day, 'I've found him!'

'Who?' she'd asked questioningly, looking up from what she was doing at the time.

'John Webb,' he'd said exaltedly: John had also worked at Tepco fitting out dinghies at the end of the 1950s, alongside Alan Platt and Laurie Harbottell. The skipper

Dolphin, Finesse 21 No. 2, sailing off Leigh-on-Sea when new in 1963. Courtesy of Vic Hardingham.

had had several chats with John Webb about Laurie Harbottell and his Finesse connections. Laurie had been a local man too, but sadly long deceased. His early life and the later part had been spent around the Southend area. The middle part had been spent at sea, in merchantmen.

Laurie Harbottell was one of four brothers. 'Laurie was a short, dapper man, of around nine stone in his prime and smoked like a trooper ...' the skipper had been told in a forthright manner: the chap had been a long-time friend too. After completing his training, as a shipwright, he'd sailed as a ship's carpenter in the days when ships sailed the seas with real carpenters aboard, or 'chippies' as they were colloquially known. Where Laurie had completed his apprenticeship remained unknown.

After leaving the sea around the end of the 1940s, Laurie had started a business venture building one-offs. His base and shed had been at Barling, a small village on the edge of the River Roach's tributary creeks. 'That shed was just about twenty-six feet by eleven and a half,' the skipper had been told by John. Another, a Leigh sail maker, had said that it was twelve feet wide. 'It set the size of boat he built ...' John had said. Laurie's boats ranged from beach boats, used along the Southend foreshore, to small yachts and dinghies. 'It was around 1952 the first "Finesse" came out of that shed ... she was a twenty-footer ... I was told by Laurie that her hull was stretched for Alan's [Platt] Finesse 21 ...' He'd paused and added, '... well, that's what Laurie told me.' While they'd talked, John had alluded to a connection with the Finesse 24. The skipper also learnt that during his tenure at Barling, Laurie had paid 2 shillings (20 pence) a week rent for his shed. That had tickled John for some reason!

In 1958, Laurie had stopped building at his Barling base and went to work for the Grisley partnership at Tepco. However, at one time Laurie had also worked for Charlie Wiggins, a boat builder at Great Wakering, Essex. It had been for only a short period and John thought it had been during 1958 too, probably prior to joining Tepco. John had been a little sketchy about that episode of Laurie's life. 'It was all a long time ago ...' he'd chuckled.

John had gone on to say, 'Laurie was a bit of an eccentric ...' and had grinned avidly as he'd remembered his old friend. 'He told the "Guvner" [of Tepco] that his eleven-foot dinghy was no good! So he redesigned it ... Made it fuller in her sections with a bluffer bow ... Before it had shipped water with three men aboard going off to yachts laid out along the foreshore at Leigh-on-Sea.' He'd chuckled. 'He just about solved that problem ... He was a clever man ...' Laurie went on to design the full range of dinghies that were produced by Tepco. In imperial measurements they were eight feet, ten feet, twelve feet and fifteen feet. The eight-foot had followed later as people wanted smaller tenders and the eleven-foot disappeared. The skipper, in his fact-finding trail, had been told the same story of the eleven-foot dinghy by three separate people ... and had been quite amused by that: it was not often that oral history flows that way!

'During the early 1960s ...' John had said, 'Laurie designed a motor boat, possibly for Tepco, and made the moulds. Then Colvic approached him for a nineteen-foot, six-inch motor boat that could also set a bit of steadying sail. The design he already had and the original moulds were purchased for the grand sum of £50.' Chuckling, he'd added, 'There were nearly two thousand of those boats ...!' John had then said, 'It was around that time too that Laurie designed Alan Platt's twenty-ome-footer which became the Finesse 21 ... It was only the hull form, though ... Alan was doing the rest.' John had also mentioned what the skipper had oft heard before – that later on, Laurie Harbottell had had a hand in the design of the Finesse 24. This, as Alan Platt had later said to the skipper, was essentially scaled up from the smaller craft, and that therefore she was his own work. About the Finesse 21 design, John had grimaced a little 'The agreed price was for 2 guineas per boat ... It never changed. Laurie was never good at business.' He was also referring to Laurie's Colvic and Finesse connection and what was perceived as 'being short changed!'

Finally, John had said wryly, 'Laurie had no other family other than a sister by the time he passed away ...' He'd added, abruptly, 'I think that Laurie's drawings and records have been lost forever. I talked to the sister, but there was nothing ...'

'To the Elysian seas to build and design forever, in peace and tranquillity ...' the skipper had thought as they'd continued to talk boats and designs for quite some time ... But that was months before his visit to Alan Platt.

Alan, while talking to the skipper, had said of Laurie Harbottell, 'You know, I got to know Laurie very well ... He was married ... They lived along Chalkwell way. He and his wife parted though.' Alan had gone on to say, 'He was a shrewd man ... And his fee was good when the deal was struck ...'

The skipper had jumped in. '... We had rampant inflation later on ...' Alan had nodded, grimaced and mentioned hard times too in the late 1960s and early 1970s. Smiling again, Alan had then talked briefly of another clinker class that was spawned in Essex. They were the Maple Leafs. He'd said that they came out of the yard in Potton Creek, near the swing bridge onto Potton Island near the Wakerings.

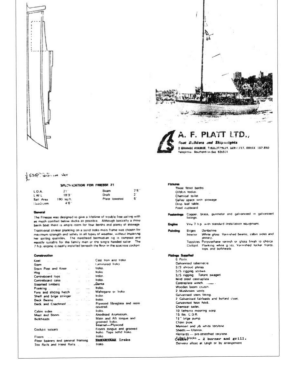

Specification sheet for the Finesse 21. This is a later version: the coach roof design has followed that of the Finesse 24. Interestingly, it had a hull outline drawing on the back cover. These later boats, like the twenty-four-foot and twenty-eight-foot craft used iroko extensively throughout the hull. Danta was used as an alternative to oak for the ribs.

The skipper and Alan had got onto the subject of some designs that closely resembled Alan's own boats. The designs on the skipper's mind had been introduced in two of Maurice Griffiths' books, *Little Ships & Shoal Waters* and *Sixty Years a Yacht Designer*. They were boats of similar proportions to the Finesse class. There was *Norma*, a twenty-four-foot sloop designed by Reg. F. Freeman of Leigh-on-Sea, a local naval architect, and built by T. H. Turner in Leigh-on-Sea, pre-Second World War. The boat had a close shape resemblance to the Finesse 21 later drawn up by Laurie Harbottell, with a shallow keel below its garboards and firm bilges. No bilge runner was shown, though, on *Norma*'s hull. She was perfectly suited to the Southend shores. The other was the first boat off of Maurice's own drawing board, which he called *Windsong*. She was twenty-seven and a half feet in length with a little more depth of keel beneath the garboards, and was launched at Portsmouth in 1929. Maurice had later adapted the design to produce a twenty-five-foot yacht with an eight-foot beam, a draft of two feet nine inches and a waterline length of twenty-two feet. It was called the Cockler class and many were built by Sea Craft at Leigh-on-Sea. 'A coincidence or what?' the skipper had said to the mate at a later point.

The skipper had said to Alan, 'With greater depth to her ballast keel she could be my own Finesse 24, *Whimbrel* ...'

Alan had nodded gently and said, 'You need a firm turn at the bilge ... the bilge runner gave protection too when grounding and lifting ... it's needed along the shore.' The skipper nodded too as he'd remembered Maurice's Cockler class with her shallow bilge stubs, but that boat had had a relatively shallow keel still. Alan had reiterated his experience of Griffiths' Storm class too.

'Boats designed for the Southend shore were obviously eminently suitable in similar environments,' the skipper had said to Alan. He'd agreed: his boats are spread far and wide.

A deeper keeled version with a three-and-a-half-foot draft and known as the Bawley class was added by Maurice and many of those were also built in the Leigh yards, especially at Johnson & Jago, and other places around the globe too. Alan would have worked on these craft. The skipper had long felt that all of these boats were part and parcel of Alan's later inspiration. Many boats in the wooden boat building era could be found to have close similarities, especially when of a similar length, draft and beam. 'It's all to do with the way a plank is shaped ... It will only comfortably take up a certain curve ...' Alan had said when they'd discussed this.

The skipper had remained intrigued, and he'd asked, 'So the twenty-four's hull ... It wasn't from Laurie Harbottell then?'

'No,' Alan had said emphatically, 'It came about naturally ... When talking to owners wanting something bigger ...' One of those customers the skipper had learnt was Vic Hardingham, who'd had a Finesse 21 for some years. He'd a growing family and needed a larger boat. Vic had wanted his new boat to be built in the same style.

Alan had smiled. 'I sketched her out ... I made a keel pattern and had it cast. Then I set her up with five moulds (stations) between the stem and transom ... And that was that ...' He'd paused, before adding, 'Building a boat is mostly done by eye, you know ...' Grinning widely, he'd then reiterated, 'As I was saying earlier, the shape of a boat's planks largely dictates the end result ...'

The skipper had nodded as Alan mentioned the possible whereabouts of drawings somewhere in his loft. The skipper had known that a local sail maker had had a sail

A pair of Finesse 21s under construction. Note the tumble home at the transom – seen on the inside face of the vessel in the foreground, which is nearing completion – and stepped coach roof. Note also the structure of the shed. Courtesy of A. F. Platt.

plan, but not a hull plan though. Later, during another visit, Alan had said that once the drawings had been used to make the patterns and moulds they'd had little use. 'An awful lot of my paperwork is scattered or lost ...' he'd said, sighing deeply.

It was the skipper's view that the Finesse 24 was clearly an amalgamation of Harbottell's concept for the Finesse 21's hull, stretched, and with improvements to the lines, especially at the turn of the bilge, of Griffiths' Cockler class.

Grinning proudly, Alan had said, 'You know that the first is still afloat and sailing ... Up the coast ... Somewhere. It was Vic Hardingham, by the way.' The skipper had known that. Alan had continued, 'He had the second of the Finesse 21s before that boat too.' The skipper had nodded.

'Ah yes,' the skipper said as he'd chuckled. 'I met the chap ...' he'd paused, 'Well the son, the second owner, anyway ... He'd said he'd had the boat for around forty years ... I challenged him and then found out the story.' The skipper had chuckled again. 'I could see that he was probably only a little older than me ... It was unlikely he'd purchased the boat when a teenager!' The meeting had taken place on a pontoon at a marina the previous season and it later transpired that he'd been three years older than the skipper, and had also been named Vic! The boat, *Delphinus*, Finesse 24 No. 1, had been based at Titchmarsh Marina for a number of years.

'Same family though?' Alan had added quickly, grinning!

'Yes ... Granted,' the skipper had added.

'That first Finesse 24 was built around 1970 ...' Alan had paused. After gazing skywards at the ceiling, into the imaginary loft of his old boat shed, as if searching his memory, he'd added, 'I'm sure it's right ...' He'd smiled before adding, and changing tack, 'I gave the cabin coach roof a stepped line. It became our trademark look from then on.'

'Yes, it's rather fetching,' the skipper added. 'The whole thing is ... The boat that is ...!' The skipper and Alan had laughed loudly together, eliciting a look from Shirley, who had been passing ...

Sometime after his talk with Alan, the skipper had tracked down *Delphinus*'s first owner, Vic Hardingham. The kindly gentleman had had some interesting information too about the Finesse 24 in particular, never mind his life story. Vic had accepted that the boat was no longer 'his', but he'd still been the legal owner ... and helped with costs. During their initial telephone conversation, Vic had said, 'I still pay the marina fees ... But she's my son's now ...' He'd chuckled, and then added with a laugh, 'I'm eighty-six now ... You know ... And I've a mass of information if you'd like to come over ...' The skipper had, a week later, travelled to the Shotley peninsula between the rivers Stour and Orwell to visit the gentleman.

The first of the twenty-fours hadn't been fitted with a centre plate even though Alan had designed her to have one. Instead she'd had full-depth steel bilge keels fitted. Vic had said, 'Alan had fitted out many Snapdragon cruisers and I knew those ... And thought that compared to the twenty-one, the Finesse 24 didn't need a plate with her deeper long keel.' Chuckling, he'd said, 'I sat with Alan on a log and we just gazed at the finished hull ... looking ... thinking ... talking. It hadn't any top hamper either ...' Then he'd laughed, '... We both got up and said "here ..." and that's where they were fitted.' Chuckling again, Vic had continued, 'I designed the sail plan layout too, for Alan, and included the pressure points [Centres of Effort] ... We got the boom

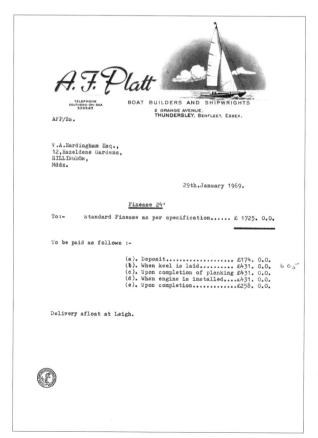

Alan Platt's letter. dated
29 January 1969, confirming
Vic Hardingham's order for his
Finesse 24, the first of the class.
Courtesy of Vic Hardingham.

and foot of the mainsail too long at first ... But it was soon sorted ... Then she sailed like a dream.'

The skipper had found during his talk with Vic Hardingham that it had in fact been 1969 when that first Finesse 24 had been built. Vic had ordered his boat in January of that year. Vic's boat was delivered ready for the summer and he'd had Alan lift her out again a few months later for winter lay-up at his yard. It was a regular feature until a home move up the coast and a mooring had been taken at Pin Mill.

The paperwork for Vic's boats had proved interesting, not only as a comparison against that of the skipper's own boat of some fourteen years later: on a website dedicated to the Finesse class of yachts there were boats that purported to have been built back to 1967–68. 'They're wrong!' the skipper had exclaimed to his mate at the time: they were dates which the skipper had long questioned. 'There's *Katrina*, which was No. 6, she's stated to have been built in 1968 ... Probably late 1970 or even sometime during 1971 ...' the skipper had added wryly. By 1972, No. 9, *Mackerel Sky*, and No. 10, *Wild Maid*, formally *Wind Maid*, had been completed. Boats were usually built in pairs and took around sixteen weeks to finish. Also, *Practical Boat Owner* magazine, a British yachting magazine, had featured the new Finesse 24 in an article in April 1970. It had had an illustration of boat number one, launched late in 1969. Interestingly, and moving on, by 1983 when the skipper's own Finesse 24, No. 64, *Whimbrel*, had been ordered, there

Above left The front of Alan's brochure for the Finesse 24: 'Finesse – Something special in wood'. Sheet dates from 1981.

Above right Finesse 24 specification details. The details relate to later boats: iroko is used extensively throughout hull.

were sixty-five on the books. (The skipper's boat and No. 65 were built alongside each other, with the skipper's inside as she was going out last – she was completed by March 1984 and was moved out to allow other work to commence.) The peak had passed by then, though, but the skipper had murmured, while studying the numbers, 'That was still around five twenty-fours a year on average ... Never mind the others ...' It had all been helped by Alan's departure from the norm, making a set of moulds for planking. He'd also used pneumatic riveters to speed up fastening work, as well as the use of spray painting, especially for varnish and undercoats.

Vic had continued, 'It all started years beforehand though. I was in bombers ... A pilot engineer ...' and pointing to a picture on his wall had added, 'Lancasters ... In the war [Second World War].' He'd gone on to talk about how he'd trained as an engineer beforehand and been in the air cadets too. After the war he'd worked up to become chief engineer with the Royal Academy and among other jobs he'd run his own company designing filters. 'I met and married my wife at the end of the 1940s and we started going to the Broads sailing ... My wife's family were connected with Hoseasons and we used to try out their new boats as they came along ...' He'd paused and laughed, then added, 'I'd spent time on the coast at Bacton as a child. It was my grandparents' place ... It was about ten miles from Cromer ...' Chuckling, he'd said, 'We continued to go back there too; my wife loved the water.' Vic had paused for a bit: his wife had passed away only the year before. 'I learnt to love the East Coast from that East Coast beach ... I'd pinch an old fishing boat and go out on the water ... We even tried herring drifting one night ... That was with my brother ... But we only caught a skate!' Vic had then talked about building a gaff-rigged catamaran out of practice ski floats for his son, young Vic, during the mid-1950s. Young Vic, it transpired, was only a little older than the skipper. Vic had also been involved with spritsail barges. The first had been the *Ethel Ada*: he had measured it and drawn a lines plan for the then owner. Later he'd sailed and helped on Tate & Lyle's *May*. 'I remember helping with her decking ...' Vic had said, proudly.

The skipper had then given Vic a brief outline of his own barging childhood and he'd soon got his research interview back on track, Vic realising that here was someone who knew 'a little' about barges ... But as with all older sailors of the 1950s and 1960s, their stories were always interesting and worth listening to. The skipper had learnt a long time ago, one can learn more when you let the other side talk ... 'So when did you get your first boat ...?' he'd finally asked very gently.

'Oh, yes, sorry, I started looking around 1960 and around the end of 1961 I heard about a new twenty-one-footer that had been built down in Essex. It was an advert in a yachting magazine ... I sent off an enquiry ... and a specification came back. We soon visited and struck up a friendship ... Alan and I, Shirley and my wife Doreen.'

'It was the engineering connection,' the skipper had said. 'It was the same with me – I've always kept in touch!'

'The boat was priced at around 600 ...' he'd said. 'Pounds that is ... All ready to go with cotton sails, galvanised rigging and a small engine,' Vic had added. 'I had terylene sails and stainless rigging ... and a sea toilet.' Pausing awhile, Vic had smiled deeply before saying, 'I liked what I saw with Alan's work ... and that was that, really.'

Vic's Finesse 21, No. 2, *Dolphin*, was launched in 1963: she was still being built in October of 1962. The price had risen by the time Vic had had the changes he'd wanted incorporated. Vic had a hand in the layout arrangements too, some of which Alan made standard. 'I wanted her right for us ... though I got a couple of things wrong ...' Vic had said laughing gently. At first the boat had been kept on a mooring off the Leigh-on-Sea sailing club where he'd been a member. It was a club the skipper had been a member of too – his parents and a grandfather also. The latter had been a rear commodore during the late 1940s. Later the boat was moved out to a mooring on the southern shore of Two Tree Island, out in Hadleigh Ray. 'She was only aground for about three hours at the bottom of the tide ...' Vic had said. The boat served for seven seasons and she was sold in 1970. Vic had added, 'I wouldn't have sold her until I'd the new one ...' His old eyes had glinted too, his mind on things long ago. 'You know ...' he'd said, chuckling like a young lad, 'Alan finished a Mirror dinghy for us too ... We raced competitively when the boy was young ... he was always wanting new sails and finally new boats. He did well too ... Everything was smoothed off on the hull.'

Of that first Finesse 24, Vic spoke of her having had only a marginal amount of tumble home running aft to the transom and that the deck line wasn't picked up, as on following boats. Her lines ran out aft, almost flat. 'Alan had been unhappy with that ...' Vic had said, laughing, '... but we've been happy with her.'

The accommodation plan was worked out with Alan. Vic had wanted a dinette arrangement, as proposed in Alan's layout vision. The galley was arranged to the starboard side. There were two bunks forward of the toilet and hanging locker compartments, all of which became the standard outfit for the boat.

The skipper himself had always liked the Finesse 24's standard and common dinette layout. It was a tried and tested formula found in many craft of the period and gave a comfortable four berth arrangement, '... And with two aboard our twenty-four is heavenly ...' the skipper had said to Alan. The boat and its layout were not dissimilar to that of the Westerly 26, strangely, a similar sized craft ... Although those Westerlys came in at least three different standard layout configurations. Both craft had a stepped coach roof with cabin sides set inwards, though the Westerlys had a little more pronounced angle. And both boats had stood the test of time. Both were comfortable family cruisers. The skipper would have liked slightly wider side decks and would, if ever he'd had another built, have asked for that.

The Finesse 21s and 24s were built with centre plates with stubby bilge runners to allow the vessels to take the ground without causing scuffing damage to their bilges. The stubs also stopped the vessel heeling over too far when grounded. Some Finesse 24s were fitted with deep steel bilge keels as well as their centre plates, while a few, like the first of the class, did not have a centre plate at all. Without doubt it was the centre plate versions that had the better sailing ability, especially on the wind and when the plate was lowered well down. The plate also made a huge difference to directional stability and helm pull when sailing hard. The later Finesse 28s were slightly deeper keeled but were not designed with a centre plate, although they would have benefited from its additional grip on the water.

Alan had explained that he did deviate from the basic specifications, but it meant time lost when two were being built alongside each other and that it was easier when only one was on order. So, some of the 24s had only three berths, the odd one or two with the traditional port and starboard berths in the main cabin. An occasional boat had changes under the mast too. That was more difficult because the mast supports

A Finesse 24,
No. 40, *Liberty*
(when built), in
the early stages of
planking up. Her
hull shape can be
sighted through the
lines of her moulds.
Courtesy of Bob
Clark.

The freshly completed interior of Finesse 24 No. 1, *Delphinus*, in 1969. Courtesy of Vic
Hardingham.

and bulkheads had been designed to coincide, intentionally. Alan had said, 'We used patterns and so made two tables ... hatches ... bunk fronts at a time.' Trying to fit in one-offs became increasingly time-consuming and difficult. 'It upset the system ... Time was money!' Alan had said, looking at the skipper wryly, adding, 'We eventually built the boats in twelve weeks. Time on one meant a delay on the other. My accountant looked very closely at all areas where money was being lost – that had been one of them!' The skipper had thought of the demise of the boat builders Dauntless, who had been based down on Benfleet Creek ...

The increased interest in Alan's boats, and in particular the Finesse 24, meant that Alan had had to ramp up his workforce, and for a decade it stood at around eight – plus Shirley, who had dealt with all the office work. Shirley typed the letters, arranged parts and dealt with finishing – berth cushions and material choices. Shirley had also carried out a myriad of other jobs too and had often given Alan a physical hand when needed. Alan had said, grinning widely (he knew the skipper's mate was not scared of a bit of rough stuff), 'Shirley did most of the internal cleaning out after the sanding work, prepping and painting ... She varnished too.'

Later, when the skipper and mate had reminisced about their own boat's conception, the mate had remarked about Shirley: she had added to her extensive range of duties by acting as a taxi service between the yard and Hadleigh. Whenever the mate had travelled to look at their little clinker yacht, it had meant a bus journey and after reaching Hadleigh, with a babe and pushchair, a fair walk. Shirley had said, 'You're not to come through the woods – please call me!' and she'd written too.

A Finesse 24 nearing completion, *c*. 1980. Courtesy of A. F. Platt.

The completed Finesse 24 No. 1, *Delphinus*, sailing off Leigh-on-Sea in September 1969. Southend pier can be seen in the distance. Courtesy of Vic Hardingham.

During the early 1970s Alan had taken one of his Finesse 24s up to an East Coast boat show. 'I only did the one …' he'd said, wryly, '… But the costs were prohibitive!' Chuckling, he'd added, 'We did do one rural industrial show too!'

The skipper had by then been thinking of the next boat, the larger Finesse 28, when Alan had said, 'We'd built those Griffiths Storm-class carvel boats too during that earlier period [1960s] and they naturally led onto my next boat, which actually started out as a twenty-six-footer. The concept initially came about because, again …' He'd paused, and then continued, '… People wanted a larger boat, but she still wasn't big enough.' And chuckling, he'd added, 'It grew a foot … before she was built.' The result had been *Tugela*, a one-off twenty-seven-footer given the number 101. She came out of Alan's yard in 1977. Ultimately the class eventually became the Finesse 28, which was drawn up by Maurice Griffiths for Alan long after *Tugela's* build. 'I kept the coach roof sides in line with the Finesse 24s and I'd changed the twenty-one cabin by then too.' The first twenty-eight was finished around 1982. Following the formalisation of the Finesse 28 design, they were numbered as a class.

For the skipper the Finesse 28 had close similarities with Maurice's own *Lone Gull II*, a boat that became a class in its own right. It too was said to have been a development of Griffiths' Bawley class, which itself had sprung from his Cockler class, which too went back to his 1929 *Windsong*. The Bawley class had a three-foot, six-inch draft and the boats were said to be twenty-six feet in length. Since they had shared the same designer, why not similarities too?

The last Finesse 28 that Alan had built had teak laid decks and was finished to a higher specification. The skipper had once met the boat's owner; he'd kept her up Oare Creek, off the East Swale. The owner, though, had expressed his disappointment with the sailing qualities of the larger vessel, and he'd had a desire to go back to a Finesse 24. 'I loved my twenty-four,' he'd said, a little wistfully. However, what the chap had eventually done the skipper was unaware of. Alan said that he'd been

The one-off Finesse 27, *Tugela*, sail no. 101, when new, *c.* 1978. She is seen moored in Hadleigh Ray, off Two Tree Island. Note two obvious differences: distance between fore hatch and mast, and greater cabin length/window spacing. She was not fitted with a centre plate. Courtesy of Bob Clark.

unaware that the chap had had a Finesse 24. Another owner had said much the same too. He'd said, 'They're dear little boats ... I do miss sailing her ...' The skipper had beamed avidly, on both occasions, and had chuckled, crooned even to his mate when he'd related the conversations to her: he'd always felt that the '24' was the best all round of Alan's boats.

There had very nearly been another class, the skipper had learnt. His local sail maker, Peter Waghorn, who had been a boat builder before transferring to sail making, had built a boat to his own design. She was twenty-three feet in length with a beam slightly less than the Finesse 24. The boat had had slightly deeper draft too, but still with a centre plate. Again, she was clinker built. The boat was called *Mystery* and was usually moored during the sailing season off the Essex Yacht Club along the Southend foreshore near Leigh-on-Sea. Peter had said to the skipper during a discussion about boats, boat builders and the future, 'I gave the moulds to Alan ... We'd discussed them being used to make a new class ... None were built though ...' Alan hadn't remembered having the moulds, but only an open question about another class. Alan had later said of this, '*Mystery* is a lovely boat ... faster ... and narrower than my twenty-four.' He'd added, 'She would have been too tender for my customers ...'

The boat, the skipper thought, had a look of something between a Finesse 24 and a Folk Boat in hull shape and form. 'She's a pretty boat for sure ...' he'd told the sail maker during their discussion.

While talking in general terms with the skipper, Alan had said, 'When your boat was built, the orders had started to fall away. Yours was the last two-boat build – she was inside and the other was the outer ... because it was going out first ...' That was during 1983–84. 'The thing is,' he added, 'our peak working years coincided with an upsurge in the desire for something built from wood, for a traditional-looking boat with no deck leakage headaches. It was a time of great interest in all things wooden.' Alan went onto say, 'Later, we did a lot of infill jobs. We had a contract working on the refitting of Hoverspeed's huge channel hovercraft running from Dover to Calais – they were pretty impressive things. Alan had paused awhile to collect his thoughts. 'I had some work on executive jet refurbishments too. It was usually out at Southend airport, but we had to go to other places too.' Alan and his small team also worked on refitting of jumbo jets at Stanstead airport. He'd concluded his enlightening information stream by saying, 'We did everything to keep the nucleus together between new boat orders. All my apprenticeship training and my time with the army, learning to become a marine engineer, all helped. I had a broad knowledge base. I had to use it. I had a family to feed … Latterly there were just the two of us …' None of that could ever be denied. Finally, with more than a contented look on his face, Alan had said, 'I retired from boat building, and by 1998 I'd closed up the company.' Pausing, he'd added, smiling, 'It was a long run and I got a life's work from something I enjoyed …'

Alan built his last boat in 1992. She was a Finesse 24. She'd had a design input from her first owners too and was fitted out with an open plan below. She had teak laid decks. She was No. 69 and was called *Emma & Kate*.

Thinking about what Alan had talked about, the skipper remembered a past conversation with the great man during a visit to obtain some pieces of iroko he'd

The Finesse 28, redesigned by Maurice Griffiths, as a step up from Alan's *Tugela*. This boat dates from the early 1980s. Note the loss of stepped coach top line and she is quite high-sided too. She is cutter rigged, which on the larger boat looks more purposeful. The *Tugela* was a sweeter-looking boat, even with her stem head rig. Courtesy of A. F. Platt.

needed. The conversation, as always, had been long and interesting, running through from boats and sailing to the state of the nation ... Alan had been quite vociferous about the loss of trade that local yacht clubs had caused him and other boatyards: clubs such as the skipper's own and the Benfleet had developed their own lay-up facilities ... the winter bread and butter of boatyards. 'Remember ... It's part of our livelihood,' he'd said with a tinge of bitterness.

The skipper had asked about Alan's manpower gradients too. And it should be said, Alan's wife Shirley was additional to the yard staff. From memory, Alan said his manpower numbers had fluctuated as needs arose:

Up to 1965	1–2
Up to 1970	8
Up to 1975	8 (This was reduced to one and then Alan alone for a short period)
Up to 1980	4
Up to 1985	4
Up to 1990	2
By the end	Alan alone

At a later date the skipper had also learnt from one of Alan's past customers that he'd been a hard man to work for. The relater had chuckled, 'He was tough on his men at times ...' That had not been a surprise to the skipper: Alan came out of a system of generations of boat builders and staff to whom the boss was the boss and, 'You did it my way or not at all ...' It was an aged philosophy, far removed from the modern ways of the twenty-first century, where discussion and other experiences could be used to make improvements. The same gentleman, a Leigh artist, had also said, 'Even I tested Alan's patience at times ...' and he'd laughed before adding, '... But we always got on ...' The chap had had a Finesse 21 and the larger twenty-four. His Finesse 24 had originally been named *Liberty*, sail number 40. The boat had had internal design changes, with

Above left The building of *Frith*, the penultimate Finesse 24, No. 68. She was built in 1988. Note the laminated coach roof beams, an early Finesse feature. Courtesy of Jonathan Oates.

Above right The partially constructed interior of *Frith*. Courtesy of Jonathan Oates.

port and starboard berths in the main cabin. It had resulted in a cramped galley working area, the skipper thought on seeing a photograph.

Back with Alan, the skipper had enquired about the yard's working life output too. 'There were nearly eighty Finesse 21s, seventy Finesse 24s and ten Finesse 28s,' Alan had said. That had included the earlier twenty-seven-footer. Then he'd said, 'What with the dinghies and one-offs, I reckon we built nearly two hundred boats up here ...' Alan had chuckled. Then he'd grinned deeply and nodded gently: it was clearly apparent that he was deeply pleased and exceptionally proud of that. He looked it: quite rightly, too.

The skipper had smiled as Alan said, 'It's a shame my records aren't in good order ... They have become a bit scattered with the upheavals we've had with the old house palaver [subsidence] and then moving here ...' Pausing, Alan had continued, 'I did once try to keep a record of all the boats ... with pictures ... but it wasn't easy. As soon as one was finished and delivered, I was onto another ...'

Alan had said, 'Most vessels were delivered locally, and for a time most of the craft were ordered around the lower Thames and River Medway areas.' Alan had added, 'The farthest north that we delivered a boat was to Newcastle ... The other way was right out to Looe in Cornwall.' Alan's boats were now spread far and wide.

On being questioned about the gaff-rigged Finesse 24s in particular, Alan had said, 'Griffiths drew up a sail plan for that. And an occasional 21 had a gaff rig too.' Like Maurice, Alan believed that the gaff was not the be all and end all for a traditional wooden boat.

There were a few gunter rigged 21s in the early days too. The Bermudian rig was perfect for the boats, whether in the cutter or sloop form, but the Finesse 21 definitely looked the part when dressed with a gaff rig. The skipper's own twenty-four-foot sloop had out-sailed a cutter version more than once, even while towing the trademark matching dinghy astern, and he'd chuckled about this with Alan.

The skipper had asked Alan on his thoughts on the designs ... 'They were all good boats. The twenty-one I've mentioned. It was a good design. They were all family boats, the twenty-four especially. The twenty-eight was more of a motor-sailor, but sailed well enough too. They were all designed for use in the short chop that the Thames estuary can produce ... and similar waters. I was very happy with them all.' Pausing, Alan had added, 'I've enjoyed seeing many of them sail and have often admired one out on the water ...' Alan had tailed away then, as if dreaming of each and every one of his creations. The skipper had wondered if Alan had seen *Whimbrel* out along the south Essex shores, but hadn't asked.

Alan then went on to talk about his passion for being creative. The skipper had gushed to the mate about that later. He said, 'Alan just went on about it, his enjoyment, his pleasure ... He was rubbing his hands. It felt as if in his mind he was shaping something, something like ... oh, perhaps rounding the edges of a centre plate turning block ... a simple little thing, functional, yet so lovely to look at.'

'I can imagine him doing that,' she'd said with an animated expression, adding, 'You made a new one of those at Bradwell years ago ... didn't you?' An answer wasn't needed.

In the early days, Alan said, he'd had all his planking timber delivered from Sadd's of Maldon ready planed. It was mahogany in the earlier craft for planking and cabin

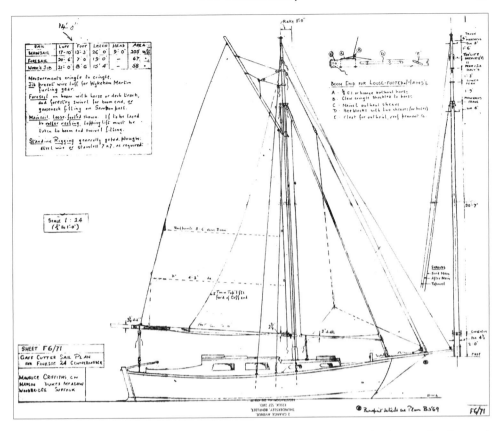

Maurice Griffiths' drawing of the Finesse 24 with a gaff rig from 1971. The drawing is referenced F6/71 – was sail No. 6 a gaffer too? Note that the cockpit coaming run is not correctly swept down from the cabin top – it is reminiscent of Griffiths' own designs. The drawing has sail maker Peter Waghorn's comments about sails and bowsprit: Peter thought these were for *Emma & Kate*'s rig. Courtesy Peter Waghorn, W Sails, Leigh-on-Sea.

sides and rock elm for the timbers. Later, when he'd taken delivery of a planing machine and a heavier-duty sawmill, he'd had logs of iroko delivered rough sawn. 'Iroko was used extensively in all later boats from the mid-1970s,' Alan had said. 'Oak and danta was used for the ribs.' (Danta was a tropical, close-grained hardwood which had a dark colour. It behaved similarly to oak.) The advent of decent electrical machinery, small enough to use outside a large facility, helped to cut his building times greatly, improving profitability. He'd chuckled. 'I've still got all of my old hand tools,' Alan had continued, '… Even an old three-foot jack plane …' The skipper had nodded, thinking of his great-grandfather's smaller-sized jack plane in his own workshop … 'We cut to size all our own timber from the cut logs.' The skipper had nodded: he remembered clearly the stacks of wood seasoning outside the yard's gates … right back to his first visit to the yard.

During the later part of the 1990s, the old build shed had been converted into a bungalow as a retirement home for himself and Shirley. Alan had had to obtain a local government change-of-use order to do this. Their old house had had to be pulled down due to subsidence and it was rebuilt. It was now occupied by a family member. The skipper had chuckled, more than once, with Alan about sitting and talking in the

Finesse 24, *Emma & Kate*, No. 69, seen out of the water at her Northumbrian base at Blyth. Her hull displays her builder's inspiration by Griffiths; compare to Griffiths' Storm class seen on page 34. Courtesy of P. Gosling.

old shed ... Alan said, 'You're sitting right where your boat was built ... Well she was a bit further over there, actually,' as he'd pointed towards a beautifully constructed red-brick fireplace. The fire was fed with logs cut from Alan's own patch of woodland that surrounded the tranquil home. On the skipper's visit during that fine autumn, it had been particularly spectacular.

Alan had also talked a little about his own sailing experiences, too. Apart from messing about on the silt-laden waters in front of the building sheds of Sea Craft, Alan had, after his army time, taken up sailing in a small way. His life as a boat builder put severe blocks on any extensive periods of messing about on the rivers ... Alan had said, during his talks with the skipper, 'We had a caravan during our early days ... and a dinghy. For some family holidays we camped in a farmer's field near Kirby-le-Soken. We walked the sea walls, explored Skipper's Island across the rickety causeway, and when the tide was in we sailed around Secret Water.' Alan had used the evocative name that would forever be associated with Arthur Ransome. 'I've had a Jewel-class dinghy too ...' Alan said, smiling, before adding quickly, 'You know ... The class is based at the Walton & Frinton Yacht Club ...'

The skipper had taken a deep breath as he'd nodded vigorously: he'd known those lovely craft and had often seen them sailing. There had been an article in a magazine too ... but he'd not been able to recollect which ...

Rubbing his hands and smiling gently, as feeling for something again, Alan had continued, 'I still have *Dawn*, my EOD ... an Essex One Design ... It's in the back there ...' And he'd pointed, from his chair, through the sitting room windows. 'It's one of my projects ... Perhaps...' he'd added, tailing off. Grinning, he'd then added, 'Though she needs a little work.' Alan had paused, and with a wry look had said, 'Not sure if I'll get round to it though ...' Alan's boat was over sixty years old. It had been built by Anderson, Ridgen & Perkins at their Whitstable shipyard in 1948.

The skipper had also talked with Peter Waghorn (W Sails) and had learnt more. (The skipper had had many long conversations with Peter over the years!) The class had been designed by Morgan Giles and was adapted from the earlier Thames Estuary One Design (TEOD). Both classes were clinker-built, with a common length of eighteen feet. The TEOD had hit the estuary with a huge splash in 1912: the boats were fast. The skipper had been told, 'Remember the boats being sailed back then – dinghies, that is – were generally heavy old things and often of the old fishermen's type ...' The EODs and TEODs were essentially a very lightly built vessel with a tall slender rig, ballasted by a heavy swing centre plate which had, in time, resulted in wringing of the hulls. The early boats were Gunter-rigged, and Bermudian soon followed. Owners essentially 'toyed' to get the best within the rules. Local yacht designer Reg Freeman had become involved in drawing up sail plans too. Then, in 1920, the Essex One Design appeared. Differences were limited to minor hull changes to the stem, the run to and shape of the transom and around the bilges. The Essex had been designed with the mast stepped aft of the foredeck, while the TEOD's mast had been stepped through the foredeck. In the late 1960s a call went out for a new boat and a GRP version. The Estuary One Design resulted and many were built during the 1970s. They were built by various boat builders, locally and beyond, but Structural Marine Plastics on Canvey Island had eventually built many of them. Interestingly, there had been a TEOD called *Dawn* too.

The skipper too had talked about his experiences racing his Finesse 24 and Alan had chuckled, his eyes alive as he'd said, 'Not many people know this.' He'd said, 'I used to regularly do the Nore Race.' Chuckling, he added, 'My first was on a twenty-one ... She was No.12 and later the same owner had a twenty-four and I went racing in her ...' Then, laughing, Alan had said, 'I was winning my own trophies ...' The preponderance of the Finesse classes locally was the main reason why the Benfleet Yacht Club had had a series of cups presented to them for the two main classes to vie for in the local annual Nore race. 'Those cups were presented by the Finesse Company,' Alan had said proudly. Alan had raced in Vic Hardingham's *Delphinus* too.

The Nore race, a Thames estuary race, had been inaugurated by the Benfleet Yacht Club in around 1925. It was initially sponsored by a local man, Mr Garon. The club (founded 1922) was based on an old spritsail barge from about 1927 to 1935. Later, in 1946, they acquired the Inner Dowsing lightship, built in 1840. In the 1970s, it and the club were still situated above the bridge at a wharf, but the building of a new fixed road bridge across the creek meant a move and the club had relocated onto Canvey Island, below the Dauntless Yard. The tidal flood barrier had also been built since too. Their old lightship was finally sold in 1984 to interests on the Medway and became a restaurant. The yacht club had then moved into their purpose-built clubhouse on the island.

'What about cruising?' the skipper had asked quietly.

'Ah yes, we ... well, I did a trip on a customer's boat once that has remained memorable – for the wrong reasons... We set out for France, Calais or somewhere.' He laughed at the memory. 'The wind was all wrong and the skipper said as we approached the shallows around the Margate Sands that it wasn't good ... We turned tail and sailed quickly back to the East Swale. It was a boisterous day ...' He grinned as he'd added, 'The boat was great ... She took it. I was pleased.'

Above left Sailing hard, Bob Clark's Finesse 24, No. 40, *Liberty*, some years ago off Chalkwell, South Essex. Courtesy of Bob Clark.

Above right Alan Platt doing foredeck duty on *Severe*, a Finesse 24, No. 5, during a Nore Race on the Thames estuary. Note the typical 1970s design of spinnaker. Courtesy of Bob Clark.

The skipper had nodded as he had mentioned briefly a couple of his own experiences. He knew too that the boats had done extensive passages across to European waters, and never doubted the boat's ability to look after her crew, provided warnings were heeded!

Alan was in flow again and there followed various yarns. One of them was about seasonal collection and delivery trips. Alan had said, 'I used to collect a motor boat from round at Brandy Hole [on the River Crouch] and bring her to Two Tree Island. The owner liked her at the yard where I could do some jobs on her ... They were cracking trips sometimes ... Others were horrible.'

The skipper knew too that Alan had sailed on a boat owned by Hall and Daphne Blanche. She was a gaff-rigged twenty-four named *Halda*. She was an early boat. A Maurice Griffiths original sail plan drawing of a gaff-rigged Finesse 24 was tracked down by the skipper. (The boat's hull and deck structure outline wasn't correct, though!) It had been drawn up for *Halda* in 1971. About that boat, another man, the owner of a small chain of marine chandlers, had expressed a forthright opinion to the skipper, 'That boat was a bit of a pig to sail in a blow ... I went out racing round the Nore in her ... We had to give up on one occasion ...' he'd said. 'Bally owner would never reef ... She kept griping up to windward. Hopeless ...' There lay the problem, the skipper had thought ... quietly ... with many sailors! Later, the skipper learnt that the Blanches also had had a Finesse 21, also named *Halda*; she was gunter-rigged. Their boat had been sail number 51 and it was apparent that the couple very quickly upgraded to their larger boat. Their 'staying with Alan's boats' was a common feature among owners. Many of the older generation of sailors that the skipper had spoken to had done so.

At the time of writing, the Finesse 24 once owned by the Blanches rested upon rotting chocks at the back-end of a boatyard in the Walton Backwaters. The boat had been viewed by the skipper over many seasons, gradually degenerating year by year. When last seen during the summer of 2010, the skipper had, as he'd walked sadly away, mouthed, 'Your days are numbered old girl, unless some saviour comes knocking ...'

Some years earlier, a man in the yard had recounted a tale about the boat to the skipper. 'Oh yes ... That boat. Well there was an old boy ... well he'd retired here or something. The chap appeared here one day and bought her. We used to watch ... All seemed to be going along well as he'd started to get her ready for the water ... She'd been out for awhile ... but what a lovely boat ... Then one day we noticed he'd stopped coming. He was usually down most days ... Well, regular like ...' The man chuckled, but it had quickly fallen away to a grimace as he'd added, 'Apparently the bloke's wife wasn't enamoured with the time he was spending down at his boat.' The man had grimaced. 'He'd just stopped coming. We heard it was a case of "Me or the boat" so that was that ... He's refused to sell her, too ... so it's just sat here ...'

'A sad tale indeed ...' the skipper had thought, thinking of his own mate's love for their boat ...

Alan still played with wood. 'I rebuilt a wooden staircase for my daughter's house ...' he said and as he'd looked around, he added, 'I built this place ... It's difficult to believe that the outside is the same as it was when it was the boat shed ... Five

Halda, sail No. 7, a gaff cutter-rigged Finesse 24. Halda currently rests ashore at Titchmarsh Marina, awaiting rescue. Courtesy of Bob Clark.

twenty-ones in here one time ...' He shook his head slowly and smiled contentedly, happy in the knowledge that he had fulfilled his life's ambition.

The skipper had left it there. He hadn't asked about how the boats were built: essentially clinker boats were built the same way they have been for hundreds of years. Differences there were, yes, but mere superficial trifles really. 'There are plenty of books that describe the construction details of wooden boats,' the skipper had later said to the mate, before adding, 'Anyway ... it would take a book itself!' knowing that John Leather, naval architect and maritime historian, had written a wonderful book about the subject – titled *Clinker Boatbuilding*. Sadly John Leather had passed way in 2006.

For the skipper, the boats were a tribute to both their builder, Alan Platt, and the initial designer of the Finesse 21, Laurie Harbottell. And, too, all who worked on them. The fact that most were still sailing around the estuarial waters of Britain would ensure a lasting legacy well into the future. Each had a charm of their own, an aura. Each had always attracted fond, admiring looks from owners of glass-fibre creations: many of those had eased past the skipper's own Finesse 24 as he'd sailed at less speed, smugly feeling a huge dose of contentment. The skipper, too, had written elsewhere about being 'chased' by a big Oyster, a yacht of some sixty feet or so. It had been on the River Orwell, some seasons ago. The crew and passengers had wanted to have a closer look at the quaint little clinker sloop that was reducing sail on her approach to Pin Mill. Praise indeed! Or was it something else ...?

A Bermudian cutter-rigged Finesse 24, No. 25, *Windsong*, seen in the Swale during 2009.

'Would you do it all again?' the skipper had asked at the end of his discussions with Alan.

Alan had looked at the skipper, smiled, and then he'd suddenly chuckled. Grinning, he'd probably been involved, he'd said, 'Remembering back to my apprenticeship. We had a cheeky lad who came in much earlier than me … When he'd finished his apprenticeship the men locked him in a wire cage and placed him outside with a label on, with something like, "I need a job …" The cage had been used for insulation and it was probably not very nice in there.' Alan had laughed, as the skipper had wondered what this had to do with his question. Then Alan had added, 'The industry was full of rough and tumble then. Working conditions were hard. You had to stand up for yourself, but if the gaffer said jump, you jumped!' Grinning, he'd continued, 'Conditions were rudimentary at most small boatyards. Many changed as health and safety rules tightened up. People now wouldn't like the conditions we had … But, would I do it all over again?' Alan had briefly paused, smiled, and then said, 'The easy answer must be yes, really. I never had a day when I didn't want to go to work.' It was across from the house. 'There were headaches, of course,' he'd said, adding with an undoubted finality, 'There always were and will be …'

Alan was still holding something in his hands; they moved … as if putting the finishing touches to …

Sometime later, while the skipper had sat with his notes and his thoughts, he'd murmured, 'Most boat builders and designers tended to be a little eccentric …' The skipper had added (it was an opinion he'd held for a long time) 'I'm not sure if Alan is or isn't … he has his woodland …' He'd spoken louder, for the mate's benefit, for she'd been listening quietly to his murmurings. 'Whatever lies behind any untold parts of this tale, or not, the plain fact is that had those two men, Alan and Laurie, not met, then the Thames estuary, and other waters too, would not have been graced with such beautiful, evocative and purposeful craft so aptly designed for their intended environment.' He'd paused, briefly, before adding, 'They were classics when they first appeared in the 1960s and they will remain so until the last, probably some fifty to seventy years hence, falls prey to the ravages of time and old age …'

It is fitting that Alan's story closes with his last Finesse in full flow off Blythe; *Emma & Kate* spreads her wings, sailing under the flag of the Royal Northumbria Yacht Club. Courtesy of P. Gosling.

A Poke Around …

'I must get those pictures!' the skipper had suddenly exclaimed.

He was sat in the conservatory of his home lavishly enjoying his toast and home-made Seville marmalade as his coffee steamed beside him. The mate had looked across at him expectantly. He had remained quiet, having heard the weatherman begin to utter the forecast …

Then he'd said, with a voice full of hope, 'It'll be bright and clear later …'

Even though it was a miserable, grey morning, the skipper, gazing beyond the protective double glazing, had looked at the murk optimistically. He was feeling quietly confident: even as early as it was, there was a hint of brightness beyond. He'd mentally discarded any thoughts of a sail. It was again windy. Boy! They'd had some wind that spring. It had been boisterous for what seemed to be weeks on end. That day was to be little different.

'What pictures …?' the mate asked after waiting what seemed an age, her glass of orange-coloured fruit juice (they all looked 'orange' to the skipper) held in mid-flight.

'Those ones I said "I'd lost" … Of the Crouch … Bits and bobs, I need.'

Some time previously the skipper had been to an old boatyard on Wallasea Island. It sat along the southern bank of the River Crouch. He'd wanted some photographs. The almost indistinguishable remains had been an ancillary yard of W. King & Sons of Burnham. King's had had a yard on the Burnham waterfront for many years and more space and access to deeper water was needed, so the Wallasea Island facility was constructed on a piece of higher ground on the edge of the river. The Wallasea site had been built to construct larger yachts being ordered from the yacht builder about one

The remains of King's slipway on Wallasea Island. Time and tide are doing their work and in a few years nothing will show of man's endeavours here.

'... Get Fred to knock the knee bolts through will yer ...' Drawn by Mrs G. D. Ardley.

hundred years earlier, and to service the type. Of course, the yard was ideally situated for the repair and maintenance of all the larger yachts in the area.

The original yard in Burnham had long closed down and it was now filled with housing in the form of 'des-res' flats – desirable residences – for the upwardly mobile crowd. The skipper would've preferred the yard: waterfronts needed boatyards, surely.

Sometime after his visit, the skipper had suffered from a computer glitch. It was a typically catastrophic one! It had resulted in some photographic losses – well, the skipper hadn't completed his protocols. The pictures had not been backed-up. 'Ah, there's a lesson for you ...' the mate had said at the time, adding more than the skipper cared to recall. Her admonishments had rung in his ears for days!

'Oh, yes ... Ah, yes ...' the mate said, looking up and fixing him with 'one of those looks' and it had reminded him, firmly, without compassion, of his folly.

The journey was, of course, made by road, not by boat! It was, as predicted, a blustery day, but the brilliant sunshine after the lengthy period of wet was companionable indeed. The showery rain had cleared earlier, but the wind had remained. It was gusty and of sufficient strength to make walking along the top of the sea wall a bit of an effort. The wind had dried the ground admirably though, leaving only isolated puddles and patches of slippery mud to contend with.

From the safety of land, walking along the sea wall, the turgid-looking water that ran in a dirty silver-grey streak between the river's confining banks had caused the skipper to shiver. It was so different from that seen on a balmy summer's day when cruising ... The skipper saw a multifarious collection of yachts whose owners had chosen to leave their pride and joys afloat, tugging at their mooring lines along the fairway. They had partially swung to the strong wind: they sat wind rode across the tide. All were visibly rocking to the wind over a tide-run-induced swell; white water welled under their bows at the end of each curtsy. Internal wire halyards clanked in a ragged tune as the clutch of masts cut arcs in the skyline. There was no other movement upon the river, and the skipper hadn't been surprised.

After a short spell of walking, the skipper had arrived at a turn inland, and he'd stood gazing thoughtfully across a patch of saltings. Outside the wall was 'his' old yard, covered in a miasma of marsh plants and rough grasses more suited to the higher

W. King & Son's yacht yard on Wallasea Island as seen from the water in 1960/61. Beyond the mainmast of a spritsail barge and sheds is the sea wall upon which the skipper slipped. Courtesy of M. Mellard & P. Pearson.

Hauling up a two masted ketch with the Burnham-on-Crouch waterfront beyond. The date is unknown, but thought to be some time in the 1930s. Courtesy of M. Mellard & P. Pearson.

levels, less tolerant to salt. He'd looked hard and tried to envisage the yard as it had been: there was little left to go on. Among remnants and tangles of old growth were the first shoots of fresh green.

Then, as if a light had been lit, the skipper's mind conjured the scene. He saw a hive of industry. Some sheds sat close to the present sea wall. There was a slipway, and beyond a wharf along the river's bank ... there were noises. The sounds of mechanical saws, the softer swish of a hand plane and the sweet, resinous scents of freshly cut wood ... of mahogany and teak. It was peppery. It was enough to set the skipper's heart pounding. Glancing across the scene, his imagination conjured the yard's noise and bustle.

A shout rang out. 'Jim, I need an 'and up 'ere ... Hey, get Fred to knock the knee bolts through will yer ...'

A fine yacht was taking shape. Her hull was completed ... Men were sanding her buttocks and the graceful curves of her planking sweeping fore and aft, and those running the hull down into her keel. She would soon go down the ways to grace this and other anchorages around the yachting coasts for years to come ...

Marvellous yachts had slipped down the ways here and gracefully entered the water for the first time. Many were for local sailors too. The skipper was able, much later, to find more about one. Her present owner provided him with some details that have been handed down with the vessel. The yacht, *The Blue Peter*, slid down into the silt-laden waters of the Crouch in 1930. She'd been designed by Alfred Mylne, a respected yacht designer of the period, in 1929. The yacht had gone onto win over fifty races under the burgee of the Royal Corinthian Yacht Club on the Burnham River.

In 1938, a moment in time of the yacht's life and just before the lurking conflagration that hung over the world, she'd been hauled ashore and lengthened. Her then-owner, Desmond Molins, wanted a longer vessel. The yacht was originally built as a typical cutter, with a short bowsprit. Her length after rebuilding was increased to 19.6 metres (64 feet 3 inches) and a comparison with old and new pictures shows her with greater overhangs fore and aft, producing a much more graceful vessel. After her lengthening she was rigged as a powerful stem head cutter. (This was then known as a 'slutter rig' – a name that had been condemned to yachting history.) The yacht was reputedly the largest yacht built by W. King & Sons; regardless, she remained a testament to her designer and the craftsmen of King's Wallasea Island yard. At eighty years old, *The Blue Peter* had recently had a total refurbishment at an Italian yacht yard under the ownership of Mathew Barker. She remained British flagged and continued to be registered in London. *The Blue Peter* was again sailing under the blue ensign, and the burgee of the Royal Corinthian Yacht Club graced her masthead, as it did in 1930. She was much loved, revered as a beauty wherever seen, serving in her role as a charter vessel, mainly around the Mediterranean.

Shaking his head and moving forward, with little thought, the skipper had tripped on a grass tussock. He'd slid into a soggy, mud-lined rut in the soft top of the sea wall and crashed down onto a knee. His bad knee ...

The W. King-built *The Blue Peter*, currently owned by Mathew Barker. The yacht was lengthened by King's a few years after her build for the then-owner, Desmond Molins. Courtesy of Mathew Barker.

'Damn!' he'd said, grimacing as he'd risen awkwardly. Flexing his gammy leg, he added wryly, 'Careful, boy ...' He'd felt quite cross with himself and could hear clearly his mate's admonishments ringing around his thoughts!

Looking out on the piece of ground before him, he saw that it had, when chosen, been well above sea level when it was the yacht yard. Now, it was obvious that spring tides inundated the site regularly, the skipper saw. The remains of a shed – well, the pillars that had once supported it – were still in place; but tides, marked by the their leavings of mixed vegetation matter and other detritus, showed that the land was well on its turn towards marsh. The remains were the yard's inshore building.

The yard's sheds, the skipper knew, had been more than typical garden varieties. They had been substantial affairs and there had been at least two. Boatyards always called them sheds – whatever their size. One had had an upper story, an office above a workshop. Another had been a big affair. It had had a removable side so that big yachts could be slid across from the top of the slipway on greasy side-ways for storage or work under cover. It had sat to the west of the slip and a large winch. *Moonbeam* had been one of the big yachts that used to be looked after by the yard. The remains of the slipway winch base and a heavily rusted ground chain – probably a tackle purchase point – sat in front of those pillars. The skipper had thought that another building had been sited inland from the big shed too ...

Beyond, the remnants of the yard's slipway ran out towards the river. The skipper saw that it had had a central carriageway, with outer ways with scalloped 'rails' either side. It ran, through a tangle of salt-tolerant grasses and sea purslane, away to the river's edge, where the skipper knew it had long ago been destroyed by time and the river. Next to a section of the central rail was a railcar. It was dislodged. On a closer inspection, the skipper saw that it had once been held in place by steelwork. It was,

Ferroconcrete yacht under construction at the yard in 1973, after King's had vacated the site. Note the winch and top of the slipway and 'cars' on the track ways. Compare with the earlier illustration showing the slip's remnants. Courtesy of M. Mellard & P. Pearson.

in many places, completely rusted away. The wood was, surprisingly, in an amazing state of preservation. The skipper had grinned and exclaimed, 'What industriousness those men had ...' marvelling with a huge grin too.

Looking beyond the ragged broken ends of the slipway, the skipper gazed for a while at the rippling waters that were by then rushing out. The tide had turned. The skipper knew that below the silt-laden flow sat the remains of a wharf. Some of its broken stumps poked above the surface, causing the tide to swirl, washing tendrils of wrack back and forth; it, tenacious stuff, was hanging on. He knew too that a barge-like vessel was down there ... 'They're all over this place ...' the skipper had thought, thinking of several barge remains a little further down river from his present position.

Gazing in that direction across the marsh, which looked golden in the afternoon sunlight, the skipper thought wryly of another visit here, again without the mate, when he had traipsed across a swathe of marsh to look at an old barge, the *Mundon* of Maldon. Her decks and sides had all but gone, 'Down to her light waterline, perhaps ...' he'd thought, for a bowsprit bobstay turning block was still attached to the gnarled and splintered stem, just above the mud. He'd thought, too, 'Her chines must be a good way down ... just short of a metre ...' There was a moraine of rotting wood and ironwork. Displayed among the sea-moss-covered mud and marsh was the old ship's rusting mast case, and close by was its attendant winch. Its spindles, with a rotted wooden barrel and gear wheels, had fallen off – the case's starboard side toothed main wheel was visible and poking out of the eroding bank of marsh. There were also the unmistakable cast-iron pipes of the patent bilge pumps fitted to these old craft, and the heavy forged iron strap knees that helped to bind the barge's structure together, when whole.

The skipper had been 'aboard' two other barges too. One, her bow, which was largely intact, showed from her woodwork that the poor thing had been abandoned long before her life was really finished. Her forward deck beams still had remains of white paint adhering and carefully carved inscriptions, such as 'Certified For Two Seamen' and 'Certified Sail Space' ... as fresh as the day they'd been carved. She was the *Harry* of London. The other, the *Argosy* of Rochester, had disintegrated down to her 'waterline' and at her stern, near the virtually intact remains of her rudder, was the remains of her chain steering mechanism. It was of a type no longer seen. On her port side, a leeboard winch sat where the deck had dropped onto her ceiling. Further forward was the mast case. It looked as if it were sitting waiting for her mast and new winch barrels to be fitted. Seeing old vessels in that manner, especially when their gear had been left in place, intrigued the skipper greatly. It took him back to his childhood, when he had been surrounded by decaying old sailormen, living aboard his active spritsail barge home. This old girl, though, was being battered by the river's waters: the marsh that had built up around her in previous years was by then being washed away, by river wash perhaps: this river had a large number of power craft zipping about, creating excessive wash disturbance.

The area where those vessels sat was now inaccessible to walkers, for they were beyond a section of sea wall realignment – part of a grand project for Wallasea Island: the sea was, at man's behest, having a large part of the island back. It had warmed the skipper's heart and tickled him immensely when he'd first learnt of it! The 'inning' of this land had begun back in the fourteenth century. That land had had to be substantially raised to current mudflat level, and a little higher still for marsh regeneration to establish itself

Remains of the spritsail barge *Harry* on Wallasea Island. This and the remains of two other barges, the *Argosy* and *Mundon*, are not now accessible to the general public as they sit within a section of land given back to the sea as part of the Wallasea coastal realignment project.

and then flourish. Further plans had been approved too. It involved shipping round the estuary material dug from tunnelling in London. It was similar material to that of the island's make-up. Huge quantities were needed to raise the island's inner land levels.

During all of that the skipper's gaze had fallen on the wreck – well, an abandoned hull of a yacht – which sat a little closer and was still accessible. The wreck, an old gentleman's yacht of the Edwardian era, had lain in the marshes for a considerable number of years. She was a narrow-gutted, finely shaped thing (a narrow beam for her length, and typical of the period). She was once a beautiful vessel and would have enhanced any waterfront of the period – 'Even now' the skipper had mused, looking at her with just a little affection.

Leaving the slipway of King's old yard, the skipper made his way out to the old ship. He knew that he would pass the 'other thing' he'd lost. In the marshes, to the east of the old boatyard, were a group of rapidly deteriorating oyster pits.

The outer edge of the marshes was being eaten away along the river's edge. The pits had been dug on what had been land that would not have been flooded during normal spring tides, yet when the skipper visited, the regular inundation was clear and its destructiveness very apparent. The salting edges had turned to a mud and sea-moss-covered terrain that ran in a gentle slope to join the mudflats before dropping rapidly into the river. The action of wash waves and such struck the skipper too.

The skipper walked round a couple of the pits, looking at them. Some still had intact sluices with plugs still in place. The sky's brightness made photography difficult, but none the less he'd recorded what he'd wanted to replace, murmuring into the strong wind, 'Some of this will be gone soon …'

That done, he'd carefully trodden a path towards the remains of the gentleman's yacht. 'Must be aware of damaging these delicate plants ...' he'd thought, and also 'Perhaps I should leave well alone ... I am being careful ...' The pull, though, to record was too great.

The yacht had always intrigued him. His first sighting of it had been back in the summer of 1980 when, with his mate, a fresher to yachting, they'd battled up the Swin against an easterly. They'd left late on the tide ... They'd had a 'spot of bother too ...' That, though, was described in Chapter One – something best remembered for the happy outcome. It had always, though, been something to inwardly reflect on ... and thank the Gods for a safe arrival, finally, in a safe haven. It had not been a glorious moment of the skipper's sailing life!

'Still fairly intact,' the skipper whispered. 'Much more of her planking has come away though ... frames are good ... just a rub down ... a fresh coat of paint ...' he thought whimsically, chortling immediately before grimacing at the thought of his mate hearing such words.

Many years before, the mate had been warned by somebody, the skipper couldn't remember whom, but he was sure it would have been one of his extended family: all wished to 'protect' the skipper's bride from any madness on his part, like buying an old barge ... It had been the time they'd been looking at boats and had ultimately bought their *Yachting World* People's Boat, built from the newfangled wooden material, plywood. Plywood had been greatly improved during the Second World War and it had great structural strength. The boat had been almost a vintage. She had been an excellent little vessel, which they'd both learnt to handle under sail alone ... The skipper had moved away while those memories had flowed through his roving mind.

A Victorian yacht lives on in the marsh, slowly decaying. This boat, photographed in 2008, had been in this, its last berth, probably, for nearly fifty years. Her sheer has remained true. Most of her frames are intact and below the mud she will be perfectly preserved ...

Coming to a stop at the edge of a rill in the marsh, he'd found an old skiff and had muttered, 'Maybe she was an oysterman's boat …' She was but a few ribs, rotting bottom planks and her gnarled transom showing clearly what she had been. She had the shapely girth of a sturdy working boat. In her transom was a deep scallop for a sculling oar. 'Look at that!' gasped the skipper. 'It's well worn …' He pictured the old boy who would have quietly gone about his work, an old battered pipe clamped in his jaw with puffs of strong tobacco wafting away downwind of him, day after day …

A more recent arrival lay beyond the two old craft he'd looked at. That one, though, hadn't been of interest.

Looking up at the weak early spring sun, well on its way down, and then at his watch to confirm his thoughts, the skipper realised that it was time to get a move on. He worked his way carefully across the marsh. It was at a height that rough grasses, when they could grow well, hid the underlying ground. Clumps of tangled yellowing tufts – trip hazards – were passed cautiously by. Reaching the wall, at a different place to that at which he'd made his way out, he found along its base a mass of timber baulks. The timbers had semicircular scallops carved down their lengths, 'They're from the old yard,' the skipper cried out, pulling a piece of mossy grass away to be sure. It was a fascinating find. 'Sat here for years, I shouldn't be surprised,' he'd thought. 'Long ago left here by a spring tide …'

With caution (the wall top was hideously uneven in that area), the skipper began his walk back upriver to his car. As he left the old yard behind him, he stopped briefly to retie a boot lace. It was at a bend in the wall. His view to the east was about to disappear, and regaining his upright posture and flexing his shoulders to settle his rucksack comfortably, the skipper had gazed eastwards again across the distant expanse of low flat land and said before turning away, 'It won't be long before the spoil starts coming down from London …' He'd grinned: not all people, sailors and landsmen alike, around these parts had applauded the decision to turn the greater part of that island into a bird reserve, part freshwater marsh, but on the whole back to the sea as a 'natural' wild marshland environment.

'It's a wonderful use for the spoil though,' the skipper had said to his mate earlier that year, when sailing on the river. From the waterside, eating a particularly nice lunch overlooking the water, they'd then gazed with awe at the then fairly recent smaller experimental project which, even after two very short years, had become a self-regulating tidal mudflat and marsh habitat. (The skipper had heard since then though that the birds had not arrived in a denseness of numbers as was expected. 'All in good time …' he'd mused.)

The mate had continued to look at the skipper over the top of her newspaper, awaiting his next pronouncement. The skipper had then exclaimed, 'At last! … Man's common sense has prevailed!' The mate's eyebrows had risen up: not all the river's users had agreed with it, especially among the Burnham-on-Crouch crowd, and before she'd been able to speak what had been on her mind, the skipper had shouted, 'Wheat to wetland!'

'Calm down …' she'd muttered before adding, 'Where's it going to come from … The spoil, I mean?'

'From the Cross-Rail project – from London – first good use for London's rubbish …' the skipper had said, laughing, raucously, while his mind had fooled with one of his pet subjects: other people's rubbish tended to set him off.

That was all a while ago, though. He'd shrugged and set off again, head bowed into the wind, intent on the distant marina. Before reaching his target, he'd stopped by an inset into the sea wall to look over a huge conglomeration of old timber floats. Some had sunk by the look of them. Waterlogging had probably reached the point where it had overcome the wood's natural buoyancy, especially with the huge amount of metal in their make-up. It couldn't have helped.

'What were they, you may ask?' the skipper murmured as he'd set off again, fighting against a wind that tugged and frapped at his coat – though the sunshine was warm on the cheeks. The skipper knew, though, that he would have some windburn later … He pulled his hat down harder.

Continuing his walk, a conversation, pure fiction of course, came to mind. But it would have taken place had the mate been with him … That he knew from long experience.

'What were they?'

'Well, they're cats'

'Come on. What the devil are they?'

'They're probably old dockyard cats …'

'Yes, but what are they though?' she would have implored, shaking her head: she'd be none the wiser.

'Let me finish,' grinning at the mate's impatience. 'They were used as fenders between moored ships – to keep them apart.'

'Oh, I see.' She would have said, her head nodding gently, remembering the skipper's days tied up to a dockyard wall or alongside another grey-painted vessel.

Grinning, and continuing to heed his mate's final words of earlier that day and watching his footing, he'd dropped down from the top of the sea wall and traversed the last part out of the biting wind.

Later, back at home, flushed and thoroughly warmed, he waited for his mate's return. While setting the table for their evening meal, she'd clattered through the door, calling, 'Did … Did you have a good time?' Then she'd tentatively asked, 'You were careful …?' before saying, 'Come on, tell …'

'Oh yes …' The skipper paused, and added, 'We'll have to sail back there some time … There's more to poke around …'

'Why?' the mate quipped and pausing briefly added, 'Not likely.'

'Oh!'

'Well …' She was grinning impishly. 'Not too soon, anyway,' she said with some hesitation. And, after a moment, she added, 'Well, maybe we'll go round into the Roach.' Her head was gently nodding, as if affirming her words. 'It's nice round there … Yolksfleet and the Havengore …'

The skipper saw that she was actually deep in thought!

'Yes please, I'd like that. I liked it round there!'

The mate, the skipper remembered, after their last visit had stated, quite emphatically: 'The Crouch is not my favourite river … Well, downstream anyway!'

He'd grinned at her, thinking, 'Was that a softening of her heart?' but said nothing.

The skipper had enjoyed his poke around. It had been just a little walk alongside the banks of a mud-edged, silt-laden river. It was on land that had had a long history of battles against the sea. It was a land that was littered by man's old ships: a little old yacht yard, many of whose progeny still sailed the world's seas.

Just One or Two …

Across the narrow channel from the little clinker yacht, along the edge of the saltings, tangled strands of yellow-flowered sea purslane were being gently caressed by soft, silken tresses, the flower heads of cord grass, waving as the lethargic breeze played with them, teasingly, on a hot, sultry afternoon.

The breeze, barely enough to flick the burgee, had hardly ruffled the water's surface between the yacht and mud edge lying close by. It was a surface that seemed liquid silver in the afternoon's brightness to the mate, who was sat propped up on cushions beneath the cockpit awning. The mate had looked up with a start: she'd awoken from a brief doze and her book, with her fingers entwined in a few pages, surprisingly, still lay snugly in her lap. She closed her book and smiled. She saw that the tide had risen markedly since her last look marshwards. She saw, too, the skipper in his lug-sailed dinghy, tucked down and masked behind the gunnels, slowly making his way back towards her: in the distance a tan sail had emerged from the marshes. She smiled. She knew he would be bubbling with excitement. 'He's just a little boy really …' she murmured, her smile becoming sweeter by the moment.

He'd gone off, some two hours before, ignoring the apparent openness upstream towards Old Hall Creek and its marshes, some recently let back to the sea too, and Boles Creek to poke deeply into a marshland channel, a twisted finger he knew that ran this way and that from Woodrolfe Creek as soon as it had begun to fill on the fresh flood. The creek ran up to a marina, trapped, between half tides, behind a sill near its head. There the creek turned sharply and ran further along the natural high tide edge. Beyond that upper part, stretching eastwards was an extensive panorama of open marsh, where yachts sat snugly in mud berths around its fringes.

They'd sailed into this place earlier. It was one of two channels off the Quarters, the quaint name given to the channels that seeped inland around the western side of Mersea Island. Those channels, though, ran in a generally westward direction before heading north. A light southerly had allowed them to creep, lazily, on the last of the ebb, past channel buoys that had lolled awkwardly, as if drunk even: they were without sufficient bottom weight to hold them upright. Murky water, being passed by, had become fingers of sandy mud that had glistened in the sunshine. The skipper, remembering the channel from many previous visits, had 'allowed' the boat feel her way. They'd passed a stationary yacht, stuck fast. She'd had the look of a deep 'keeler', far deeper than their own shallow-draft, centre-board sloop. The skipper had said, 'They'll be alright – bottom's soft – the ebb's about done too.'

'I remember … We have to keep close to that shingle bank,' the mate had said, looking across at her smiling skipper.

'Yes, that's where we cut across when the tide's up – to the west of it!'

Anyway, it wasn't long before the dinghy had closed with the quietly anchored yacht. The fresh flood was, by then, nearly half done. It was running at its fastest and the skipper saw that it created a miniature wash at the stem as it flowed innocuously by. Little else affected it. The mate filled the kettle and lit the gas, then watched as the dinghy slowly ranged alongside. It kissed the fenders softly and the skipper tied off the painter and lowered the sail. It had been quickly stowed. She watched as the skipper had wound the sheet round the sail and its two varnished spars, before unshipping the rudder and dagger board. At that point she'd heard the beginnings of a whistle, then the more strident 'I'm boiling' song of the kettle.

'Ah, tea,' the skipper had enthused as he alighted deftly from the dinghy, ranging it astern of them.

He'd started before any question had been asked … 'There's a barge – well, hulk actually …'

'I would never have guessed,' the mate said teasingly.

The skipper grinned. It was a grin the mate had seen many times and loved …

'I crept in with the tide' he said, bubbling with excitement. 'All along the mud line there were audible pops emanating from worm and crab holes as the water reached them. I just let the tide take me …'

'I love that sound,' the mate said, 'on a quiet day – like on our home mud mooring.'

'The tide was edged with a froth of dried mud. Scud! It's like soap suds. I watched as it crept up the shallow sloping mud banks until the dinghy moved on. When the dinghy stopped, more scud collected around me, until it escaped before I moved again

'… tipped the dinghy …' Drawn by Mrs G. D. Ardley.

... The tide was visibly rising upwards ... all the time. It's amazing to watch at close quarters ... Like a miniature estuary. I poled the dinghy along the tortuous channel, though by the time I left I sailed out. I'd tipped the dinghy over onto her bilges to slide round the bends,' he said laughing, as the mate had glared at him briefly!

She had said nothing, but looked lovingly across the cockpit table, spread with their afternoon tea. She thought, but had not said, 'He's in one of those moods ... He's about to start ...' But he'd already started!

Since passing out their tea, the mate's book, held covetously in one hand, had remained closed. It was carefully, reverentially almost, put down. She slowly poured the skipper's tea, taking her time, enjoying the skipper's long pause. She'd chosen to have a cool drink, not understanding her skipper's penchant for a hot beverage in the heat. Even though she knew he was right in his assertion that a hot drink, and tea in particular, had an extraordinary cooling effect on the body. The tea poured, the skipper was away again.

'There's a myriad of hulks,' the skipper said. 'Old craft, barely recognisable, except for one ...' His eyes had glazed over, a little, as if deep in thought. 'I knew straight away,' he said, pausing.

'What?'

'The barge in there was ... no, is the *Saltcote Belle*.'

'Oh yes ...'

The skipper believed all of these old ladies kept their names until their last rotting timbers had departed from the surface. Even then, their graves would contain their bottoms for a great many years. The bottoms were constructed of English elm attached

Off Woodrolfe Creek sit the sad, rotting remains of a once graceful lady. She's the *Saltcote Belle*, 49nrt, built by Howard in Maldon in 1895, and was originally the mill barge from Saltcote Mill, near Heybridge. Abandoned in 1985, she slumbers in peace as time and tide do their work ... Photographed in 2004.

to oak floors with oak trenals (treenails – wooden nails). Elm, in particular, was a particularly durable wood, if kept wet. The skipper had known that barge from an earlier period of his life and his heart had missed a beat on seeing her as he'd found her. She'd always looked resplendent – her sides painted, yacht-like, in black and grey.

'Her stern has collapsed. It's very badly rotted. Some pipe work still ran below her sagging decks ... Main hatch had dropped, though. But the mast deck was still up high – be the struts beneath – holding it all up – for now.' He paused, then added, 'I couldn't get past at first – some debris stopped me!'

'Don't forget your tea ...' the mate interjected.

'No!' And picking his cup up, absently, he continued, 'The top of her stem seemed rarely to be immersed by spring tides. Her windlass bitt heads seemed new – well, they were before the old girl was abandoned. They've collapsed recently.' He took a pull from his mug and followed it with a mouthful of cake, working quickly to free his tongue. More tea helped. Spitting crumbs, he added, 'Her fore hold hatch was still in place – it looked weird – had a layer of mud on its top, like cake icing drooping around the edges – oozing fresh cream even! The forward end has dropped down with the collapsed fo'c'sle deck – you know – where you used to "go below" on the *May Flower*. Beams have given way ...'

The mate had nodded. 'How long has she been there?' she asked, trying to remain interested, but generally not sharing her skipper's fascination with the ghostly rotting remains he was always so diligent in finding in various waterways around the estuary.

After looking thoughtful for awhile, he said, 'About twenty years ... I think,' but with some hesitation. When the skipper had first seen the hulk she'd been abandoned for around nineteen years. He'd been trying to find her for several years before that though. The skipper then said, grinning broadly, 'There's another round here. She's up the next finger.'

The *Memory*, 65nrt, built at Harwich by Cann, 1904, as seen in 2004. She was abandoned in the marshes off Woodrolfe Creek after a fire below while being used as an accommodation barge by The Fellowship Afloat organisation, based on the old lightship moored on Tollesbury Marsh. She was abandoned around 1990.

'Oh, right ...' she said. 'More tea ...?'

'She's the *Memory*,' he said, as if ignoring the mate's question about tea. Then he added, 'Yes please, it's been a thirsty afternoon ...'

'Didn't she belong to the Christian outward bound lot on the lightship?'

'Yes!'

He remained quiet, thinking. It had seemed a long time but wasn't. The old barge had been used for accommodation. Before that she had belonged to a trust that had originally set out to keep a barge trading in the carriage of goods and not as a charter barge, as was the employ of the remaining few sailormen, but after an accident the barge was declared unfit for purpose. That story had been told in *A Fair Wind for London*, by John Kemp. The trust eventually became the East Coast Sail Trust. The trust acquired the *Thalatta* after her cargo days were over and she was re-rigged around 1966, making use of some of the gear from the *Memory*: her sailing days were finished – a surveyor had condemned her structure – well, her floors (bottom frames). For many years following her reincarnation the *Thalatta* was used to take thousands of schoolchildren around the East Coast, giving them a taste of the trading routes, and of the workings of a barge. However, by 2005 it had become acutely apparent that time had caught up with the old girl. Her hull and structure were rotting away. Repairs were needed; those were initially to be dealt with in a large refit. As was usual with old barges, this spiralled uncontrollably into a major rebuild – the only way to deal with an old barge after a hundred years of life, bearing in mind that most were not expected to go beyond fifty. During 2008 the rebuild of the *Thalatta* had stalled, funding had run dry and she had languished at St Osyth on her steel pontoon, her fate in other people's hands. Additional heritage funding during 2009, thankfully, allowed the work to continue: her last forty years have been honourable indeed. 'And, too, she's a worthy cause,' the skipper thought. By August 2011 the barge had been relaunched.

The finger the skipper was talking about had moorings round its inland perimeter and he'd run the dinghy in for a look after leaving the other hulk. On the way in he'd been hailed by a familiar voice. From the cockpit of a powerful Sadler yacht, the face of a club colleague grinned avidly across the water at him. The hail rang out again: 'Come on over ...' Across the quiet water it had sounded loud and out of place. With the sail lowered, a few swift strokes on the oars quickly brought the dinghy alongside and before the skipper knew it, a glass of wine was being proffered. They'd sat chatting for a while, well a long while. It was this in fact that had taken up the bulk of the skipper's time away from the mate, but she hadn't known that!

Upon bidding his leave, the skipper had rowed over to the old barge, climbed onto the marsh and carefully worked round to the *Memory*'s forward end, taking care of his footfalls to avoid wanton damage to the marsh plants. Her sides were by then riddled with rot. The rot, damage typically from repeated crushing, would probably have been due to regular sliding through lock gates at Ipswich and the London docks during her long trading days. Her rudder had caused the old girl's stern post to fracture: the rudder had dug into the bank and the barge had slid a little as she'd settled. Strangely, her hatches were still covered by the remnants of tired green tarpaulins.

'As I departed,' the skipper said, 'I rested on the oars briefly and said, "Shame ... But your fate has been no different to many others ..." Then I sailed away.'

The *Memory* by 2010. Twenty years after being abandoned, her hull remains virtually intact, but her tired fastenings show signs of fatigue. Soon her rotting timbers will collapse.

The skipper had then remained quiet. A contemplative look had spread over his face, though. The mate had grimaced slightly. Wanting to get back to her book, she asked, 'More tea?' adding, 'There's a drop left.'

'Err, yes. Yes please,' the skipper said, adding what was to be one final comment, a comment that had come from his short contemplation. 'They're … just one or two … of many.'

'Yes … Yes, I know!' the mate interjected, firmly, before draining the pot into the skipper's mug and adding, 'I'm going to finish this book now … Quiet!'

Grinning, the skipper had added, cheekily, 'Then have a nap!' They both laughed as she had leant over and ruffled his hair. The skipper settled contentedly with his book. Briefly, as he opened it, he'd thought, 'The mate's had enough … For now.'

A silence then shrouded the cockpit. That was, apart from the intermittent gentle flip and flap of the ensign hanging loosely from its staff. In the quiescence it wasn't long before the skipper's eyes had closed … his mind remembering a host of things … back to the 1960s … his childhood years. Was he asleep though?

The skipper had fond recollections: many years before, he'd witnessed the *Saltcote Belle* sailing in the Thames and Medway barge matches. He'd watched her on this river too, up at Maldon. She'd sail up past the strand to berth at the Hythe, under sail alone. He'd knelt on the decks of the *May Flower*, leaning on her rails, as a nine-year-old.

The *Memory* too was a feature of the skipper's childhood. There had been only one survivor from that age which had sailed regularly over the intervening years. She was the *Marjorie*. Another, the *Henry*, had been refurbished, but rarely sailed. Seeing her during 2009 at Standard Quay up Faversham Creek, the skipper was saddened by the look of neglect that pervaded her decks. Her sails were ragged and her rigging was weathered and slack. She'd looked forlorn.

A watcher would have seen the skipper stir, but he wasn't awake ... And too, a faint smile etched his face.

There was about to be another resurgent spritsail barge. The *Edith May*. Her spars had recently been shipped aboard, her gear raised, striking the sky, proudly, where her fluttering bob crackled in the breeze. And, 'She's been measured for a new suit of sails,' he'd heard.

The skipper had visited the old dock where the old barge had been ensconced during her decade of rebuilding to look her over. She sat afloat: the tide was in. The dock was open to the wide mere, a shallow sea that was fed from the River Medway beyond. At her berth, the echoes of her fluttering bob as it crackled in the breeze could be heard as they rebounded off the ancient stone walls of the waterside church that sat close by.

The skipper was still smiling, the mate saw, yet seemingly still in another little world. 'His own little world,' she silently thought.

'Sailors ... along ... along the barge coast ... will see her ... in sail again ...' the skipper had murmured. 'She'll ... she'll make a grand sight,' his shallow voice had quivered too.

Barely awake, becoming alert, he'd stuttered: the mate heard him. 'For now ... vessels have escaped ... fate of those two in the marshes ...' and rubbing his eyes he'd then murmured, '... For now ...' as he became aware of his mate's look cast fondly in his direction from her position, as she lay back on her cushions, across the cockpit.

The mate was smiling gently at him. She closed her book and said, 'You've been mumbling ... again. Good dream was it?'

Across the cockpit he watched as his mate had swung her legs down to sit up from her cushions. He saw that her eyes had twinkled, mischievously. A thought occurred to him, 'She just doesn't understand ... She thinks I'm daft ...' He'd remained silent, it was best, while all the time gazing back at her with more than a modicum of wry bemusement – pity even!

The *Memory* in her prime off Leigh-on-Sea, taking part in the 1964 Southend-on-Sea barge match. She was then operated as a trust barge endeavouring to continue freighting. The project failed. Courtesy of Keith and Marian Patten, from an original print by Leslie G. Arnold.

Walloped in the Wallet

The mate was sat back against the cabin bulkhead, resting comfortably on some cushions. Her eyes were firmly engaged in traversing the pages and eating up the words of the novel that was propped in her lap. The skipper was watching her. He too was sat back in the cockpit … His gaze moved out across the placid calm. It was so quiet that the soft gurgles of the last of the ebb as it flowed sluggishly past the clinker lands of the yacht's shapely hull seemed to sing a song to the skipper. The yacht was sat, resting, tethered to her anchor in Yolksfleet Creek. Across the uncovered mudflats on either side of the yacht the sea walls rose from a fringe of salt marsh that looked almost hazy in the late afternoon warmth. Along the sea wall top, long straw-coloured grass waved gently as it was caressed by the soft air, and the simplistic wavy lines often drawn by artists to indicate rising heat displayed themselves: the stems of taller grasses seemed as if to wriggle in the heat-laden atmosphere. The burgee was all but limp; the dinghy's trailing ribbon pennant curled and flicked gently …

Looking up and speaking, the mate disturbed the skipper's thoughts, cutting off the trail that was weaving in his mind. It made a change! She'd said, 'It'll be like this … when we sail down the coast to the Swale … won't it?' It came with a slight stutter. Their plan had been to depart from that idyllic spot and make a passage down the Swin and across the estuary to the East Swale, or the Medway.

The skipper hadn't immediately answered. How could he tell? And in any case, a skylark was singing from some point, high above them … Watching its nest, perhaps. Finally, after a lengthy interval that had seemed to the mate as if he'd been ignoring the question, he'd said, emphatically, 'I hope so!' adding, 'We do need a breeze though …' looking inquisitively at her, yet inwardly knowing the question's reason.

'But it won't be like the Wallet will it?' implored the mate, losing a little colour in the memory of it.

'We won't go,' he said gently, with a quiet firmness that he hoped would reassure his mate.

'It was bad,' she said, looking serious. She was referring to a recent passage down the Wallet that had started in sublime sailing conditions, even if it they'd needed to do it in two legs out towards the Gunfleet Sands. A chunk in the middle had been 'Bloody'.

Reflecting, he'd chuckled. 'Yes,' he said. 'Even for me it was bad.'

The mate had nodded and smiled wryly – her skipper admitting something … 'There's a thing,' she thought!

Nothing was said for a while. It was as if both were deep in thought, dozing.

Yes, the skipper had become quite concerned at the rapid deterioration they had found at the lower half of the Wallet on that particular passage. It had been wind over tide, of course. The wind, forecasted to be nothing more than a gentle south-westerly three or four, became a vicious five to six, gusting more, he'd felt, whipping up a horrendous melee.

The Wallet could be likened to a wide venturi between the Gunfleet Sands and the Tendring coastline. It is wider at its northern end, into which the tide pours, whereupon it becomes squeezed. As it approaches the narrower southern end, a faster running flow spews out over the Colne Bar and Eagle shoals, and strikes the northern edge of the Buxey Sand, whereupon it spills into the rivers Blackwater and Colne. It sluices out across the Dengie Flats too, but before reaching the Dengie it deeply scours the bottom, hard to the Buxey edge, creating a deep hole, the Swire Hole. With all of these difficulties, it was a latent menace. All East Coast sailors had had some experience of its nastier side. The whole area, with the swatchway across the tails of the Buxey and Gunfleet sands, was a tidal gateway for vessels departing and arriving from all manner of places up and down the coast.

The skipper murmured to himself, softly, 'Even on a calm day the runs and swirls are impressive … Water becomes coloured by millions of sand particles … boiling like jam nearing its setting point.' They'd both recently 'admired' those forces in action – when all had combined to make life a misery. It was a tempering reminder to the two sailors of the uncontrolled fury that lay within the waters: given the chance, they could be hideous. He was aware of the mate's eyes upon him.

'Yes,' he said, with some gravity, gazing across the cockpit, 'That day was something else … It didn't go on forever.' Very quickly, his voice had lightened considerably, he'd continued, 'It was only part of the passage … It was a relatively short part too …' He stopped; he had a penchant for understatement! The mate was looking at him … 'But boy, it bashed us about,' he'd added quickly. Grinning wryly at his mate, he'd said, 'It was the worst passage we've ever had, too.'

That, from the skipper, was music to the mate's ears. She thought, 'That's twice in a few moments …'

It took a lot for the skipper to admit he'd had a bad passage. But, as they'd both agreed at the time, it was a case of knuckle down and get on with it. To the skipper, the episode was as vivid to him as the present, quiet solitude that surrounded him would be in his mind later. Both were worth savouring – for different reasons …

On the day of their poor passage, they'd left the Walton Backwaters with a useful south-westerly on their starboard quarter. The previous evening's forecast had been good. They'd looked forward to a pleasant and untroubled sail down to the Blackwater areas. The mood was amiable. The mate had never had a penchant for the coastal side of sailing and always felt a little uncomfortable at the start, before quickly settling. The skipper knew this and gave her the helm on that short leg down the buoyed channel. It kept her busy.

Nearing the outer red buoy that marked the tail of the charted drying spit, the skipper took the helm and edged over and in some two metres brought the boat round onto a southerly course to clear the Naze. That tack, hardened further onto the wind once clear of the Naze shallows, took them across the Wallet towards the Gunfleet's old tower. While on that passage the mate had made bacon sandwiches – she wasn't too enamoured by hers though, watching with a little disgust as the skipper had enjoyed his with customary gusto.

A forecast came out across the VHF radio. It was from the coastguard station, not more than a few miles across the water, and visible too. They had both listened, intently. It concurred with the earlier words from the local radio station.

'Not another forecast from La La Land,' the mate had chirped, smiling and adding, 'I hope …!'

The mate, the skipper had seen, seemed to be content though. He'd not responded to her light-hearted, but for that season apt, comment. They were going well and it had been easy and comfortable sailing up to that point, so they'd chatted, as was the way.

Later, closing the Wallet channel buoys, the Essex Skillinger smack *Pioneer* crossed their bow. She was on a long fetch down to somewhere off Clacton. They'd watched as a youngster had danced on the bobstay, catching wave splashes with 'his' feet. The skipper had said, cheerily, as they'd cleared the fine old (new: how much was there of the original?) vessel, 'We'll hold this until we can see the sands … and follow in her path …' at which the mate had immediately peered at the chart, sending an indignant look his way.

Looking up from the chart and looking around, she said, 'Is it me … but isn't it lumpier out here …' The skipper smiled. He'd known that. He'd felt the greater heave earlier, but had chosen to say nothing. They were well on their way … a few miles from halfway.

Looking at the chart himself, the skipper thought, 'That's a long leg in towards the Clacton shore … clear the point … bear away for the Nass … much as we thought discussing it earlier …' He'd looked at his mate, grinned and said, 'The Wallet's renowned for that …' Little did he know, but the Wallet was about to wipe away that eminent grin!

It hadn't been long before the skipper had called out, 'Ready about …' and soon after settling the boat on her new course, the mate had begun another trick at the helm.

Looking around them they saw that a huge number of craft were either on a leg out towards them sailing, or hugging the shore going along under power. The other thing that had become noticeable was the waves. They had been fairly slight, but had begun to progressively build up somewhat and were beginning to break along their crests, leaving streams of stringy white froth.

As yet the froth wasn't being blown by the wind, the skipper saw. 'Tidal forces,' he'd thought, thinking of the power of nature and its penchant, given a chance, to humble man.

Some distance down that leg it had become obvious that the mate's apprehension was well placed. The sea had built up appreciably. The troughs were still long, but the peaks were breaking nicely … The skipper had made a decision. He'd said, with a serious tone, 'I'm going to put a reef in the main – we're going along well – well over halfway,' but smiling had added, 'No need to press her …'

'Clip on …' the mate had said, quickly, with some earnestness too.

'I am.' He'd smiled, too.

'Too right you are …'

'Excellent ship's safety officer, I love you!' The skipper had thought, as he'd gone forward, while the mate eased the main sheet to feather the sail. The reef had soon been accomplished. A few seasons earlier, they'd changed from roller to slab reefing and since then, reefing had been so much simpler and the sail set superbly too. Other people had suggested that perhaps they should think about a roller headsail too …

Back aft, the skipper and mate had had a short discussion on the deteriorating conditions. It was getting very lumpy. Turning back had been mentioned as a resort, but dismissed. Waves were by then seen to be breaking too and spume was drifting and being whipped away by the wind. The wind though, although it had freshened, was not particularly strong. Later it became more gusty. It was the motion more than anything, at that point. 'Look,' the skipper had finally said, voicing an earlier thought, 'We'll tack once we're past Clacton pier … get to weather of the bar … then bear away for the Nass.' The mate had nodded, it was a passage made so often before, but the skipper saw that she was far from content. Concentrating, she'd continued gamely at the helm.

As they made progress on that leg, which was quite rapid, they'd watched the antics of other yachts around them too. Some were big vessels in comparison to themselves … all were shipping water across their bows, as they were from time to time. Water regularly sluiced down the side deck too as steep rollers ran by. The skipper had begun to consider that – though there was still a reef left to put in the mainsail, the boat wasn't being pressed.

Spray had gone beyond merely an occasional hazard; it was almost constant, shimmering in the sunshine as it streamed across the decks: the sun still shone! The mate's face, though, had long lost its shine. The skipper had grimaced from time to time, but it must be said, both had developed grim looks. The mate had gone quiet too, a bad sign, her colour had become wintery-looking – pale – yellow even. The skipper had begun to work hard at being cheerful. They'd plugged on. The greater distance outside had been accomplished.

At some stage the mate had made a comment about the windmills, a wind turbine farm, which was springing up like a sea of daffodils along the run of the Gunfleet Sand. Some were bare stalks, some higher than others, a few had their seed-pod-like turbine gear houses; of those, a sprinkling had their petal-like blades attached.

The skipper remarked jovially, 'They'll be up and running next summer …'

The mate had nodded, and after staring out across the water at them for a while longer said, 'Gives the impression of land enclosing us on both sides – sort of comforting – yet knowing it does nothing to quell the raging forces that are locked up in this Wallet …' The skipper had nodded. Another crew earlier that season had made a similar observation. It was just a short time after her last comment that the mate had suddenly cried out, 'I don't like this.' She'd then said, 'I don't want this …' with a look that screamed, 'Can't I go home …?'

The skipper had squeezed his mate's arm and smiled warmly, hoping to comfort her, and murmuring, in a manner borne of years of togetherness, said, 'We're doing fine … do you remember the time you sang to me …?' A hint of a smiled briefly washed across her face.

The skipper had taken over the helm as they'd passed some distance to seaward of Clacton Pier. Soon after he'd tacked, they were on their last leg away from the shore and the skipper had had to concentrate on nursing the boat through some boiling water with steep, nasty lumps coming out of nowhere.

The mate was looking over the cabin top, on the up side of the cockpit – the skipper hadn't liked her position – he'd mentioned it – but she was always happier there. 'Look at those ... waves...' she'd shouted. Her voice had trailed off rapidly as she'd seen some craft, away to leeward and seaward of themselves, rising and crashing over some more rollers to briefly disappear in the spume. Astern of them the dinghy, on a long line, dived between the waves.

Then it had happened; their boat had been walloped by several short, steep walls of water that had appeared from nowhere. The boat was thrown awry. She'd almost stopped dead. Water sluiced along the lee deck and spewed into the cockpit. Not a good thing! The mate had yelped loudly, in horror, as the grasp she'd had on her handholds were severed. She had then been thrown bodily across the cockpit. She struck the coaming – hard, the skipper had seen. She'd crumpled into the corner, hurt, but safe from further movement. From below there'd been a crash and the tinkling of breaking glass.

'Hold on!' the skipper had shouted, putting an arm out, to reassure her, 'I'll just steady the boat and I'll be with you,' he said affectionately and firmly. The boat had needed attention; she was the skipper's first priority.

'I'm alright ...' came a strangled cry, 'Really I am ...' It was obvious she wasn't.

'She's being very brave,' the skipper thought. 'Where's it hurt?' he'd asked, looking at her keenly before casting his eyes briefly below, too, thinking, 'Nothing much amiss there ...'

'She struck the coaming – hard ...' Drawn by Mrs G. D. Ardley.

'My side … my bottom …' she'd stuttered, not knowing whether to cry. 'But nothing seems to be broken.' She winced and then grimaced, her eyes on the skipper. He'd felt the look keenly too.

'Good!' The skipper paused. He'd looked round towards the tall cardinal buoy that marked the Eagle shoal, then earnestly at his mate. 'Five minutes more and we'll tack for the Nass …' He stopped, and then grinned at her: she'd started to sing. They were special – cheer-up songs. 'What a girl …' he'd thought, 'cheering me up – when she's the one that's hurt …' It was then that he'd realised that a little earlier he'd had more than a heightened feeling of anxiety. 'You're going to be black and blue,' he'd said, grinning at her.

'That's better,' she'd said. 'We're alright …' Then the mate had smiled… 'I always bruise badly … you know that … I'm alright … can you carry on for a while?'

'Yes, just sit there. We're coming round soon.' And he'd added, 'There's some broken glass on the cabin sole – think it's a lamp glass – must have been the bouncing. I'll clear it up later …' The mate had nodded, affirming her understanding.

It wasn't long before that moment, the moment to tack, had been reached. Bringing the boat round, the skipper had immediately eased the sheets to settle the game little sloop onto her new tack. She, the boat, found this eased course a little more comfortable – as did her occupants. Looking astern, the skipper had seen that the dinghy was up on a plane. A foaming wash seethed under her airborne forefoot. The skipper had, it should be said, looked at the little boat from time to time during the previous two hours – there she had always been, tugging gamely at her painter!

They'd soon crossed the Colne Bar; its buoy lay to seaward of them, bent to the forces of tide swirling around it. The skipper had seen the satnav show a reading of over eight and a half knots … He hadn't said anything. The mate hadn't noticed either event. She was, though, by then looking around and taking an interest in the world around her again. The motion had eased appreciably, the lean had gone from the boat and the waves, flatter, were more or less on their beam. Shortly after, the mate, bless her, had suddenly said, 'Look, I'll take her now …'

The skipper had not wanted her to do another a trick – it wasn't necessary. He'd looked at her earnestly, while easing the sheets a little further. 'Are you sure?' he'd said, looking at her earnestly again. Her colour, he saw, had returned a little. He smiled at her, but before he could add something on his mind, the mate had made a move.

'Come on – you've been at the helm for longer than you should – I want to – it's only fair … You get some of those cereal bars … keep our hunger pangs at bay …' and she continued to ease herself into a position on the windward side, to helm. The skipper generally preferred the leeward side. He relinquished the tiller after briefing her on their position, required direction and boats around …

'Food,' he'd thought, 'she must be feeling a little better – wasn't sick though …' and said, 'Food, yes that'll be good,' and briefly disappeared below to fetch the tub and clear the shattered lamp glass.

The mate, it was obvious, hadn't taken on board that they'd passed the Colne Bar, because, strangely, she said, 'When do we cross the bar …?'

The skipper had looked at her, inquisitively, before saying, 'It was ages ago … that's the Bench Head,' pointing to a buoy that was reeling in the distance away off their port quarter.

'Oh, right ... I wondered ...'

'We'll be off the Nass in a short while.' So they were. Their buoyant home had become progressively more comfortable as the water flattened and the wind had taken off further.

Soon the Nass was passed, at what had seemed a fantastic speed, and the wave from a passing powered craft barely caused more than the usual scrunching of the clinker planks as they'd met the water. It had been music to their ears. The skipper readied the mainsail ties and at a prompt to the mate, he'd gone forward to the mast. At a nod from him, she'd rounded into the wind and he'd quickly doused the sail. It was soon stowed securely. The boat's speed was immediately slashed and Cob Marsh Island had no longer seemed to be rearing up at them as quickly.

Closing with the tail of Cob Marsh Island, the skipper had started the engine and said, 'I'll stow the jib and set the boathook mooring line ... Engage when you're ready.' His jobs were soon done. Moving on down the line of moorings under power, the skipper, from his position on the cabin top, soon spied an empty buoy between Cob Marsh and Packing Marsh islands; pointing to it, the skipper said, 'Round up and come back – I'll do the hooking.' He'd seen the mate's nod.

Soon after putting their own line to the buoy and completing the tidying of the sails, the mate had called, 'Soup! Come and have it now ... while it's still hot ...'

'What a wonderful person you are ...' the skipper had murmured quietly upon entering the cabin, his senses savouring hot soup. He'd also seen the first real smile from his mate for nigh on two hours, or so. It cheered him. The smile hadn't disarmed him, though: his eyes had seen that the mate had furtively shovelled something away ... Another odour attacked his nostrils. Softly smiling, his eyes sending messages, he'd said soothingly, 'What's that smell?' Another, more bitter and tangy even, rose above the soup's pleasing aroma. Then a realisation had hit him, right between the eyes. That odoriferous pungency – it had been a bruise ointment ... The mate had said nothing ... So that was what he'd seen her slipping away ... it was an embrocation. 'You're bruised,' he'd said quietly ... kicking himself for 'forgetting' the earlier incident ... and as he'd taken his seat opposite her, he'd added, 'It was the fall ...'

'Yes. A bit ...' she'd said, her lips puckering, ever so slightly, as she'd answered both questions, then, smiling thinly as a tear had welled, she'd quickly said, 'That was bloody awful ...' adding, 'Here, come on, let's have our soup ...' The skipper had apologised ... commiserated and much else besides ...

'Ah yes ...' the skipper murmured softly, slowly coming to, and thinking, 'She'd not been referring to the soup either ...' He rubbed his eyes and looked across at his dozing mate: she remembered that day all too clearly ... and looking around at the gentle backdrop of Yolksfleet as it framed them, it was hard to believe in such sails. The pacific breeze, which still had in it barely enough strength to flutter the dinghy's blue masthead ribbon, hardly ruffled the water's languid surface. The skipper murmured again: the mate heard him, 'Ah yes,' he'd repeated, 'that baffling Wallet ...' He paused and stuttered, 'Hmm ... yes ... we were ...' as he'd looked across at his mate, locking eyes as hers had fluttered open, and had added, '... Walloped in the Wallet ...'

Follies in the Marsh?

'Ah yes ... There's ...' the skipper had murmured as the mate worked her way aft, having set the yacht's big Genoa, '... there's those things I was telling you about ...' They were leaving Maldon behind ... It was after they'd spent a sleepy couple of days parked in a mud berth up alongside the town's pretty hythe. The town was a place often visited, by sea or road: it had an aura, something special. And it had yet to become twee.

'What's that ...?' the mate had quipped as she'd stepped into the cockpit. 'Hold on ... Let me adjust the sheet ... Now, what are you warbling about?'

The skipper had grinned; his eyes sparkled. 'In the marsh over there ...' the skipper said, pointing towards Northey Island as his voice had trailed away. His mind had flitted to the set of the sails, though, and he'd eased the headsail sheet a little more, for he was steering round Herring Point – almost on a free run before a pleasant and warm south-westerly air. Beyond the hard sea-walled nose at Herring Point was the Heybridge wetland reserve, set among disused gravel diggings that ran back towards the old village of Heybridge a mile to the north-west. The skipper's thoughts dwelt upon the point for a short while, watching too that they were in sufficient water: they were punching the last of the flood. He briefly mused about the ship breaker that had used the 'nose' too: it had 'deepish' water right up to its edge and many old naval vessels had ended their days in that rural spot on the edge of the water. The yard had closed years beforehand, yet some of its detritus still infested the environment. It was of a minor nature, though, but many would be unaware, the skipper thought, that the leavings, concrete blocks, were for the feet of a crane, or that they had had something to do with the gravel extraction ... Nothing else remained to tell a walker along the sea wall, or a sailor, sailing by, of the industries that once profited upon that grassy spot. The skipper, miles away, had then become aware of his mate: she was hopping from foot to foot.

'You with us,' she'd said, with just a little sarcasm, adding, 'I've been looking, but, at what ... what's over there?'

Looking up, the skipper sighed, 'Ah ...' Then he'd thought, '... She's still waiting ...' but only uttered, 'Oh yes' as he'd looked again in the direction she'd been looking. 'We're closer now,' he'd said as he'd again pointed, but in a different direction, for they'd moved along somewhat. Then, in answer to his mate's growing impatience, he'd said, 'That old barge over there. Behind the sea wall ... Look, you can see her stem head and rudder top ... I've read she's a folly ...'

'Can't see a barge or anything that resembles a barge ...' the mate had muttered indignantly: she'd been kept waiting, and added, 'I'm sure you imagine half of what you see ...' And she'd nearly inserted 'most'. All she'd wanted was for a little quiet, a period of reflection ... space to enjoy the late morning's sail ...

'Stand on the cockpit seat ... look ... just above the wall ... No, no, to the east, east of the house on ... Northey Island. I can see it clearly ...'

'You would, you know what you're looking at ... You see things that aren't there ... I'm sure ...' repeating the gist of the remarks she'd made a little earlier.

'Oh, yes!' The skipper had exclaimed, feeling a little hurt. He'd seen, though, that her expression had been tinged with 'What, another old wreck ...' quite early in this 'conversation'. So he'd grinned at her, thought, 'They're old vessels ... they have souls too ...' and with that look he oft displayed when about to launch into a knowing monologue, said, 'My old ...'

He was about to mention his old childhood home, but alas the skipper hadn't a chance: the mate had jumped in with a comment, as she smoothly eased towards him, pecked his lips and cut him off. 'I enjoyed our stay in Maldon ... Here, you put the kettle on, I'm taking over. And ...' she'd paused, grinning broadly, and almost laughing, said, 'I'll remember not to cut the corner by Hilly Pool ... like you did last year ... bumping over the point ...' At that she'd slid into the helming position and 'nicked' the tiller.

The skipper had meanwhile gazed across the water, reflecting on the heavily treed shoreline, trees that almost enveloped the two houses on the island. The tall house had at one time been the home of Sir Norman Angell. Another house, barely visible and lower, was now used by a National Trust keeper: the island had been passed to the Trust.

Leaving Maldon behind on a quiet morning.

Accommodation was also available for holiday let too, the skipper knew. He remembered briefly the long letter he'd received from his old bargeman friend who lived in those parts. He was a man who was a fount of information of huge depth, about barges, their history and their last trading days. Turning towards the cabin, he'd said, 'I'll tell you all about them later,' and disappeared below to be the galley slave, thinking, 'What I know … anyway …'

Meanwhile, the mate had enjoyed an enchanting sail down to Hilly Pool, past the bustle of Heybridge Basin, before coming onto a broad reach down along the marshy eastern banks of the island. Those banks were deeply indented with guts and channels that cut through once-rich sheep grazing land. Remnants of the island's broken sea defences poked in grass-tufted mounds above the high tide that had soaked the marshes. The skipper's barge sat as if marooned, far away, close to the house. The mate had looked in that direction, but saw nothing. She'd sailed on, enchanted by the open sky that carried typical summer fluffy clouds. It was a view not so often enjoyed that year. The sky added to the allure of the watery world. It seemed to her that the boat only required a tweak of the helm, casually now and then, to keep her roughly on their heading towards Stansgate Abbey farmhouse, deep in the distance.

The mate's reverie was abruptly broken by the skipper. 'Here,' he announced, interrupting her period of delightful reflection, mimicking those around them, 'your coffee,' and handed it to her as he'd stepped into the cockpit clutching another brimming and steaming mug and the biscuit barrel.

Sighing, the mate had said, 'I'm steering roughly for the abbey,' adding without expecting any answer, 'We're going into Lawling … aren't we?' The skipper had merely nodded, smiled in acquiescence and not replied, so she'd settled back and continued to enjoy her sail.

A little later, the skipper had seen that out in the open the wind was more of a westerly and eased the sheets, grinning at the mate as he'd done so. It had picked up a little, too: a rustle, gurgle and occasional gentle slap had begun to rise from the waterline. His thoughts, it must be said, were still on those lonely remnants from a mightier yet harder past which sat marooned within the marshes, inside the broken walls of Northey Island. The poor old barges had been built as workhorses. There was never any intention for them to last forever, or for as long as they had, although there was not much left of one, and the other was a crumbling hulk; but it was the same for many old craft.

The skipper had mused, 'I'll have to make a trip to the island to get a closer look at the more intact one …' and slowly shaking his head, he'd left his thoughts to themselves: there were other things going on around the yacht as it was steered, expertly, downriver. Inwardly he'd glowed with pride, though: he'd seen how much the mate was enjoying her sailing. Running and reaching were fine he knew, 'but …' he thought, '… she hated tacking …'

'Seen those two barges', the mate said quietly, reverentially almost, looking closely at her skipper. He'd nodded, but the mate was left wondering what it was that her skipper was thinking …

The two barges, the *Hydrogen* and the *Thistle*, were on their way back upstream with a gaggle of people swanning around their decks. They had departed earlier than the skipper and the mate had: gradually, since the berths at Maldon had been dredged, the yacht pontoon had become almost marooned on a sea of mud that had steadily built up. It had recently caught many a yachtsman out on falling tides ... A Dutch yacht had had trouble getting clear, they'd heard earlier that summer. On one of the barges the skipper saw that many of the ladies were clad in colourful, floaty dresses better suited to the church bazaar. He'd grinned: the sight was at odds, in nautical terms, with the nineteenth-century look of a spritsail barge. The women mingled with suited men, chatting among themselves – a wedding party, perhaps. All had seemed to be having a good time, enjoying a glass or two. Voices drifted across the water and arms were raised by several of the passengers – the mate responded in kind. On the other barge, the crowd were more suitably clad, he saw. And the skipper had mused, 'It's a pleasant day to see the river ... to enjoy its panorama and get a little taste of barging, too.'

Passing Osea, the skipper had gazed around at the panorama: it looked particularly fetching in the dappled light of high, passing clouds. It wasn't windy, so the passage of high summer's fluffy cotton balls was slow across the sky. The island's colours changed slowly too. Greens, yellows and browns were heightened and darkened in a leisurely fashion, as were the blue-greens of the surrounding waters, while the facets of gentle wash waves glinted in the sunlight as it had flickered intermittently. White sails, cream sails, tan sails and multi-coloured concoctions moved around them slowly, some far away, others within the intervening span. Far away in the distance, where once fleets of tan-sailed spritsail barges and smack sails had predominated, and for a time innumerable numbers of rusting ships were laid up during the 1950s and 60s (past and later decades too), the skipper saw the *Pioneer*, a rebuilt ketch-rigged Brightlingsea Skillinger smack. She was somewhere off Bradwell. Beyond her was the silhouette of a spritsail barge, black against the distant horizon. It was all extremely evocative and the skipper felt a zinging excitement. It had cheered him somewhat. He'd become less thoughtful. He'd a happier look.

The mate had seen the skipper's features soften. 'Back to his gentle smile,' she'd thought, watching as he'd swilled back the last of his coffee. 'Surely by then cold ...' she'd murmured ... but had continued to leave him alone.

Suddenly the skipper had then smacked his lips and thrust his mug under a side pocket in the cockpit, out of the way, where it clinked against the mate's mug. Looking at the mate, he'd said quietly, 'Do you want me to take over, you've had an hour ... or so ...' as he'd also covetously glanced towards the tiller; his hand strayed, too, the mate had noticed ... They were nearing the point where a change of course was needed.

'If you like,' the mate replied, glancing across at a buoy which had 'The Doctor' stencilled upon its side. The buoy slowly revolved as it moved in the tide's flow, washing its weed-infested skirts to and fro, a little beyond the yacht's hull.

'Um ... We turn at the next red ...' the skipper had muttered.

'Oh, here ... Yes ... You take her,' the mate had said hesitantly, and reluctantly relinquished the long, smoothly varnished tiller to his caresses.

'On our next visit to Maldon we'll have to walk round to the causeway and visit Northey Island,' the skipper commented as he'd manoeuvred the boat across the 'fairway' towards Mundon Stone, the shingle and shell headland that sat at the eastern end of Mundon marshes. 'Follies ... Indeed ...' he'd muttered, too.

The mate had been remembering a chilly bottom of the tide the previous week, when they'd scrubbed weed from the boat's underside … Shivering, she'd muttered, 'Oh yes,' adding enquiringly, 'Can you go on it? … Thought it was private …' It was kind of private: it was owned by the National Trust, but visits could be made. 'What's the island's history?' the mate added: other than a little about the Battle of Maldon, she'd known little. She realised, too, that it was probably the island that the skipper had been thinking about earlier.

'Over lunch …' the skipper had said in answer to her question. The mate had nodded: they were rapidly approaching their chosen anchorage, in a freshening breeze too. It would be a late lunch. A repast of succulent pork pie from a rather nice butcher they knew up Maldon's interesting and lively high street. The mate had procured other tasties too, olives and such, for later in the evening.

Soon after, in an area that the skipper knew was safe to anchor in, he'd tracked the yacht across a stretch of water that had looked wide, yet at low tide was barely half the width, with shallow edges. Before turning back a few boat lengths, he'd quickly briefed the mate, handed over, gone forward and dropped the headsail, clearing it off the deck. No words were spoken. The mate had rounded up and the anchor had splashed overboard. He paid out the chain, snubbing it in the usual fashion. At a sign, the mate saw that the skipper was happy. 'All's well,' she'd thought as she made her way to the mast to lower the mainsail. The boat had quickly swung to the tide. No sooner had it done so, the mate, with a glance at the skipper, murmured, 'I'll get lunch ready …' leaving him to tidy away the sails and set their anchor ball aloft.

Nodding, the skipper stood briefly, then released another few metres of cable. He'd watched it jerk, grinned and turned to deal with the sails. All around them were a hornet's nest of dinghies with multi-coloured sails, fighting the ebb and each other as they battled into the creek. They were happily engaged in racing. Support craft buzzed around, watching, waiting, ready to help. It would have been a quiet day for them with the light breeze of earlier, but it had strengthened appreciably. It would drop again later, all knew, and it could be rapid, often necessitating the help of a support boat to get home. 'Be alright today … Wind'll hold out …' the skipper thought, turning away to tidy the mainsheet and set the cockpit table up.

Lunch was a lazy affair with a beer to wash it down. A snooze beckoned the mate, but the skipper had other ideas … 'Right,' he'd said, 'about those barges … and the island too …'

The skipper knew that it had been said that there were three known remnants of spritsail barges on the saltings inside the old seawalls of Northey Island. Passing by many times over the years, he'd often gazed over the expanse and looked quizzically at various old yacht bottoms that rotted away along the edges too. One of those barges was the *Gillman* of Rochester, a vessel built in 1865 at Lambeth. She was a small barge by latter-day standards and became a timber lighter with Brown & Son, timber merchants based in Chelmsford. She'd spent her last years working between the Osea Island anchorage and Heybridge Basin carrying wood. The old girl had had a decade sailing in the Parker fleet down at Bradwell during the time the skipper's childhood home had been owned there too. The poor old girl had fallen off the register by 1928, though.

'It's said …' the skipper had murmured, '… that the barge was placed in the marshes as a folly,' mumbling somewhat – he'd felt uneasy.

The *Gillman* of Rochester, as seen in 1962 by Patricia O'Driscoll, who at the time was one of two female barge mates. The other was Marion Carr, who eventually became a civil servant. Patricia later co-authored a barge history, was editor of both *East Coast Digest* and *Bygone Kent*, and has continued to write. Courtesy of Patricia O'Driscoll.

Picking up on his comment, the mate's interest had been rekindled; she'd looked up sharply and had enquired, 'When was that?'

'It was around 1950,' he murmured: there was some doubt about that date. 'It's what I've been told anyway ... There's not much of her left, I understand.'

The mate nodded and awaited the next ... She watched and continued to wait while the skipper had sipped a little of his beer. Then he was away again.

'Then there's the *Mistley* of Harwich,' he'd said. 'She came a decade later – I've been told – around 1960. The barge had spent about twenty years with Brown & Son, lightering timber in the canal.' Then, grinning, he added, 'She came to a sticky end though ... It was off Southend in December 1940 [the 6th, actually]. There was a great gale in the estuary. Barges and ships got into difficulties ... Anyway, the *Mistley* foundered. Her crew were rescued by a lifeboat. Soon after, the barge was raised and ended her days as a lighter.' The skipper had paused. 'But,' he added, 'she's still around ... up in those marshes ... a long, lingering death ...' Feeling a little choked for some reason, the skipper sat briefly, smiled and added, 'She was built up at Harwich in 1891 ...'

'Built a little after your old home,' the mate had whispered, smiling tenderly.

'There was a funny thing about her that tickled me ... after being bought by the mill people [R&W Paul] of Ipswich.' The skipper had chuckled, 'They re-registered her in Ipswich – my barge pal gave me all the stuff about her – as I said, it tickled me though. She wasn't ever an Ipswich barge ...' The skipper was thinking, too, of an ancient and historical animosity that had rumbled for centuries between those two ports!

Looking thoughtful, the mate had murmured, hesitantly, 'Didn't ... Did you say there was another?'

The skipper nodded saying, 'Yes, but little or nothing is known of her, I'm told.'

The conversation seemed to peter out and both had sat back and nodded off. By the time any consciousness had returned to either, the tide had neared the bottom of the ebb. All around them, close to low water, young common seals frolicked in the shallows. Some slid and wallowed about on the shinning, wet, muddy slopes … 'Just like human children,' the mate had giggled. Others lay in a typical banana shape displaying their sides, almost russet brown on some. Their hides, apparently, were dyed with pigments picked up in the estuarial mud. It was sheer magic. And that magic had continued into the evening. The mate's larder of nibbles was broached and enjoyed while a tasty chunk of lamb bathed with fresh (almost dried) rosemary – from their garden – was washed down with a glass or two of red wine. Both were in a happy mood as the sun set over the marshes that edged the land to the west of them. The thrumming tones of a harvester could still be heard running back and forth across the unseen fields deep below the protective wall. Soon, the seals were on the move too after a period of quietness: the tide had turned and a fresh flood was bringing them their supper. The mate had also murmured something about their bunk …

'No, not yet … It's a night to savour awhile,' the skipper had said soothingly. The mate had ignored the comment, but had briefly stayed put.

'There's a whole load of dead oaks over yonder, somewhere – died after an inundation of salt … They stand like eerie ghosts …' the skipper had whispered. 'The last inundation was in 1953.'

'I expect so … I'm sure … Come on …' the mate had said quietly, and added firmly, 'Bed …' with the merest of a glint in her eyes, the skipper had seen. So he'd followed her below …

A year passed by and again the skipper and mate had sailed up into Maldon, up the barge river. On that visit they had eschewed the yacht pontoon at the Hythe, for it was all but useless. A look as the tide fell had confirmed their knowledge … They'd moored instead at the friendly little place that had once been a sail making establishment – the skipper's father had had a sail made for the *May Flower* there in 1965. The sail makers were established on the site in about 1870, replacing a granary, and some of the buildings were thought to date from the earlier use. From 1919 until its closure in 1969, it had been run by the renowned Taylor family.

During their stay the pair had had a walk round the edge of the Blackwater, past a depository for old and decaying vessels, past the site of the battle of Maldon and then across the causeway onto Northey Island.

After a lengthy perambulation round a pretty lane fringing the island's edge, habited buildings were reached. After checking with the warden, they'd been told, 'There are guests here on the island … Sorry … You can't look at the house.'

The mate had nodded and had replied, smiling, 'Oh, that's alright …'

'The family still use the old house too,' the warden's wife had said, jumping in. The wardens, a husband and wife team, were found to be very friendly and extremely approachable. It transpired that a great-niece still 'owned' the house. This had intrigued the skipper immensely.

'Oh … Who's that then?' the skipper had enquired, slowly and deliberately.

The lady had smiled sweetly and said, 'Oh that's Sir Norman's … His nephew's daughter …' as the skipper's mind had wandered down a family tree!

The original house on Northey Island, now used by the National Trust wardens. Courtesy of Alice Everard.

'Right,' the skipper had quickly said. 'I only want to look at the old barges ...' he'd added enthusiastically.

The wardens were extremely interested in the skipper's desire to search out and see the old barges. The mate had soon got into a convoluted talk about the skipper's writing ... embarrassing him greatly!

'Ah,' the lady had said, disappearing and calling out, '... Hold on, I can give you an address ...' The skipper was given the address of Sir Norman Angell's great-niece ... and with requests to stay off the marshes – or at least be careful – they had gone in search.

The skipper had grinned impishly when they'd been told to mind the marshes, and he'd said, 'Been wading in mud and around marsh all my life ... Know what I'm doing, but ... yes, I'll be very careful ... I promise.' Both wardens had looked at him.

It hadn't been a search really: the skipper knew exactly where the two main remnants were. The skipper had already spotted the exact locations of both barges earlier and had decided to visit the *Mistley*, the more intact one, first. Traipsing along the top of an old sea wall, through rough grass often inundated by the sea, they made their way carefully. At a point along the wall's top, the skipper had left the mate sitting in the sunshine and made off across a patch of rough grass that quickly petered out and fell away to saltings and a muddy gut. As he'd gone, the mate had called out, 'Remember what the warden said ... No wading across mud ... It's dangerous ...' thinking, 'It's pointless telling him ... He'll do exactly as he wants!'

It was pretty obvious to the skipper that if the *Mistley* had been a folly, then she'd been poorly placed. Her position just hadn't looked right. Years before, her bow had,

The *Mistley*, as seen in 2010. The creek in which she was poorly moored runs astern of her shattered hull. Note her windlass barrel, and the chain running up past the access hatch in the chain locker's remains and over the top of the rotting bulkhead.

he saw, hung over the marsh edge and dropped sharply. Without any support forward, her back had been broken under her mast deck. Her sides were curved in reverse to her original sheer line, planking that had split away had flicked back up, relieved of the opposite twist they'd had for some forty years. And he'd also heard the folly had been on blocks ...

The skipper had moved to within spitting distance, looking more closely into what was once her fo'c'sle, and had gazed at the barge's windlass barrel. It lay in the mud, aft of her decayed bitts. Her anchor cable, still wrapped around the rotting wooden staves of the barrel, rose up and hung over the ragged and weathered top edge of the forward bulkhead and down into the chain locker's remains. By the barrel, the chain pipe poked from the moss and glasswort-covered mud ... Her decks forward of her chain plates were gone. A fore hatch coaming sat propped on a beam, inclined to the mud at one end with its other still sat on a perfectly preserved angle iron ...

For a while, the skipper had stood looking ... These sights had always tugged at his heart. Feeling the eyes of the mate on his back, he'd called, 'It's hard underfoot,' adding, '... Just going to look if there's any sign of her particulars.' A barge's particulars, her net registered tonnage and official numbers, etc., were always carved into the aft face of the aft sailing beam that supported the mast waist deck. There were signs, but they were well wasted.

Standing and looking about in the main hold, the skipper had heard a plaintive call tailing off: 'How long you going to be?' He didn't answer immediately, for he was gazing aft at the barge's shattered stern. The poor old girl's transom had gone, leaving her rudder standing ... The skipper had mouthed, 'Yes, there's nearly always a rudder ... If shipped when an old barge was abandoned ...' He chuckled: 'What ... another rudder,' mimicking the mate's usual comment when he'd returned from a wreck trek with a sketch of what he'd seen!

The presence of the mate had gone from his mind, so entranced was he inside those remains, then remembering her call, he'd waved. Turning, he'd called, 'Coming ...' and made his way back to the sea wall.

'Done ...?' the mate had asked flatly, with an unsaid 'Time we're moving ...' and 'I'm bored ...'

Well, yes, here, anyway,' he'd said, grinning. 'But I still want to see that one over there,' pointing across the saltings to what looked like a chunk of driftwood sticking up from an area of rough grass that was higher than the surrounding sea of purslane. The mate had stayed put on firmer terrain that time, too: a rudder poking out of mud and marsh had never excited her!

Remembering the warning imparted by the wardens and another marsh foray, the skipper had felt his way cautiously across the rough terrain: he'd fallen into a metre-deep chasm once before. That had been a year or so back at St Osyth, when looking at an old West Country vessel tucked into the edge of some saltings. At the time he'd not known anything about her, but later had found that she was indeed probably a Taw & Torridge estuary sand barge. Her particulars agreed. She was around forty-five feet, wide-beamed and had carried around forty tons of sand or gravel when trading. The vessels were thought to have been schooner rigged, without a bow sprit. The hulk seen had remnants of only one mast tabernacle, though. The poor old girl had obviously been somebody's pride and joy, sailed as a yacht.

However, reaching an obvious rise, the skipper felt that he was aboard the *Gillman*. He'd stopped and stood. Around him he visualised her hull rising up around him. He was in the fo'c'sle area. He would have been staring down her long hold, aft to the skipper's cabin bulkhead. Moving carefully, edges of her sides could be felt, and towards her aft end and rudder broken frames poked wickedly from the purslane and long, tufted grasses. Looking from astern, at her rudder, the rise from her bottom towards the turn at her lost transom could still be seen above a lingering patch of wet mud lurking beneath. There, the skipper had stood and sketched, while the mate had stood and waited, patiently. 'Bless her,' he'd whispered into the breeze, while looking her way with more than a little affection, and waving when she'd waved!

Closing his sketch pad, the skipper had sighed as he'd made his way back to the mate. Reaching the position where she stood, she'd said, 'Come on, we've shopping to do later this afternoon.' Well, the mate had. They were leaving on the next morning's early tide. The skipper was planning to go off on a little jaunt into the top of Heybridge Creek to look at whatever was there later too. He'd offered to help shop, but with a gentle cuff had been sent on his way. First, he'd had a poke around the local yards while waiting for the tide to rise.

Later in the afternoon, and luxuriating in the bottom of his dinghy as he'd sailed upstream, the skipper had recalled some years before, when with the boy ... In a different dinghy they'd visited the little backwater he was again headed for to look at an old Maldon-built barge, the *Beaumont Belle*. The old girl had been built by Howard, who'd mainly built yachts, and all of his small number of vessels had the

The author's sketch of the *Gillman*'s aft end – her rudder and stern post – 2010.

same fineness built into them. The lovely *Mirosa* was one of his, too … East coasters would know her! On this later visit, though, he saw that the vessel's tired old hull had almost completely collapsed.

Across the creek another old sailorman, the *Edith & Hilda*, built up Milton Creek in 1892, mouldered too. Remnants of her life as a home sat poking above the shallow water: a stove, what looked like a cooker and various pipes … She sat among a host of 'tore-outs and ris-ons' being lived on as houseboats. (Ris-ons were old boats with a varying amount of top hamper to make living aboard more comfortable … The term was originally given to wooden lifeboat conversions of the early to mid-1900s.) Along the marsh edges were a myriad of abandoned hulls. 'It's all rather sad,' the skipper had mouthed, though. The dinghy sail was hectic at times: the breeze frolicked around the hillside, which ran down to the upper river's edge. It came in baffling directions as it was fed around the many cornered buildings of the mills. It rattled across the saltings between the creek and the main river, causing the skipper to be responsive and vigilant to its wiles. The sudden lurching of the boat as he'd endeavoured to use his camera had made life frenetic … but fun! The mate had returned from her shopping and long stowed the stores before the skipper had hove in sight. She'd been watching for his return.

Their departure from Maldon the next morning was a very quiet affair, with barely enough wind for steerage. The tranquillity of it wasn't shattered by their chugging engine either: it was only used to clear the tight spot in which they were berthed. The boat's sails did the work: there was enough of a zephyr for them. Maldon from the water at that time of the day and tide looked sublime. The town's waterfront church up on its crest was mirrored with the lofty rigs of some spritsail barges. Colours, too, were perfectly transposed … It had been enchanting. Bit by bit, as Maldon was left astern, the breeze began to ruffle the surface until a faint rustle fetched up from the forefoot and a noticeable gurgle emanated from around the transom. 'It's funny,' said the skipper, 'one doesn't normally notice it ...'

The mate had murmured, 'What's that,' as she'd gazed around, mesmerised by the scene's serenity and stillness. Ashore, only a couple, a man and a woman, with a small pooch moved. That had been down by Maldon's memorial to her defeated warrior, at the end of the town's long promenade. The skipper had shaken his head, indicating that he'd not spoken: the voice had floated across to them from one of the two people ashore. It's strange, but true: few landsmen realise the power that water has in amplifying voices ... It could be interesting sometimes!

Later that evening, in the quiet of the Mersea Quarters, the skipper had ruminated about the previous day's visit to Northey Island. Looking across at the skipper, the mate had cajoled him. 'Come on,' she'd added, 'you've got the great-niece's address ...' murmuring quietly, 'write ...'

'I will,' the skipper had said in a hushed tone. The quiescence of the evening had enveloped them by then, and the skipper felt the marshland atmosphere deeply and shivered.

A little later the mate had murmured, 'Come on you ... Our bunk calls.' The coffee mugs had been drained. Curlews and oyster catchers, gulls galore had begun calling to one another over Cobmarsh Island: the tide had turned. The mate added, 'Enough of your follies and foibles!' And after giving him a hug, repeated, 'As I said, you can write to the lady when we're home ...' So, below they went.

'I will ... I'm intrigued ...' he'd said as the hatch shut out the worst of the rising cacophony greeting the fresh flood.

Towards the end of that summer the skipper had indeed written to Norman Angell's great-niece, Alice Everard. He'd visited her, too and met her husband George. Alice was the daughter of the island's last private owner and the skipper had learnt much from her. 'What a lovely couple ...' the skipper had said to the mate later, 'I was royally treated ... Her father was Sir Norman Angell's nephew ...' The mate had nodded slowly as the skipper enthusiastically bubbled and burbled about his day ... hopping from foot to foot as quickly as he'd darted around the subject.

The mate had been confused from the start ... She'd soon stopped him and said, 'Slow down ...'

Sir Norman Angell was an early recipient of the Nobel Peace Prize. He was born in 1872, in Holbeach, Lincolnshire, and was given the names Ralph Norman Angell Lane. During his life, Norman dropped his first name, Ralph, and Lane, the last part of his surname – why wasn't discovered – and became Norman Angell. He was knighted in 1931. His father had had a raft of shops and retired after selling up to become a gentleman farmer and magistrate, spending his time in study and reading. He was a pretty typical late Victorian gentleman of leisure of the time. He'd encouraged his son to do the same – read and study, that was ... Ralph later became one of Britain's and the world's great political thinkers, producing many books, especially on the futility of war. It was largely for this that he had been awarded the peace prize in 1933.

Norman bought Northey Island in 1923 from a Vierville de Crespigny, who had apparently been a bit of an eccentric. The land included a selection of run-down farm buildings and a cottage, apart from the expanse of land lost to marshes some years

The house that Norman Angell built, photographed in 1928. The new building was built against the original house and had panoramic views over the land and recently flooded marshes. Courtesy of Alice Everard.

earlier. Also, Alice had said, 'There was an abandoned spritsail barge to the east of the dry land ...' She had also alluded to the island's poor farming proposition, for although it had been around 300 acres, a little over 80 of those acres were viable. And of the higher and wall-protected areas, some, in Norman's time, would wage a constant battle with him and were a drain on his meagre resources. 'Norman wasn't well off ...' Alice had said, with a look of seriousness. The skipper had nodded as Alice, chuckling, had said, 'Norman was always known as 'N.A.' within the family, and by friends too.'

Alice had then talked about how the island had been discovered ... 'Norman wanted a secluded base from which to write ... He discovered the place while sailing lazily by in his yacht ... He saw a "for sale" sign,' said his great-niece, and she'd added, 'He'd found it.'

Incidentally, the yacht is thought to have been a converted whaler type of craft, much in vogue during the post-First World War years. His great-niece had continued, 'N.A. loved his sailing ... he loved his island and the house he built there ... he was bombed, too, during World War Two ... and he was on the Germans' hit list, it is said ...' There she'd chuckled, 'Something to do with his anti-war stance and earlier warnings ...' Pausing, Alice had then hopped back to N.A.'s yacht and continued, 'I didn't know that boat ... But I did know an old motorised fishing boat he had later, when I was a little girl. And of course, the family used to holiday on the island. It was wonderful for us. I loved it. I was very lucky.'

The skipper had asked Alice about her father. Alice said, 'My father, Eric Lane, was Norman's nephew ... as you know. He and my mother, Nora, bought the island from N.A. in 1946: he lived in America at that time. Father added South House farm, across on the landward side of the causeway ... It was needed to make farming and living on the island viable.' Alice had stopped briefly. And then she had quickly added, 'Father still had the farm up in Lincolnshire. It was still my home. The house was empty most of the time.'

Norman Angell's yacht was moored near a rickety staging that ran out over the mud where his dinghy was kept. Courtesy of Alice Everard.

Eric Lane's purchase unified the two significant land parts of an important chapter in English and British history. The island had then become Alice's own holiday home, but it was a place she'd known well from an early age.

The island was the landing place for the Vikings (Danes), who had been based on the Isle of Sheppey during the late 900s, for an attack deep into Essex in 991. It was a time of constant changes in leadership and allegiance when the Anglo-Saxons spent around 200 years fighting off the Vikings. Ultimately, the bulk of what is now England was finally divided on a north–south spine in the hope of peace. It led to attacks from kings from what are now Norway and Sweden and the Vikings began to settle their part of the land, establishing themselves at Yorvik (York). The defeat and infamous act of 'fairness' by Brythnoth, the Earl of Essex, in inviting the Danes over to firmer ground to fight was tragic, as it led to payments being demanded to buy off the attackers. This was known as Danegeld. For a period around 1013 the land was ruled solely by the Danes, while the Anglo-Saxon court found succour with the Normans. King Æthelred the Unready (a corruption of *unraed*, meaning 'no council') had endeavoured to wrest the kingdom back in 1014, but he was defeated by Canute who then married Æthelred's widow, Emma: the king had died shortly after. Canute then became the undisputed ruler and ruled for some twenty years as King of Norway, Denmark and England. His death led to infighting and the return of the heavily 'Normanised' Anglo-Saxons. Finally, it led to King Harold's defeat of the Norse under King Harald Hardrada in 1066 at Stamford Bridge near York. He'd then had to march to Sussex to meet Duke William of Normandy ... where a stray arrow caused an utter change in British history, largely making us what we are today.

Alice had continued, 'There was just one old sailing barge ... near the house ... It wasn't in a good state when dad bought the place.' Alice added, 'That's apart from the one that has all but disappeared to the other side ...'

'It's to the east, past the land that was flooded some time ago ...' Alice's husband had chipped in, 'I know where it is ...'

'Ah,' thought the skipper, 'So, that other barge is visible … if you know where to look.' He knew that a barge book had discussed the fact that another vessel was known to rest in those marshes. He'd smiled, though, but had remained silent.

Alice had continued, 'It's said that my uncle used timbers from that old barge, the earlier one … when building his house … He was a bit of a "bodger" and used what he could put his hands on … he hadn't much money then.' Alice had also shown the skipper a photograph showing a barge being broken up on the beach near the house (and the house barge N.A. had), so it was likely he had used timber from more than one vessel. The house had been built very shortly after Norman Angell came to the island and was a very higgledy-piggledy affair, but none the less charming, with its high, turreted upper story that now poked engagingly out from among many trees. The trees had all been planted by N.A. during the 1920s, early in his ownership. Alice said, 'He dragged the timbers from that barge across the saltings. The beams are still holding the building up.' She'd pointed to a picture.

On a further visit to Alice – luckily for him, it had been to the house on Northey Island – he'd seen that the ceiling joists on the lower floors were indeed barge timbers. N.A. had used the floors from the old barge and treenails poked provocatively from them; most were still captured and looked as hard and fast as when first hammered home when bottom timbers were fastened to them.

The skipper hadn't been able to enlighten Alice on the history of that 'lost' barge, the one she'd referred to as the 'haunted barge'. She'd also said, 'We used to walk out over the marshes, with an adult, and I remember it as being covered in weed.' The barge had been placed across a water course, she thought, and it seemed that her purpose could have been to block a flood channel … An attempt to reclaim the land by N.A.'s predecessor, or before.

The inside of Norman's house. The vertical supports are tree trunks. The main beam had once come from a barge but had recently been renewed. The ceiling joists, barge floors, are original. There are treenails in them which once held a barge's bottom together. Courtesy of Alice Everard.

The skipper had known that the barge's history had been lost in the mists of time. It was possible even that the hull had come onto the island during extreme flooding that took place in 1897, when the outer walls to the river and those to Southey Creek behind Northey Island had failed. That disaster became known as the 'Black Monday' flood. It was then that the major part of the land had reverted to salt marshes. There was another big flood in 1901, and there were others during the 1920s too. 'Who now knows …' the skipper had murmured to the mate, some time later.

Remembering something, Alice had grinned; looking back at the skipper, she'd said, 'I remember that on the way out to that old barge we used to pick up winkles. We used to take them home for mother to cook.'

Then Alice had said, 'Family lore says the *Gillman* had been left at the edge of the creek where her remains now sit. A gentleman had asked Norman to look after her for a while for him. The chap never came back, though. He was going to do it up … or something. We never found out the real story, though …' There Alice had paused. Smiling, she'd then said, 'It was here when father purchased the island from N.A. in 1946. When it came? I have no idea … But she was in a poor way then.' That seemed to back up a piece of information supplied by an old barge mate the skipper knew … She'd stated that the barge had come onto the island in about 1927.

The skipper, though, had been told by another barge historian that the old girl had been placed on the island around 1950, to be used as a folly. That had been news to Alice, and she'd exclaimed, 'Follies! No … There weren't any follies.'

'What about the other one, the *Mistley*?' the skipper had asked quickly, for he was keen to keep to the subject, and had added, 'I've been told that it was a replacement for the *Gillman* … as a folly too.' Alice had then showed the skipper an aerial photograph of the island from June 1960. It showed the *Gillman* only. Her starboard side and decks had gone by then, too.

Alice had laughed sweetly, and smiling had, it seemed, been searching her memory. She'd then said, 'No, she wasn't a folly either … Father bought that thing in about 1964. It was a sixtieth birthday present for my mother. Strange really, I don't know what they were planning to do with her. Anyway, the barge wasn't looked after … It was never tied properly …'

'Moored,' the skipper had added, grinning.

Alice had continued, 'Yes! So, on a high tide she went up on the saltings. Father never got her off, so the barge stayed put.' Laughing, she'd said, 'The channels were quite deep then …' She'd paused, 'We had names for them all …' and laughing again, had added, 'We used the channels to sail and row out to the river. I loved being on the water.'

'I'd wondered,' the skipper had said, 'because the position of the barge doesn't fit with being a folly. To me it looked as if she had sat over the edge of the marshes and broke her back … under her mast deck,' he explained. 'The banks would have been steeper then I think.' The skipper had then added, 'A folly would have been placed on an area of flat saltings … surely?' The skipper had summarised to Alice what he had seen when he'd looked closely at her hulk earlier that summer.

'There was one other vessel on the island, but it has long gone,' Alice said. 'N.A. had a barge moored out by the dinghy beach … It was chocked up on blocks to keep it level … When I remembered it … it was right up at the top of the beach. He used it for accommodating visitors when they came to see him … students and friends alike … during the 1930s. They all loved it.' Alice had waited patiently while the skipper had quickly found a picture of the barge, a lighter-shaped vessel, then she'd added, 'Was it a sailing barge then?'

The skipper had shaken his head, and pointing at the picture said, 'No, doesn't look likely – probably just a plain old wooden lighter. There used to hundreds of them … like that one. It might even have worked over at the Basin.' The vessel's name seemed to have been *Friends*. It was the skipper's opinion that it had been that barge that had infused the myth of Sir Norman Angell's follies, of barges set up on blocks, especially as the island had contained two recognisable barge hulls by the mid-1960s. Alice had not disagreed with that theory.

Alice had nodded: she knew Heybridge and its commercial past. 'By the time we moved to the island it was pretty derelict,' she'd said, 'and I remember using it as a den to hide away and read … It was wonderful.' She'd stopped briefly. Looking at the skipper, she'd smiled and added, 'It was my haven of tranquillity and solitude. It was absolute, because no one could find me there!' The skipper had grinned at this: he pictured himself in the same boat, doing the same thing … or his mate for that matter. The manner of that vessel's fate was not known by Alice, but it would be pretty safe to assume that she eventually went to pieces in that relatively exposed position and was probably used for firewood.

Sir Norman had had one strange, yet futuristic idea. When the family visited the island for their holidays, all the children had to transplant shoots of Spartina Grass out on the saltings and mudflats that had so recently been grazing land some twenty or thirty years earlier. Alice had said, 'N.A. found this grass growing down in Southampton Water. It was along the shores where he'd been sailing with a friend … it was somewhere down near Hythe. He pulled some up and took it home to his

Norman Angell's lighter, No. 527, *Friends*, in about 1930, which he used to house students and visitors during the 1930s. She was moored on a flattened 'table' on the beach opposite Heybridge Basin. Note the vessel to the left – she is being broken up. Courtesy of Alice Everard.

The final position of Norman Angell's accommodation lighter. It had been jacked up and positioned where it couldn't, or could rarely, float. A folly indeed! Courtesy of Alice Everard.

island to grow.' Alice had chuckled and added, 'He wanted it to build the land up … To make his island bigger … Visions of rebuilding the sea walls …' She'd again added, 'But it didn't grow very well …'

The skipper thought about this. 'Perhaps it was on mud that was too low … the grass is only a salt-tolerant plant – not a seaweed,' he'd said wryly. Looking across at Alice, he'd then added, 'He was way ahead of his time,' and then added, 'Well, it does now. It's cord grass … an American strain was introduced, but it hadn't taken very well … it did something strange, though. A self-generated natural genetic engineering occurred. It cross-pollinated with our English variety [*Spartina angelica*] and produced a hybrid [*Spartina townsendii*].' He'd grinned, 'An emotive subject, that … genetic engineering … Then it soon started to spread like wildfire. It has choked many creeks since …' Alice had nodded.

The skipper had also told Alice that, in his view, 'The saltings at the south-eastern end of the island are creeping eastwards so Sir Norman's dream was really happening – don't think the land will be reclaimed though!' There weren't, the skipper had read, many areas where the original English grass grew: the hybrid had succeeded almost as well as the grey squirrel had in the animal kingdom.

An area of land had since been let back to the sea. This was to the eastern side and was a university project to see what happened (George had thought that it had been carried out under the auspices of the University of East Anglia). It had quickly reverted to salt marsh and it had, like the saltings within the greater part of the island, risen with the rising sea level. Following the example of that project, many other such projects were now taking place around the Blackwater estuary, and other areas around the East Coast.

Finally, Alice had said, 'During the 1960s, father was getting on and he was afraid that the island would become a caravan site or be dug up for its deposits of shingle.' Pausing and looking at the skipper wryly, she'd added, 'I'd ultimately gone off to university and then later married too …'

Across the river, Alice's father had watched as acres of land were excavated for its substantial shingle deposits during the 1950s and into the early 1960s. Before that, during the 1920s and 1930s, the Heybridge shore had had a ship breaker's business. Now the area was cleared of industry and its resources were spent, yet it had found a useful purpose. It had been converted into a semi-fresh wetland. It had quickly

Alice, Sir Norman's great niece, and George Everard outside Sir Norman's house in 2010. The house has had some alterations over the years. The conservatory in the bay has been added, as has shiplap cladding to the upper stories. Trees now surround the buildings, adding to the feeling of tucked-away seclusion.

become a bird reserve and, with a maze of footpaths that threaded through it, a place for people far and wide to enjoy.

Smiling graciously, Alice had finally said, 'The island, with the mainland farm, was passed to the National Trust in 1978.' Alice had added quite fervently, though, 'It wasn't sold. I keep hearing that it was …' The family had, though, retained use of the house that Sir Norman had built beside the original farmhouse, on lease from the National Trust.

Alice's nephew had continued to farm at South House farm, as well as up in Lincolnshire. South House was leased from the National Trust and the land included that on the island where only cattle are grazed, leaving the land as natural as possible. No ploughing was allowed under the lease. 'The pastures are for the birds …' Alice had added. The skipper was left with the impression that Alice had other thoughts.

The island had remained a place of solitude, a place of natural beauty and a place recognised for the richness in its diversity. It was a place very much both land and sea; it largely sat betwixt them … During spring high water, the land was a mere dot in a huge lake fringed by its low outer broken walls. It was a natural habitat, a salt marsh wilderness. It was as important in that respect for the ecology of our land, and for its sheer beauty, as the valleys, hills and dales, mountains, and lakes of Britain's more northern areas.

'Yes …' the skipper had reflected knowingly to himself as he'd turned towards his car when leaving Alice. 'And … a National Trust treasure …' he'd added cheekily as he'd driven away.

Wending his way home across Essex, towards his mate, the skipper had exclaimed, 'A folly … No, never!'

The Shifting Sands of Time

The skipper and mate were running serenely up the River Deben's lower reach, having recently crossed the bar that besets its entrance. The mate had said happily – she'd always expected the worse there – 'That was an easy entrance …' and, for good measure, had added, 'It's changed from the last time we were this way … hasn't it …?' including a question in her comment.

The skipper had nodded, but had remained silent. His silence remained for what seemed a long while: the coast had changed, and it had been changing ever since the land bridge to Europe had finally sunk beneath the North Sea's waves some 8,000 years beforehand. It was a time span of finite proportion compared to Earth's life cycle … but that momentous event would eventually mould the region's early coastal traders and sailors. And, later, the Corinthian sailors, forerunners to people like the skipper and mate.

That new coast line of about 6000 BC appeared after the cataclysmic upheaval that occurred as melt water from the last ice age burst out from behind its terminal moraine. It carved its way through the South Downs, cut Britain off from mainland Europe, and rerouted the Thames and the Rhine from their northwards-leaning final runs into their present positions. Those two rivers had previously run out across the land bridge northwards, entering what is now the North Sea roughly on an east–west line from the around the Wash. The Thames had, it was thought, run from somewhere in Wales, then more or less along its present route to around west London before travelling across Essex and out through what became the Walton Backwaters and the Naze, with an estuary that probably included the Rhine's before becoming sea. The present Naze was laid down in that period too, it was known: sediments and stones show that they had originated in Wales. The whole coast was therefore relatively young, and it was also fast disappearing into the sea – wherever man had not intervened.

The mate was still looking at him. She'd thought, 'What on Earth is he thinking about now …' but, characteristically, let him be!

The skipper's thoughts, though, had led him to think privately about the estuary's more recent evolution, too. There had been many quite major changes in the lifetime of just three or more generations: he could remember his grandfather telling him about one such channel that had essentially disappeared, except for its name. That had been the Rays'n Channel, down off the Dengie peninsula and entrance to the River Crouch. Finally, though, he'd suddenly said, 'Well … Yes it has … But it was the same a few years back …' He'd paused briefly to reflect before adding, 'Well, more or less anyway …' raising his eyebrows provocatively!

The Deben's entrance channel and its outer sand and shingle banks moved around under the influence of the coast's long shore drift and nature's storms – usually winter easterlies. It was the same for the bar at the entrance to the Ore and Alde, a little further north; and also, it seemed, for the even more northerly Blythe, beyond Orford Ness: there, the sea was attempting to change man's fixed coastline at the old haven's river, at Southwold. Was it nature's plan to reopen Blythe Haven? For now, the skipper had heard, man was intervening to maintain the status quo, but what of the acres of 'inned' marshes upstream below the town of Blythe that had been retaken by the sea in recent times. What of those inner forces?

The mate had picked up their pilot book (*East Coast Rivers*) and pointed to the chartlet and said, 'Here look …' The passage in from the Haven, past the East Knoll and to the Mid Knoll, had been a little east of south-east … while their passage had been a little east of a north–south line. The mate had grimaced and shivered too.

'Ah,' the skipper had said, 'that's why I always print the latest information before disappearing for the summer …' There was a website that had chartlets provided by the actions of a few good men from Felixstowe, with the help of Trinity House too … 'My grandfather would be amazed at it all …' the skipper had added, chuckling at the tale he'd heard of his father's lengthy spell on the Pye Sands after ignoring good navigational advice …

'Your father, too …' the mate had said: the skipper's father had passed on before the internet and web revolutions that had changed man's world so dramatically.

During the following days they'd spent a night at Ramsholt, and then there had been Woodbridge, where a delightful stay had been enjoyed. Having departed from that place, they had tucked themselves into the anchorage off Felixstowe Ferry on a spare mooring before a planned early departure out of the river the next morning, Pin Mill bound – where, passing through Harwich Haven, the skipper would again ponder upon the coast's changes, both man-made and by nature's efforts.

Following a slow meander down the coast, poking into one river after the other, exploring creeks and generally amusing themselves, they'd sailed into the Crouch, a river not visited for a while, through the Rays'n Channel.

By the time of their arrival back in their home waters they had also passed by the Columbine, and the Ham Gat, where they'd swept majestically into the East Swale. The skipper had said, 'There's another swatch that has disappeared …' as he'd pointed to a patch of choppy, poppled water as the Gat buoy had been left trailing in the boat's frothy wake: the tide was sweeping across the shallows. Finally, after a week or so bumbling around the Swale and Medway, they had sailed slowly into the Ray Channel, west of the Southend-on-Sea pier.

The mate had said, 'Don't tell me …' and she'd chuckled teasingly, 'but I bet there have been changes here, too …' The skipper had ignored her jocular remark and smiled knowingly back at her … He'd a section of an old chart at home, borrowed from a yacht club pal, an old seafaring hand – a former ship's captain to boot. It was a small section of that chart from 1836, corrected to 1870, that had initially started his quest for a look at what it was like for the early Corinthian sailors from about 1880 onwards: in that time, the estuary had changed immensely. The mate remembered the look the skipper had exuded earlier in their travels and thought quietly, 'He's at it again …' But for the time, it had rested.

The mate, however, wasn't to really know what the skipper's thoughts were until a day, many months later, when he'd bumbled through to where she was quietly minding her own business. He'd enthused profusely about a digital copy of a chart he'd got hold

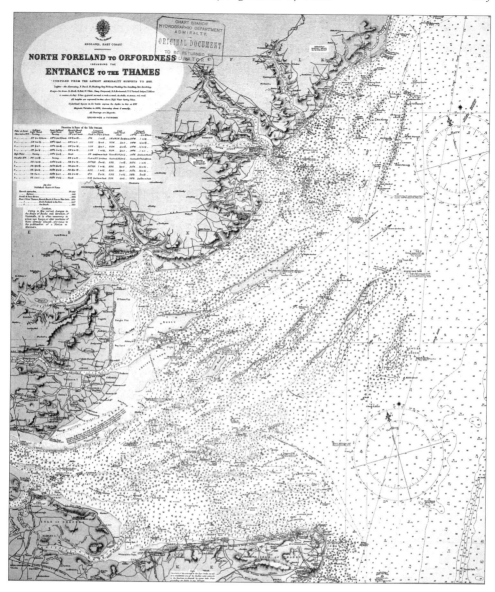

East coast chart, North Foreland to Orfordness Entrance to the Thames, of 1898, with latest surveys to 1892. Cat ref: OCB 1610 – C13. Courtesy of the UK Hydrographic Office.

of (from a kindly gentleman at the United Kingdom Hydrographic Office in Somerset). He'd also clutched a sheaf of papers, small areas of charts blown up, showing greater detail. With these, the skipper had dived headlong into the past ...

'Look ...' the skipper had bubbled excitedly, 'the entrance to the Ore was like this ...' He'd gone on to explain how the tail of the spit had fluctuated back and forth over the period from around 1892 to 2010.

In a survey of 1893 on an 1895 chart of the Harwich Approaches, the tail of Orford Beach out to North Weir Point had run south to a little north-east of the northern Martello tower. By the time of Irving's 1927 pilot book, *Rivers and Creeks of the Thames Estuary*, the tail had moved northwards to a line east of a colonial college (now Hollesley Open Prison). That situation was also the case by the time of Coote's 1960 pilot book too, but what was evident by that time was the way the river was threatening to disappear down into Bowman's Creek, behind the coastguard cottages. Bowman's Creek had had a name change and was known as Barthorp's Creek. The more northerly Woolmer Creek had become merely a shallow run into the remaining remnants of marsh. The breakthrough into Bowman's Creek and a new exit, of course, hadn't happened. The skipper had thought – he'd recently been into the Ore – 'Yes, there wasn't much left of those marshes ... The two creeks were somewhat indistinct, too ...'

By 2003 (Harber's pilot book) onto 2010, the entrance had moved southwards again. What was very apparent was the way the river had eaten westwards into the remaining marshes, giving the final seaward run a more pronounced banana shape. Those landward edges had been 'secured' behind substantial walls during the latter decades. Over those 120 years, the southern tip of Orford spit had halted its path southwards and had in fact retreated, from 52 degrees 1 minute north, one nautical mile northwards. (Note: modern charts are set by satellite fixing) It had in earlier decades been further south on its travels, too. The Ness itself had not grown either, and it was in much the same position as it had been in 1895, at around 1 degree 35 minutes east. Of course, the land of the Ness had gradually consolidated during that time, and had typically followed the evolutionary process of new shingle-based land. A channel, Stoney Ditch, that had very nearly cut through the outer edge, shown on the 1895 chart, had since turned into a muddy creek running north-east into the marshes. The ditch was in all probability the remnant of a previous coastline lost as a storm had swept sand and shingle round the Ness many years before.

'Well, it hasn't really changed that much ...' a perplexed mate had warbled, a little unimpressed. The skipper had nodded and grinned wryly, but his thoughts had already run on ... He was coming into the Deben, leaving the Ore behind. 'What about the other river?' the mate had added after a momentary pause.

'Well ...' And he'd gone on to explain ... The northern point of the river was largely fixed by the solid geographical feature of Bawdsey, although the sea regularly attacked the soft sedimentary nature of that land. The river was a different beast to the Ore: the Deben was essentially a 'canal' running at right angles to the coast. Exiting at Felixstowe Ferry, opposite the Bawdsey shore, where the river took a sharp turn southwards, constrained by its shingle bar. The exit topography had changed over the previous 120 years, with the loss of land beside two Martello towers and a row of coastguard cottages. A huge pile of gigantic rock boulders had been placed along that bank to

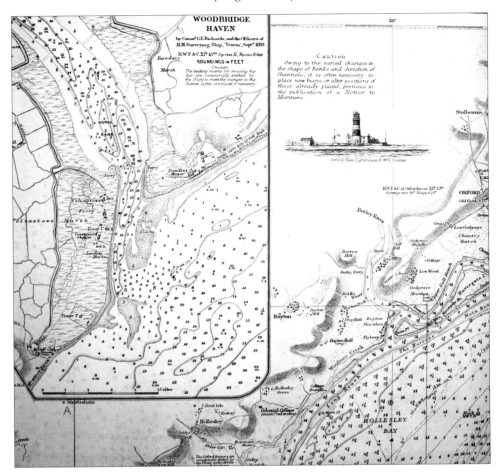

Section from an 1895 chart of Harwich Approaches, with surveys to 1892 and Woodbridge Haven survey to 1893. Cat ref: OCB 2052 – B12. Courtesy of the UK Hydrographic Office.

prevent undercut and erosion and to stabilise it. Back in 1893 the southern tower was a cable inland, the northern a half cable. Both now sat virtually on the shoreline.

Glancing at the mate, the skipper had explained, 'The point of exit has moved around, though ...' It had, too: in 1893 and 1927 the approach had been from more or less on an east–west line before turning north off of the beach at a position between the two Martello towers. By 1960 the entrance had moved to literally right under the end of Bawdsey Point. There had been two other channels shown, equating to earlier and later passages. By 2003 the channel ran out in a similar position to that of 1893 and 1927, but with a south of east approach. And in 2002 it had been hard along the shore, with the spit 'licking' towards the land. This had, of course, moved and by 2010 it had an almost north–south run. 'Interestingly ...' the skipper had thought, 'the position of the northern route in Coote's 1960 pilot book was still evident ... Ready for a change when forces dictate ...' There was a deep gully in the shingle spit on the river side, and the skipper had witnessed its use by local fishing craft.

The mate hadn't initially said anything; she'd looked at the papers and run her finger along the passages. Her thoughts had been on an occasion a few years earlier when, while leaving the river, she'd 'submerged' the skipper, who had gone forward to hoist their jib … Watching him closely, she'd absently turned the boat into the cross seas outside … 'Hmm! The skipper hadn't been impressed,' she'd thought and then smiling, she'd said, 'Not much of a change though … Is there?'

'Ah …' said the skipper, chuckling, 'I suppose not … But those entrances dance to nature's tune …' And surely, '… they will continue to do so.' The other thing that the skipper had noted about the lower end of the River Deben in particular was the mass of marshes that had been consumed by the land, 'inned' by man for farmland, and as a means to shorten sea wall runs. From Felixstowe Ferry south to a golf course (still in existence), the marsh had been in the order of three cables in width and was now dry land: 'But in our present times, with a rising sea level … For how long …?' the skipper had pointedly thought, thinking of an emergency shoring-up scheme he'd known was taking place in the autumn of 2010 to protect the golf course from the sea's undercutting.

'Didn't you say that the inning of land changed the flows in rivers…?' the mate had tentatively asked.

'Ah yes … It's all to do with the dynamics of hydraulics … Flow speeds, mass of water … Time …' He'd left it there: the mate's eyes had glazed over.

'What about this one, then? The mate had, by then, been looking at a section of an old chart showing Harwich harbour – the present Haven Ports part of the world. It was a section of a 1900 chart, with latest surveys to 1899. It was from an original, dated to 1845, of the harbour and rivers Stour and Orwell.

'Well …' the skipper had said, 'interesting isn't it?' By golly, what changes had taken place there. It was a little off-track: it was man-made change, and not anything to do with shifting sands. It hadn't stopped the skipper, though!

The differences between the details shown on the skipper's 1900 chart and Coote's 1960 pilot book were minimal. Above Languard Fort, up to Colonel Tomlinson's Felixstowe Dock, a Royal Air Force seaplane base had been built, and that had been after Irving's 1927 pilot book, too. Above the dock was an expanse of mudflats the area of a small town, and along the edge of the Walton and Trimley marshes there were a number of oyster pits used by the local oyster farming industry. The Martello tower was out on its own island, but had become incorporated into the shoreline by 1960. Since then, well, as all East Coast sailors know – and many land people too: there have been television programmes featuring the area – of the huge and extensive topographical changes to the coastline made by man to create the country's largest port facility for container ships.

As the skipper had opened out their old 2003 copy of *East Coast Rivers*, the skipper and mate had looked aghast at each other. 'Look,' the skipper had said, tracing a line across the page, 'all of that has been buried under concrete …' It was now the Trinity Container Terminal, with over two kilometres of wharf front. And the old Felixstowe Dock had recently been consumed in the building of additional berthing. The skipper's finger line, the actual line, ran just north of Languard Fort up to Fagbury Point, and there, for good measure, the upper end of the reclaimed land jutted out into the river … 'The channel [of the Orwell] has been forced over … There's less mudflats on the Shotley side now,' the skipper had added, thinking of its once being a traditional anchorage, especially for spritsail barges, in the days of sail trading.

'We used to anchor along that shore,' the mate had said, interjecting. 'Do you remember that time when we were there in a blow and there were all those barges … Several, I remember, waiting like we were for the wind to drop and go round a little …'

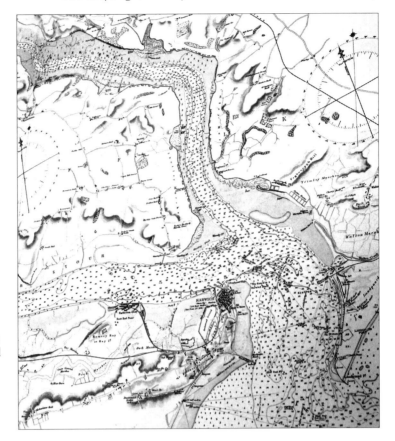

Section from a 1900 chart of the Orwell and Stour rivers, showing Harwich Harbour, originally drawn in 1845 and corrected to 1899. Cat ref: OCB 2693 – A7. Courtesy of UK Hydrographic Office.

The skipper had nodded. The Port of Felixstowe had still been relatively small then, but rapidly expanding. Its position had been perfect for the new transport system that had been exported from North America during the late 1960s. There was flat land, and an expanse of marsh and mud. There was deep water. There was a railway ... The rest was history. On the other side of the Haven, at Harwich, and into the mouth of the River Stour, huge reclamation schemes had filled over marsh and mudflats. An island, Ramsey Ray or Ray Island, had disappeared under Parkstone Quay. The quay had existed before the 1900 chart, though, but the rail links ran out over causeways – not even a road was shown! By 1927 a new town, Parkstone, had appeared on the island. Ramsey Creek had run inland for some miles, with a dock a little north of Upper Dovercourt.

'Ah well ... That's progress, they say ...' the skipper had warbled flippantly, before chuckling. The mate had grinned at him as he'd flicked a sheet over, skipping by the Walton Backwaters, a much-loved marshland-dominated world: he was interested in the sands further down the coast, where the real changes had occurred.

'Hold on ...' the mate had said, grabbing the previous sheet of paper, '... What's all that?' and she'd pointed at an indent in the land near Levington. It had been the area of marsh surrounding the edges of Levington Creek. Even up to 1960 the marshes hadn't changed greatly, but large areas of it had since been inundated too often by the rise in sea levels and had become mudflats. The area was in need of a little coastal realignment ... Below it, since 1960, a huge chunk of land had been consumed by a new scheme, a marina, and it had flourished with several periods of expansion. The marina, of course, was the Suffolk Yacht Harbour.

'And ...' the skipper had muttered, concurring with that methodology, '... marinas should be excavated from dry land ... not eat into the remaining belts of marsh ... But let's move on.'

In the skipper's view, another marina was needed on the Orwell, not for more craft, but to remove craft from the river itself. He'd felt for many years that the river had become too cluttered. It would free water for sailing. Instead of huge numbers of yachts bunching in the ship channel, as so often occurred, they'd be able to spread out ... The river's natural beauty would be restored, too. Whimsical thoughts, perhaps! All the while he'd absently proffered the next chartlet ... it was a cracker ...

'Goodness! Look at that!' the mate had exclaimed, grabbing the skipper's sheet of paper ... with an enlarged area off the Dengie.

Chuckling, the skipper had said, 'Well, there's the place that's probably changed the most.' The skipper and mate were looking at a section of a chart of the Thames Estuary from the North Foreland to Orfordness from 1898, surveyed to 1893. It was from the sailing period of Jones, Cowper et al. and their earlier contemporary McMullen, that pugnacious, irascible even, man of the sea and more besides. The skipper had quickly put his finger on the Rays'n Channel, a channel that had entered in the folklore of East Coast sailors.

At the time of that 1898 chart the channel had been as wide as the East Swale was at high water off Harty Ferry, or as wide as the Crouch at Holywell Point. That was around half a nautical mile. At low water it had had a least depth of two and half fathoms (between four and five metres), whereas in the run of the Whitaker channel, east of a buoy marking the entrance to the Rays'n, there had only been between seven and eight feet of water. That channel, barely half the width of the Rays'n, had narrowed appreciably as it had run past a sandbank, the Swallow Tail, where the venturi effect had scoured a depth of up to five fathoms.

Moving to the Spitway, the skipper had said, 'See, you could have walked – well, waded – across there ... Only three to four feet of water ...' and thinking, 'Maybe, rather you than me': it sat some eight miles offshore!

'Look!' exclaimed the mate, her eyes glinting. 'Those two buoys ... The only one with a name is the Swin Spitway ... the other was just a buoy.' And she'd added, 'Do you think it's why we all call the passage the Swin Spitway ...?' (She'd asked that question before ... in *Mudlarking: Thames Estuary Cruising Yarns*.)

The skipper had shrugged and said, 'Maybe.' He was thinking of something he'd read and had dashed off ... Returning with a copy of *Swin, Swale and Swatchway*, he'd thumbed to a marker ... Jones had written in 1892 about a passage from the Crouch to Brightlingsea and had mentioned a missing Ray (fishing) Beacon that had sat between the Crouch and Buxey Beacon within the channel. The passage had been chosen because it was the logical one. The tide was falling, and it had also dropped far enough for them to be wary of the Bachelor Spit to the north of the Swire Hole, into which the Rays'n ran. The Spitway would have been too shallow for Jones's yacht at half tide, and in any case it was eight miles out. This was a decade before Messum's *East Coast Rivers*, published in 1903, and changes were happening by then.

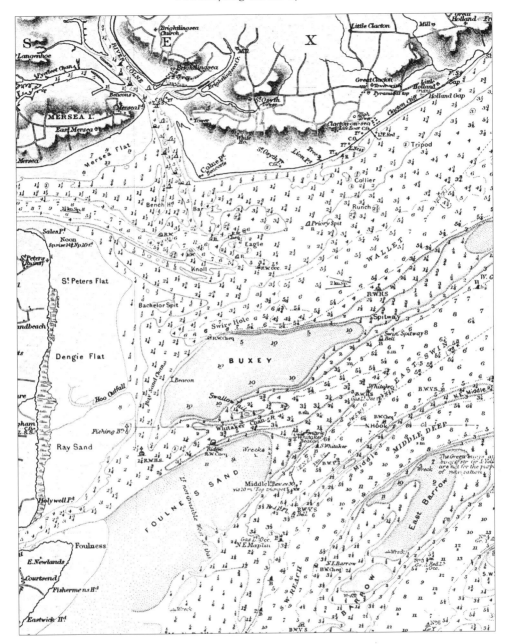

Section from chart, North Foreland to Orfordness Entrance to the Thames, of 1898 with latest surveys to 1892. Courtesy of the UK Hydrographic Office.

The skipper had found his piece ... Jones wrote:

The whole of the bay off the Mouths of the Crouch, Blackwater, and Colne is rather awkward and tiresome, demanding the utmost attention to soundings, buoys, and general look-out; and as there is generally plenty of wind, and often a haze which makes it hard to see the buoys, the navigation of these parts is difficult, and this makes it a good training ground ... An acquaintance of ours slept on top of the Buxey one night in a three-tonner, feeling jolly anxious as to the weather ...

Both the skipper and mate had sucked in deeply, feeling the memories of their own sojourn on those sands sorely (the episode described in chapter one).

By 1927, Irving when discussing routes to and from the Crouch and Blackwater areas in his pilot book, said, 'The northern approach to the Crouch, by way of the Rays'n Channel, which is undoubtedly closing up ... At its narrowest point this channel is a bare 200 yds. in width and carried [1925] only 2 3/4 ft. least water at LWOS ...' LWOS was 'Low Water Ordinary Springs': Irving was referring to mid-range tides. The Spitway had, by then, a little more depth than thirty years earlier, and was around a fathom (two metres), which hadn't altered greatly by 2010. Irving hardly mentions the Spitway as a passage, referring to cross-sands routes. The importance of the Rays'n was shown by the fact that a North Buxey buoy had sat at its northern end, marking that corner of the treacherous Buxey Sand.

Chuckling wickedly, the skipper had elicited a 'What's that ...?' from the mate.

'Oh ...' he'd quipped, 'can't see many of today's GPS-driven sailors sailing straight across sands ... Can you?' The mate had, by degrees, shaken her head slowly back and forth, as if wondering whether or not to agree with him. He had been looking at a chartlet from Irving's pilot book of 1927 showing cross-estuary routes, right across the top of the Buxey!

According to a 1938 Admiralty chart of the estuary, the Rays'n had been enclosed within the one fathom contours, with a least depth of not a lot! 'My grandfather and father used that channel many times before and after the Second World War,' the skipper had said wryly as he'd pulled a face to match, and thinking too that even then they'd have had to wait for the tide to rise. Archie White, sailing in those times too, wrote *Tideways & Byways in Essex & Suffolk*, first published in 1948. Within the book he had a sketch chart of the Blackwater and approaches and the Rays'n Channel. He showed a depth of three feet (at chart datum, it must be assumed). It was the skipper's belief that this sketch was adapted from the current pilot book of the time by Irving.

Then, looking at his 1960 pilot book, the skipper had seen that Jack Coote merely mentioned 'the very shallow Rays'n Channel'. It had then had around two feet, a shade over half a metre, at low water. It had since been known to empty, giving a dry path onto the Buxey, should a walker choose to walk that way ... Coote had also warned of target debris.

The Royal Air Force, bless them, had used the Dengie Flats as a dive-bombing range, mainly during the 1939–45 conflict, and none of that wreckage littered the flats in those pre-war days of the 1920s and 30s. There were now two sets of beacons marking larger target wreckage. Coote said, in 1960, that there were two large derelict motor craft and a target left on the flats, and that the area had not been swept. In the 1950s and 60s they

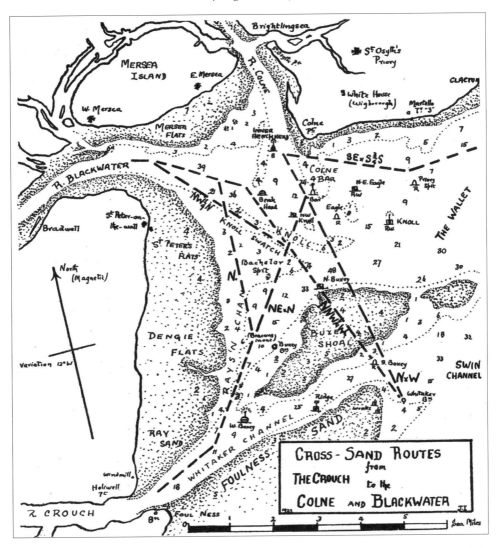

Cross-sand routes from the Crouch to the Colne and Blackwater, from *Rivers and Creeks of the Thames Estuary* by John Irving, published by *The Saturday Review*, 1927.

would have been a hazard, but by 2010 many of the items had wasted and rotted away. Time and tide had healed many surface obstacles, but, the skipper had murmured, '... the Ministry of Defence should have cleared the area of their waste, surely ...'

Why the Rays'n Channel virtually disappeared in such a short length of time had never been discussed, as far as the skipper had been aware '... though it must have, surely!' he'd often thought. He'd heard rumours of a book that detailed the history of the estuary, but had been unable to trace it ... it may have been enlightening. However, the skipper had long held an opinion: that when the progressive inning of salt marsh on the Dengie had reached a certain point, there had then been a sufficient reduction of the eastward run-off across the flats joining with the flow out of the Crouch to upset the area's hydrodynamic balance and cause a decrease in the Rays'n's flow, resulting in its slow demise. Loss of flow through the Rays'n had then resulted in a greater flow and deepening of the Whitaker Channel, leading to it being the main and only real channel. In the late 1800s there was a deep channel, the Hoo Outfall, wider than Paglesham Creek, running out of the flats into the Rays'n. 'Interesting ...' the skipper had thought, 'but the Whitaker appears to be closing again ...' He was thinking about the growth of Ron Pipe's tongue as it licked out from the Buxey in a similar position to that detailed on the charts of 120 years earlier ... 'What's going on?' were his thoughts.

The mate had sat and looked at another piece of paper while the skipper had had his own conversation ...

'Oh well!' the skipper had suddenly said as he too had moved on, following the mate, who was by then looking at an expanded section of the 1892 estuary chart showing the East Swale ... She was tracing a passage across the estuary that the skipper and mate had regularly undertaken over the years.

'There was a wide gap inside the Columbine,' she'd indisputably uttered, '... and look,' running a finger into the entrance of Faversham Creek, '... there was a creek running in here too!' At the entrance to Faversham Creek, and to the east of the ferry hard, was a mass of marsh islands with a waterway running west into what was now Oare Marshes. The chart was interesting indeed and they had both pored over it, exclaiming this and that from time to time. Not even the ammunition works had been built, or the dock and wharves along the Uplees shore.

The skipper saw that the creek now known as Conyer Creek had been called 'Conyers Creek' and the hamlet of Conyer itself hadn't been shown, hadn't existed even, as a true place. He'd known that it had: a section of an 1893 Ordnance Survey map, adapted by Richard-Hugh Perks, showing 'recent' inclusions – dwellings, brick, cement and barge works – had been included in a book, *Just of the Swale*, by Don Satin. It and the 1892 chart showed the creek snaking, for some three miles, inland in a generally south-westerly direction, reaching a mill and its pond at Tonge, by the London–Dover rail line. The creek's mouth was wide and open and wharves and docks dotted its length.

'Look,' the mate had exclaimed, 'Harty was an island then, too ...' Harty was then separated from the mainland by a waterway crossed by a roadway that ran south from the Eastchuch to Leysdown road. The creeks were New Creek, to the west, and Cable Creek to the east.

The skipper saw too that Windmill Creek still ran wide and deep up behind Elmley Island. It was a place that had once been a paradise for wildfowlers. The skipper also knew that at that time Elmley was a place of industry (see *Mudlarking: Thames Estuary*

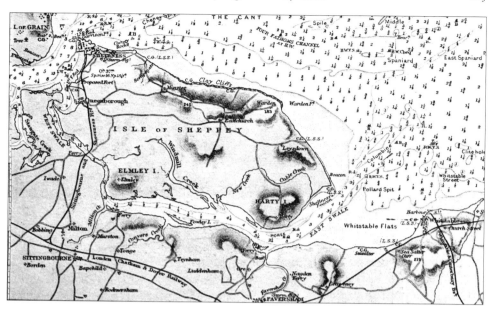

Section from chart, North Foreland to Orfordness Entrance to the Thames, of 1898 with latest surveys to 1892, showing the Ham Gat swatchway. Courtesy of the UK Hydrographic Office.

Cruising Yarns). Fowley Island, at the entrance to Conyer, along the South Deep, was several times longer than in 2010, and it had had grazing fields upon it then, too.

'The Columbine ... well, the Ham Gat,' the skipper had said, getting back to what he wanted to show the mate. 'Yes, it has closed off ... though a friend of ours was seen to use it a few years ago ... well, try to ... you know who ... we were told about it, with much mirth,' the skipper had chuckled, then added, grinning, 'It's all part of ditch-crawling.' However, the skipper wouldn't say who'd been seen, but that the yacht's owner had worked for a bespoke yachting magazine!

In 1892 the Ham Gat had had a clear channel inside the Columbine Spit which had been marked at its northern end by a buoy, known as the Ham Fishery. The buoy was shown on a sketch chart by W. Edward Wigful in a charming article about yachting round the Swale written in the early years of the 1900s, and reproduced by Maurice Griffiths in *Sailing on a Modest Income*. Irving had written the passage up in 1927 too, though he had added a cautionary note about a gunnery range close by and wreckage on the passage's best route ... Irving said, pointedly, in his pilot, about coming from the Thames, '... its use involves little saving in distance ...' A buoy, the Ham Gat, that still existed, essentially marked the southern end. A spritsail barge, the *Colonia*, sank in the Gat around the 1950s and her wreck was still marked on charts. The channel had then still been in existence, with around four to six feet of water; however, Coote's 1960 pilot book did not show the northern buoy. It had since failed to receive any useful mention, and seemed as if it had never had any real use, anyway!

'We're nearly home,' the skipper had jovially said, nudging the mate in the ribs ...

It was as if they had been re-enacting the path of their summer cruise of earlier that year: he'd also pushed under the mate's nose a copy of an old chart of the Ray Channel, the stretch of water off their Southend-on-Sea shore.

'Blimey!' the mate had exclaimed lustily, nudging the skipper's ribs in return, 'Look at all those channels ...'

The chart, or section of it, was the 1836 chart (corrected to 1870) that had set the
skipper off on his estuary voyage. It had shown the entrance to the Ray a little further
to the west of its present position. There had then been two channels running inside
Marsh End Sand, the sand that ran out from the eastern end of Canvey Island. The
outer was the Ray Gut, which led to Smallgains (Oyster) Creek and the passage to
Benfleet; and the inner was The Slade, which led to the Leigh Swatch and thence the
creek to Leigh-on-Sea. A couple of cross-cuts or rills were shown connecting the two
east–west channels. Amazingly, the tail of Canvey Island had then run out marginally
east of Leigh old town. The chart, actually based on a survey of 1836, had a quality
of detail that put present-day charts firmly in the pale.

'Southend didn't exist ... well, in the form it later became ...' the skipper had
commented. 'Look, there's Old Southend ...' which was to the east of the pier '... and
New Southend ...' which was a collection of buildings at the pier's landward end.

Jones, in his *Swin, Swale and Swatchway*, said that a brickfield lay to the west of the
Crowstone. It was then used as a 'marker' to going in from the Low Way buoy, that, in
1892, sat virtually directly south of the Crowstone. There were by then two passages

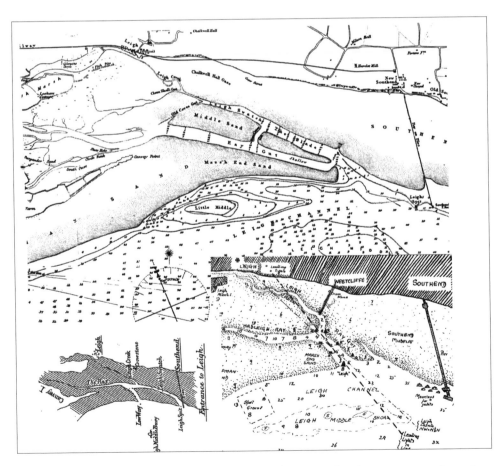

Top: section from a chart of River Thames, sheet 3, Sea Reach, of 1836, corrected to 1870,
showing the Ray channels off the Leigh-on-Sea shore. Left-hand side: Lewis Jones's 1891 sketch
of Ray Channels. Right-hand side: Lt-Com. Irving's chartlet of Ray approaches from 1927.

into the Ray, which had become a single channel. The other entrance was directly west of the pier, via what was called the Leigh Swatch, which had taken the place of the Slade. To complicate matters, Leigh Creek's entrance lay to the east of the western passage, too.

Interestingly too, on the 1836 (1870) chart there had been a buoy marking a spit immediately west of the pier. It was from there that the 1892 Leigh channel was shown. And some years later, in Irving's time, there had been a cluster of mooring buoys around that position placed for the big 'J'-class yachts that raced off the shore during the interwar years. Irving's 1927 pilot had then showed that the Ray, a single channel, opened out through Marsh End Sand. It ran in a little east of a north–south line to the Crowstone, straight through into Leigh Creek roughly on a north-westerly run. A remnant of the Leigh Swatch was shown with a spit. Marsh End Sand had since wandered back towards the pier, but along its edge there had remained a major rill that ran deeply into the sand roughly around that old way through …

The skipper had wondered long and hard about all of those local changes … Several things had been going on locally, though. Firstly, brick making at Chalkwell: mud may well have been extracted from the area. A major development had been the pier. It hadn't long been built. Construction in wood had started in 1830. By 1848, it had reached the low-water mark. It was replaced by the present iron pier, built between 1877 and 1889, and a final extension was added in 1897. It was probable that it had taken several decades for the local channels to sort themselves out after having a sieve-like dam built across the run of the coast. The brickworks site was part of an area of low land, later reclaimed, east of Chalkwell station. The London–Southend railway line had originally run out over the shoreline from Leigh and its old station, around Bell Wharf and along under the cliffs before coming ashore by the present Chalkwell station. Land reclamation had changed that shoreline and recently an area of 1920s housing has been protected only at huge expense. The other happening was the coming of the railway when the London and Tilbury line was extended to Southend in 1856. From west of South Benfleet to Leigh-on-Sea, it was built over marshland below Hadleigh Downs. It had been then that the sea wall was constructed, running directly down the waterway. It had enclosed the creek's northern saltings, separating at a stroke a swathe of salt marsh with its huge area of tidal run-off, greatly reducing the tidal flow volumes through the Ray channel.

Slowly, as if coming up to an anchorage in a dying sea breeze, the skipper had intimated that he'd come to the end of his run around the edges of the Thames estuary, but there was still something quite startling. 'Look,' he'd said, pointing at the compass rose on his old chart. 'Look how variation has changed, too …' It had. Within the Thames estuary, it had reduced from 16 degrees west to 2 degrees 25 minutes west over the period of that 120 years. They'd glanced at one another and mouthed, 'Sixteen …' They hardly took it into account locally!

Out in the estuary, there had been many such changes. One had been a recent one, too: the North Edinburgh Channel, once a shipping route which had silted up to the extent that it was no longer buoyed. It had followed the earlier demise of the South Edinburgh Channel … and so it could go on. 'There we are …' the skipper had said, feeling poetic, 'those changes have always been taking place and will continue to do so, ad infinitum.'

Grinning, the mate had added, slowly and deliberately, while looking intently at the skipper, 'Yes … And let's hope there will always be sailors …'

'… Among the shifting sands …' the skipper had finished for her!

Alone Around Suffolk's Edges

It was hot. Not just hot, but unbearably hot. It was sultry, sticky and stifling. Close in, even out on the water, wafts of prickly heat drifted from the land. It had been building for some time. Sleep at night was a fitful affair and refreshed morning feelings had receded into the dim past. The skipper had begun to live a lethargic existence around Suffolk's edges.

Before that, the skipper had had a crew, two 'Jolly Boys', a brother and a cousin, to keep him company on a voyage from Canvey Island to Pin Mill. That had been a three-day 'men's' trip taking in the two days before the previous weekend. It had been frivolous and full of bonhomie! Their trip had ended at the Royal Harwich Yacht Club, where the mate had joined ship, and after a convivial family luncheon she'd taken the skipper's cousin into Ipswich to catch a train home: his presence was needed on the Sunday! The other crew member had disappeared off in the yacht's dinghy to explore the Orwell shores downriver, to wend through Pin Mill's eclectic mix and poke up into Levington Creek before returning in time to dish himself up for a dinner evening at the club.

That had seemed an age away as the skipper looked forward, with a leaping heart, to the arrival of the mate on a hot Saturday morning. It was a morning that had warmed from the start, from a level one would normally have expected during the day ... It had only promised more heat. He'd found a spare mooring a short way into the Twizzle, off the Walton Channel, deep in the Essex Backwaters. After tidying the sails, he'd scooted about the cabin to wipe through with disinfectant and such to make everything shipshape before setting off to row ashore to, as he'd thought he'd have to do, hop from foot to foot to await the arrival of his mate. He'd been wrong there: midway to the shore, his telephone had burst into song ... Resting the oars and plucking the strident tones from a pocket, he'd been met with, 'Where are you ...?' in an expectant voice. Then, 'Oh, right, I'll wait for you here then ...' the mate had burbled excitedly.

Some ten minutes later, after the skipper had walked what seemed like miles along a floating pontoon, he'd found the mate loitering near the steep gangway from the pontoon with a mountain of baggage ... The hugs and kisses (and tears from the mate) over, they'd lugged the gear to the dinghy. After it had all been stowed, the mate had said, 'There were a few things I found on my list ... Stuff that hadn't gone to the boat before you ran away from home ...' she'd added cheekily, as the dinghy left the pontoon behind. Sitting back in the stern sheets she'd then murmured, 'Ah this is good ... cooler, too...' and pulled her floaty skirt up round her thighs, causing the skipper's heart to flutter mightily and his blood pressure to shoot sky-wards. Grinning at the skipper's look, she'd muttered, 'It's horrible at school ... Even the kids have had enough ...' The skipper had smiled: she'd seen his look ...

'... her floaty skirt up
around her thighs,
causing the skipper's
heart to flutter ...'
Drawn by Mrs G. D.
Ardley.

A little while later they'd departed from the Twizzle and gone round to their favourite spot, deep up Landermere Creek. It was always found to be quiet there. It had been a gentle sort of sail too, nothing difficult, and once clear of the Walton Channel the mate had enjoyed having the helm on a comfortable quartering breeze leg. Passing the entrance to Oakley Creek, the mate had spied a colony of seals sunning themselves on the last of the mud before it was covered by the rising tide.

Watching her, and waiting until she'd soaked the sight in, the skipper had said, 'I sailed to the top of the creek the day before yesterday ... there was a freighter up there ... then tacked out...' He'd grinned as he'd seen a delicate, yet noticeable, shake of the mate's head ...

Reaching Landermere's first reach, they'd tacked in and then the mate had sailed the boat up to their proposed anchorage, rounding up for the skipper to lay out their anchor. The rattle of the chain as it had run out over the bow roller had filled the mate with fresh thoughts of this different world. It cheered her immensely, washing away work! The jib had already been dispensed with, so she'd left the mains'l to the skipper and tidied the cockpit instead. 'Beer?' she'd called. The skipper's grin was broad as his head had nodded vigorously.

'I'll set the awning up ... It'll allow the air to move ... and keep the darned sun off ...'

'Right ... I don't need that sun bearing down on me ...' the mate had implored, adding, 'Here's your glass.'

The skipper had grinned, lifted the glass and murmured, 'Cheers!'

Settling down in the cockpit, the mate had said, '... Right, what have you been up to since I saw you off last Sunday morning? ... Come on, tell all. I know we've talked ... but I didn't take any of it in!' She'd paused. The skipper's thoughts were of his mate, clad in light yellow, the breeze ruffling her skirts, standing, watching, probably tearfully, as he'd sailed away ... he'd momentarily felt guilty ... 'Didn't you come here?' she'd suddenly asked, breaking his self-reproach.

'Yes, later, last night in fact ... But I had two nights in the Twizzle at the beginning of the week – remember it was breezy – well, it blew hard on the Monday ... horribly ... then it went.'

The coaster the skipper saw when he sailed up Oakley Creek to the wharf at its head. She is the *Mungo* of Nassau, Bahamas.

The skipper had had one of those glorious sorts of sails, with a full-sail breeze, a bit of spray and had fetched the tides about right, too. Grinning, the skipper said, 'Leaving the Orwell ... the colours around the Suffolk hills was a stupendous sight ... There was some cloud and the sun ... they were mottled. Then there were all the different sails ... barges, gaffers and a host of yachts skittering about.' The mate had initially coloured, but then smiled: she'd thought the skipper was going to mention the roundness of those hills: which he'd a penchant for.

The skipper had had to beat out of Harwich. There were long and short tacks up the narrow channel that led to Hamford Water, and then a dead beat into the Walton Channel. He'd continued past Stone Point to stow sails before the moorings. A number of motoring vessels that had had an apparent lack of sailing-rule knowledge had been an eye-opener to him – frightening on several occasions, too. Grinning, he'd said, 'On the way in ... one motor vessel, a big thing, came up fast on my port quarter ... it kind of slowed ... would have been better if he hadn't ... the wash was enormous ... it slammed into me ... the boat wallowed and rolled back and forth, slamming the boom about. That really got my goat up ...' He'd had a serious look. Then, chuckling at another memory of the sail, he'd said, 'Beating in towards and past Stone Point I went in over the shallows, there was plenty of water ... to keep clear of the more torturous section ... I was tacking outside the buoys ...' Pausing, he'd added, 'I got shouted at ... I mean ... really bellowed and gesticulated at ...'

'Why?' the mate had asked, indignantly.

'It was something about going aground ... Chap was going like this ...' and the skipper had raised his arms, as if to indicate a depth ...

The mate had laughed loudly ... then said, 'We always go over the shallows ... we know those waters ...' And the mate knew that the skipper would have had an eye on the depth with the jib ready to let go ...

'I found our old Leigh friends in the Twizzle ... had their boat on the next-door mooring to the one I borrowed ... they'd hired it for a month ... and we supped ashore together on the Monday evening.' Grinning, he'd added, 'It's not the same without you ... They looked after me!'

Whimbrel in 'her' anchorage up Landermere Creek. She was joined by another ditch-crawler, a Leigh bawley, the thirty-two-foot *Enterprise*, LO 218, said to have been built by Reed of Burnham-on-Crouch in 1905 but not remembered as a Leigh boat (she may even have been a Burnham bawley). The old boat has been rebuilt several times and has been maintained in use as a yacht for many years.

'Bet they did … You'd be happy with anybody …!' the mate had exclaimed, chaffing her skipper.

'Oh, yes.' And he'd grinned avidly. Disappearing into his own world for a while, he'd been quiet …

On the Sunday, the skipper had met a group from the Holbrook Royal Hospital School. They'd sailed in during the afternoon in smart little gaff-rigged craft … they'd been well reefed down and had moored along a long pontoon outside the marina. The little ships were all crewed by pupils from the school. Passing their little fleet of craft, the skipper had smiled as several crew members had stepped back to let him by, saying, 'Good afternoon, sir …' He'd nodded in appreciation.

The boats had been shepherded by a rib and a cruising yacht. The leader had been very enthusiastic with his prodigies. 'It's an end of term treat …' he'd said to the skipper when they'd met at the marina bar later that evening. 'They're putting their sailing theory into practice … busy planning their next move … wanted to go to the Deben … doubt if it's still their plan … I'll see soon!' It wasn't: the skipper had seen them coming down from Ipswich later in the week.

The skipper had thought 'If that school can do this … why can't ordinary senior schools? … But of course these were boarders and captive to the system … extracurricular activities filled the gaps – no family constraints …'

And so it had gone on. The skipper had skittered back and forth between Pin Mill, The Backwaters and the Stour for a whole week, thoroughly enjoying his time. A lazy night on the Stour was his highlight … And looking at the mate, he'd murmured, 'I went up to the Stour after leaving the Twizzle … Thought it would be interesting to poke up into Holbrook Creek too – that was fun.'

The skipper had found a waiting buoy out in Holbrook Bay, some way in past the northern beacon. 'It was out from a new line of buoys marking the way in towards Holbrook …' There he'd moored and gone ashore in the dinghy. He'd found the creek fascinating and full of small craft moorings. 'There were boats as big as ours … It

Across the creek from the old hard is the slip and boathouse of the Royal Hospital School; both sit on top of an old barge wharf. In the middle ground is the sea wall severing the creek from its source. It 'protects' a stretch of land, covered in scrub, that falls away on the inside.

was no different to our creek really,' he'd said, adding, 'I don't think there are many visitors, though ...'

The mate had continued to sit, quietly listening, watching ...

As the skipper had sailed ashore in the dinghy, he'd passed a rustic clinker day boat that had originally hailed from Faversham, many miles down the coast. Later that boat had been passed again, under sail, while the skipper had been beating out of the creek. The creek was full of an assorted number of craft. Many were old, hailing from the 1960s and 1970s, and perhaps seeing out their last days. Others were quite modern. And there was also a profusion of day boats and weekenders; all, doubtlessly, gave their owners pleasure. All had shared a common trait: they were shoal draft and well suited to their sailing environment.

The skipper had tethered his dinghy to a weed-covered walkway, leaving it to bob on the tide beside a hard. A tree-lined path had taken him into the village, whereupon he'd walked up to a public house at Harkstead to slake a thirst, along a road that overlooked the water with views across to the dappled Essex shore. The way had been full of the scents of cottage gardens. A profusion of pink roses had flourished in many gardens along the way too, serenading him with their perfume ...

The old creek had long since been closed off from the sea. A fierce sea wall sat astride the natural run. Inland, the course could be clearly seen. 'If only,' the skipper had muttered, when looking at this, '... if only this was still open ... the creek would be deep and navigable ... That land cannot be defended for ever ...' It lay, deeply, beneath the wall. Seemingly high up on the seaward side sat an old lifeboat conversion, dating, probably, from around the 1940s. She looked forlorn and lonely. Her paint was dulled and peeling; her cockpit covers were old and rotting. Weed had hung from the lands of her planking in long tendrils. The boat hadn't had a visit from an owner for some time, it seemed. Later, on the tide, the boat had floated. It was a tide high above the land beyond.

Over to the western side of the run into the creek was a huge area that had once been enclosed for a short period. A brick pier and length of drain, once part of that land's

Only now found up creeks such as Holbrook's: a ris-on, a boat adapted from the use it was originally built for. She lives on, just, awaiting her fate, or a new owner, perhaps. This boat was a ships' lifeboat from the age of the wooden type and probably dates to around the late 1940s. With her sisters, they were once a common sight.

system, stood out in the middle of nowhere when the tide was up, signifying man's attempt to defy the sea. Later, when leaving the creek, the skipper had gone across in the dinghy to have a look. He'd thought perhaps that a building had once stood there too. The lost land, the skipper had heard, had once been part of the Holbrook estate. Further round, the skipper had sailed close in to the remains of Stutton Wharf, once part of a speculator's plan to mine for coal … none was found. Above it, on the soft wooded slopes, was the imposing structure of Stutton Hall, set in manicured grounds.

Within the creek, also on the west bank, was the concreted slipway used by the Royal Hospital School with its angular boathouse. It looked as if it were Fort Knox. When talking to the master from the school down in the Twizzle, it transpired that the wharf had run the full length of the inner creek. 'Most of it is below the concrete now …' he'd said. The bricks needed to build the school had been shipped into that wharf too. Muck was shipped into the creek for use on local farms as well. Hay and straw were loaded as stacks for London, and later, after the school had been built, locally made bricks were sent away to wherever needed. All signs of the works had been obliterated, like so many other places.

On the eastern side of the inner creek, above the hard where his dinghy sat, the skipper had looked for an old coal house, long ago used to store the needs of the community when delivered by barge, but look as he had, he'd failed to find signs of its foundations. He'd previously read of its existence … 'The ground's probably wasted away …' had been his thought. From that side, he'd noted, the Royal Hospital School's heavily barbed-wire-fenced hard had looked incongruous as the backdrop of an eclectic range of dinghies, some battered and long in tooth, tethered and unprotected upon the ancient hard. All were numbered: somebody obviously collected mooring dues …

'Oh yes,' the skipper had said, suddenly looking at the mate, 'there was a mill locally, too. It had been in operation since around 1657. Originally it was driven by a water wheel, but later a water turbine.' He'd paused to let that sink in ... 'And finally, before closing in 1926, it had been converted to be run by a steam plant – bit like the mill at Battlesbridge ...' he'd added.

The mate had nodded.

'There was a board of interesting information ...' the skipper had muttered. 'Pity more places don't do things like that ...'

'Such as ...?' the mate had enquired.

'Well ... There was some of what I've been telling you and other interesting stuff about early human settlements ... Neanderthals lived in the area ...'

'They lived in lots of places ....' the mate had quipped. 'The line of the river wouldn't have been greatly different ... easy access to the shore ... with fresh water running down into the creek ...' The skipper had nodded: it had been thought, on the board, as she'd said ... The land had been much marshier along the banks – and would still have been, had man not walled it off!

'Later,' the skipper had said, 'I sat out the cool of the late afternoon on the visitors' buoy – to see what happened – wanted to see how far I'd go aground ...' The boat had gone aground, of course, but not for too long. Upon refloating, he'd pottered out to deeper water close by for a quiet night under a myriad of stars.

'It was fascinating sitting there,' the skipper had said. 'From time to time – well, extremely precise times, I suppose – a bell from the school clock struck the hours and tinkled the fifteen and thirty minutes as they went by ... it was amazingly tranquil and soothing. It was like looking into a rural idyll from outside the frame ... Through it all I was either reading or watching the world go by ...' Pausing for breath, he'd sat smiling across at the mate ... Then he'd added, 'Those bells ... They were so sweet ...' and he'd chuckled.

'What about them?' the mate had enquired.

'Well there was a little dong, ding, dong, dong, for the quarters ... Then a ding, ding, dong ditty for the half hours ... Then a much grander overture before the hours were struck ...'

'How did the boat sit?' the mate had suddenly asked, thinking of the time on the mud, '... and it was evening by then, wasn't it?'

'Well, she fell over a little ... but she sank into the gloop nicely ... felt like she was afloat ... I managed to cook myself some pizzas with anchovies, olives and capers ... bedded on loads of cheese ... They were lovely – washed down with a glass ...' Grinning, he'd added, 'It was too sticky for anything else ...'

The mate had nodded. Her interest was waning a little, too, in the present afternoon's heat ...

'The other thing,' the skipper had said, '... those children were out playing on the fields until it was getting dark ... Their voices travelled clearly across the wide open expanse, happy and full of life. The stronger adult voices and whistles were there too, cajoling and refereeing in the cool of the evening.' He was referring to the school.

The skipper had watched as the sun had set. It left the wet mud pink in hue. The voices had died. It was atmospheric. 'I missed you too!' the skipper had added as his thoughts had returned to Holbrook Bay: as the sun had set towards the hilly horizon, the tide had come rushing back over the mud, licking round the boat and lifting her gently upright. It had

Across the mudflats, the remains of Stutton Quay sat beneath a picturesque, sunlit Stutton Hall.

been a while before she'd swung on the mirrored surface of the night's calm, though. All around there had been a cacophony from a myriad of waders, arguing over diminishing areas of mud. It had been stupendous. Then the arguing had noticeably receded, away to the more distant shoreline. The mud had gone. Ashore, too, twinkling lights had appeared, peering out from wooded slopes on both shores: Essex wasn't so far away. The skipper had thought, remembering that by day, '… It had looked as beautiful as Suffolk's …' But as that night had come on, the last shafts of light had risen up from behind a low bank of distant cloud, shrouding Suffolk's darkened hills. That light had smothered the hills of Essex; they had glowed in patterned colours, conceding them greater beauty.

'So you didn't get back to Pin Mill, then?'

'Well, yes, I'd gone round to Pin Mill … it's such a lure … after a run up to Mistley the next morning.' But that was another story, though …

'Yes …'

The skipper had kept to Suffolk. 'I sailed round that Suffolk finger … close in past Shotley and up the Orwell. I watched the world go by. I read,' the skipper had murmured to questions on his other activities … 'At Pin Mill, I saw the *Hydrogen* under full sail, too – now that was a sight … I'd not seen that since passing her in the Swin some seasons ago, when the boy was with me.'

After that hot weekend with the mate, he'd had a few days back home. Then the skipper had had nearly two weeks of other people crewing before finally meeting the mate at Bradwell. There had been their son, who'd had a few days; a family friend, the original 'Jolly Boy'; and the skipper's sister, an experienced sailor who usually sailed in warmer climes, abroad, and had had south coast channel experience too.

'There was a funny though,' the skipper had said, sitting in a much cooler cockpit. They were by then moored up Tollesbury Fleet, awaiting a window to go southwards to their beloved Swale. The weather had changed too. They'd had a period of grey, showers and winds in the wrong direction …

'When was that, then?'

'Well, it was when my sister was with me ... up in Suffolk ... up the Deben.'

'You went up to Woodbridge three times in that week ... all your crews ...' The skipper had nodded wryly: he'd had a lucky week ...

The skipper had been walking with his sister to Sutton Hoo: she'd wanted to visit the place. It had been hot, like the visit the previous year with the mate. On the way, at a boatyard, the skipper had stopped to ask a man, craggy-looking and getting on in years, if he'd known any information about one of the three barge remains that lay along the pathway by a line of house barges with their pretty waterside floral displays. He'd got the answer wanted, sort of, and more besides ... They'd talked barges and such. The skipper had told the man, a yard manager it seemed, all about the *Cambria*'s rebuild at Faversham after a question about her ... The skipper had said, too, 'You can look her up on the web ...' and the chap had scribbled himself a note.

Then the man had said, 'I used to work at Woolverstone ... down on the Orwell ... back in the 1960s, it was... The *Cambria* used to come upriver, tacking through the moorings. The old bugger didn't mind the yachts – jus' bounced 'em off ...' and he'd laughed out loud. Owners of vessels had long complained of Bob's activities, but Bob had believed the river should have been kept clear of moorings ... the skipper was of that view too; well, certainly clearer than they presently were.

'That was Bob Roberts,' the skipper had said. The yard man was sorry to hear that ol' Bob had died, far back in 1982.

'Oh, he was that ... Lived in Pin Mill, too, and laid his ol' barge on the hard to brush her up, sometimes ...' The chap had paused, remembering. 'Our guvner gave us instructions that whenever we saw that ol' girl coming up river, we was to get out there in the yard launch and get a rope aboard. "Never mind what ol' Bob says, you jus' do it ..." So that's what we did.'

The skipper had laughed.

'Ol' Bob would go mad. Clumping up from his wheel, he'd shout, "Now you jus' git orf my barge ..." But we didn't. There was nothing he could do. His damned dawg would yap away, snapping at us ... and we jus' plucked her along ...' Of Bob's mate, the skipper failed to ask.

The skipper's eyebrows had risen a little while the man had talked, and in a pause had grinned as he'd recounted that when a boy on the *May Flower*, his father had carried onto a moored yacht on the Medway, trapping a leeboard round the mooring ... Tar and pristine glass fibre were not a good mix!

The chap had chuckled and then continued, 'On his way out ol' Bob never got past us either ... We'd see him coming out of Ipswich and we'd be waiting ...' and he'd laughed mightily!

Laughing too, the skipper had added, sagely, 'People think of ol' Bob as being a Suffolk man ... He wasn't, though ... He came from Poole.'

'Ah, but ... His mother's family were Suffolk people, though ...' the chap had said, grinning impishly. And again the skipper had laughed too, at the memory of all of it.

The mate, who had also been recalling the skipper's Suffolk tales when up in the Backwaters a few weeks earlier, had been gazing distantly over the marshes and mud banks where curlews and other waders poked about, minding their own business. She'd not responded to the skipper's last words. She'd smiled, deep in thought: she'd been musing, '... The skipper was never alone ...'

Wood from the North

'This is nice,' the skipper had said, looking across the cockpit towards his mate. 'Look, there's another barge coming down past Heybridge.'

The mate had looked up, wondering why 'a barge' should be the cause for disturbing her. Her look said it all, but she murmured softly, saying, 'You said there's a match tomorrow ... not surprising ... be some others later, too – perhaps,' and continued to smile, as if interested in a vague way.

He'd nodded as he'd gazed across the water. The tide was almost done. A barge, engineless, had crept into the anchorage at a gentle pace, with barely a ruffle at her proud upright black-painted stem. Her bowsprit jibs had been set until the last metres were nearly achieved. With a poetry of motion, sail had been shed; her foresail ran down its stay and was cleared away from the bitts by a foredeck hand; her topsail head had slivered down the slender, forward raking topmast to settle on the mainmast cap; her mainsail was slowly picked up on the main brail winch, leaving the upper cloths full; she'd glided to a stop, then the anchor had splashed through the glassy surface, her cable rumbling her windlass audibly; she snubbed, and she was still. 'It was beautiful,' the skipper had thought. He had a feeling too, 'I shouldn't break the silence ...' It was a warm silence. It enveloped the boat in a sleepy aura.

Some time around mid-morning, the skipper and mate had departed from the wilds of Pyfleet, a gentle marsh-fringed creek to the north of Mersea Island, where they'd sat for two days, enjoying the creek's remoteness. Its remoteness was accentuated by miles of open low grazing land to the north of the waterway, occupied by the military for training. There was about two hours of the ebb left to run as they, too, ran out some way towards the Colne Bar, before cutting across the Mersea flats to pick up the fresh flood into the Blackwater. The tide had helped them all the way. The passage to their anchorage was slow. A lazy northerly had made it a typically unheralded one and its one major attraction, worthy of note, was watching – a speciality of the skipper's, in particular. All through that lazy morning, barges, old yachts (not classics, in the manner described by the hoi polloi, but then, what was a classic?), smacks and the usual hotch-potch of local modern craft had been heading in the same direction as they were – upriver! Finally, in the middle of the afternoon, they'd anchored beneath Osea Island, in line with a medley of yachts, not far from an enticing shingle beach where youngsters were at play and adults walked or stood nattering. The beach was fringed by a stand of trees and within it a number of bungalows and an old country house stood. It was truly a pretty place to be, and with the wind from the north, thoroughly protected too.

As the afternoon wore on, under a sky that eventually unleashed a blazing sun unencumbered with any protective clouds, the skipper had begun to feel drowsy. The mate had made tea some time ago. Another piece of cake had been enjoyed. The pot had

The barge the skipper saw creep into the anchorage under full sail, barely stemming the early ebb.

been drained, twice. The mate had fought her eyelids to finish her novel. She'd watched the skipper's head, nodding. He wasn't far off that final point. He was in a tranquil mood. They'd had a couple of fine weeks, and after the barge match had planned to drop into Lawling Creek for a night before a night or two up at the marina that sat near its head. In his mood, a 'floaty, dreamy state', his thoughts had drifted too, to the past ...

The anchorage had been used by Norwegian barques, laden with timber. The timber was offloaded into dumb barges, and spritsail barges usually between their normal works such as the carriage of cereals for the Maldon millers beyond the Hythe up by the Fullbridge. Some of the work was done by old spritsail barges, stripped of their gear and used as lighters. That trade had continued through the previous two centuries until much more recent times. Latterly, that trade had been direct to a wood merchant and mill, next to the flour millers upstream, in coasters. That, too, had died. The barques, dumb barges and spritsail counterparts had long gone. All had disappeared, except the tan-sailed spritsail barges; many of those last few had been assembling all afternoon. The skipper's gaze had often alighted upon one after the other, sizing them up and commenting, only to himself – in his mind – on the modernity of their looks, especially their rigging and such. His own memories were of rugged, tanned flax sails and hemp, manila and sisal ropes. Thinking hard, he could still feel the roughness of the sail material, the stickiness of the sails when stitching, pushing the sail needle through the layers, and the sharp prick of the three-sided needle (that ran out to a fine point) when his other hand got in the way ... or the pain as a needle slipped off his palm and dug into his thumb muscle ... 'Ouch!' he'd yelped in the memory of it ... it was an involuntary action, and he'd looked cautiously across at the mate – she had nodded off. Her book lay on her lap!

In his mind's eye, the skipper saw a barque; well, there were several of them, clustered off this island, Osea, anchored in the wide expanse of relatively deep water that lay to its south, and the Stansgate shore. Barges lay around the barques, anchored, waiting. Some were preparing to fetch across; their windlass pawls were clanking as they ran over rows of cogs round the barrels, as the mate wound a heavy forged handle. Calls, guttural Nordic calls, from a captain or mate, in English, heavily accented, floated across the water.

Another barge was drifting down on the last of the tide; her shape was familiar. She had a bowsprit; it was steeved up, out of the way for river work. She rounded into the flow, sliding with the tide until her anchor had taken a hold. The head of her topsail had fluttered down as the barge had swung, ensuring it had fallen to starboard. It remained sheeted to the sprit end, though. The mains'l, previously set only to her sprit, was loosely brailed away in a trice. Her foresail lay on the deck, clear of the windlass. It was obvious they were waiting for an expected call. Her name, *May Flower*, carved in a waving sweep across her port transom, became clear as she swung with the tide. 'Must be between her regular runs to London or Ipswich for wheat or barley ...' the skipper's sleepy mind had frivolously thought. He'd smiled, too. Perhaps his mind had wandered back to that barge's cargo books. They were her mother's books now, and there'd been regular periods of such activity, the skipper knew, during the 1930s, when the barge had been owned by Green Brothers of Maldon.

Many unrigged spritsail barges were used to tranship the wood into Heybridge basin, too, where the cargoes were again transferred into purpose-built canal barges – open 'flatties' – for shipment up the canal to Chelmsford. Coal and chalk were other cargoes taken into the basin and transhipped too. The coal either came directly

The motorised barge *Lady Helen* loading timber in July 1959 from the German freighter *Dixy Porr* off Osea Island. On the horizon is a fleet of laid-up merchant ships, probably awaiting the call of the breakers. The *Lady Helen* was eventually hulked along the sea wall near Heybridge Basin, *c.* 1992. She was built by Short Brothers at their seaplane works above Rochester Bridge in 1902. Courtesy of Patricia O'Driscoll.

from the north-east coast, by coasting barges, or from colliers anchored in the river. Chalk was taken upstream to the outskirts of Chelmsford, where it was used to make lime, a much-needed product in the centre of Essex for the building trade, and, importantly, for the farming industry: it was used to break down the heavy clay soils that predominated. The chalk was shipped in from Kent – the only chalk in Essex was at Grays, but was used locally for cement production.

The canal, the Chelmer and Blackwater Navigation, to Chelmsford was completed in 1797 after four years of work, but it was originally proposed as far back as 1677. It had several further aborted starts, like many of the time. When it was complete, Maldon was by-passed! Even with the coming of the railways, a direct route from Chelmsford to Maldon was not built. Why was a very good question: it would have made Maldon more important as a port than it actually became. The link between the two was by branch line from Witham (and that was closed by Dr Beeching in his 1960s demolition of Britain's rail network). Chelmsford, for a while, became an industrial powerhouse, creating much employment, and a need for housing too. Early electrical industries set up in the town. Much later, Marconi came, too, with his newfangled invention, the radio, but by then the navigation and water-borne transport on inland and tidal waterways was on the wane. Housing, however, created a need for bricks, so those became another commodity transhipped from spritsail barges in the large basin by the sea lock – once a busy place. Up at Heybridge, a stone's throw away from the main river at the Fullbridge, mills and ironworks sprang up. The mills, though, had been on the River Blackwater earlier than the building of the waterway, and because of their need for water the Blackwater was rerouted to supply water to the waterway, controlled by weirs up at Beeleigh.

The *Lady Helen* seen a little later, her cargo near completion. The motor barge *Kethole* is astern. Alongsde the *Kethole* is the ex-sailorman *Adriatic*, upon which Patricia O'Driscoll was mate. Alongside the *Lady Helen* is another ex-sailorman lighter from Brown's Heybridge fleet. Brown's were a large wood importer based in Chelmsford, inland up the canal. The *Adriatic*, built of steel at Beverley in Yorkshire in 1900, now rests in the barge graveyard at Hoo in Kent. Courtesy of Patricia O'Driscoll.

Following the end of the Second World War, motor coasters again anchored off Osea, loaded with timber, and for a while transhipments by unrigged barges took place. Many of those spritsail barges survived because of that trade, to be re-rigged later during the upsurge of interest during the mid-1960s. Three of those barges, the *Mirosa*, *EDME* and *Dawn*, were still sailing. They survived mainly because of their size: they were too small to be economically viable as motor barges, yet were big enough for the work of lightering. Many similar-sized and smaller barges were either dumped, broken up, sold as floating homes, or, luckily for some, retained in sail as yacht barges, as happened to the *Venta*, *Henry*, *Violet* of Maldon, *Falconet*, *May Flower* and many others. Some sailed on in that fashion for only a short while, others for a little longer, and one for twenty-five years of regular use under the same family (the skipper's). Virtually none of the yacht barge group from the 1948 to 1960 period that had been lived on as sailing homes had survived. The only exception was the *Henry*, and her survival had been rather erratic and at times fortuitous. 'Even now,' the skipper had thought, 'her survival is in the balance': she'd deteriorated badly over recent years. The skipper had sighed, audibly, but had not disturbed the mate. The skipper, though, had remained in a dreamy state – half in the world and half in another – the past … predominantly … his favourite place!

'Those "flatties" were pretty robust craft,' the skipper thought, as he lay in his never-never land. 'There was one up at Maldon a few years back … She was ashore … being worked on at Cook's yard … downstream of the shed … Didn't have a camera with me, though …'

The skipper's memory was correct. The barge, the *Susan*, a vessel of fifty-nine feet with a beam of nearly fifteen feet and a displacement of thirty tonnes, was designed to carry twenty-five tonnes of cargo. The barge was only built as recently as 1953, and was a direct descendant of the original craft. She was fitted with an engine, the first not to require horses for her working. The barge was built by Prior's, at their Burnham-on-Crouch yard on the foreshore in the centre of that town. Since the closure of the navigation to commercial traffic the poor old *Susan* had had a chequered history, tumbling from one society or museum to another. Presently she belonged to The Susan Trust, with the long-term objective of keeping the vessel in commission. To ensure her future, works were planned to begin during 2010 at the barge repair and yacht yard at St Osyth – a thriving place that could be found up a winding mud creek deep within the bottom of the Tendring peninsula.

'Of course …' the skipper had thought, '… when the lock at Heybridge was widened in 1966, motor ships, which had superseded those barques, barges and early steamers, could go straight into the basin and unload … into lighters for Chelmsford … or even motor lorries.' The skipper had loosed a prolonged sigh. 'Lorries …'

Even after the widening of the lock, the local wood trade soon came to an end. In 1972, the final cargo was transported by water to Chelmsford. The cargo was taken up to Brown's timber yard in the Sprinfield basin (presently used by Travis Perkins' building materials firm). It had had nearly 200 years of commercial use, but like many of Britain's inland waterways, it had fortunately remained in use for leisure. Small coasters continued to go up to the Fullbridge above Maldon for a little longer before it, too, became a haven purely for spritsail charter barges, yachts and the like.

The skipper had felt a little languid after his long muse, but a flicker of a grimace had crossed his face at his final thought … 'The canal craft …' It spread into a grin as he'd said,

A Chelmer barge of a type similar to the *Susan*. Drawn by Mrs G. D. Ardley.

'I must go and see the *Susan* ...' After the demise of the waterborne trade, the majority of the flat barges fell into disuse, were tucked away in little backwaters and slowly rotted, especially the wooden craft. Steel vessels would have been hauled out and cut up ...

Close to the canal basin, a mill was located. It was up a little creek that barely indented the land. Once it would have meandered inland but the sea wall had crept out, finally closing its marshy interior. Now it was a marsh-filled lagoon. In the time of the skipper's daydream, it had been a thriving a busy place. Barges came and went – wheat and barley in, flour out. The mill owner had his own barge too – she was the *Saltcote Belle*. The creek still held a barge; it sat, her hull virtually buried in mud and marsh. Close by, another was known to rest too. People who saw those rotting pieces of wood probably wondered what they were, or even, more likely, took little notice. Their world had gone, it lay in the past. Yet the skipper firmly believed that those old and gnarled remains would know, feel even, by some process unknown to mere mortals, that their sisters still sailed up and down the river beyond their muddy resting places.

At that point the mate had stirred, looked across at her skipper, and with a faint smile heightened by a twinkle in her eyes, she'd quietly slipped below thinking, 'He's away ...' The thought was incorrect – yet he'd been quite unaware of her going!

Meanwhile, in the skipper's mind, the *May Flower* had picked up her anchor, and under topsail and a bit of main had sheered across the last of the ebb to berth alongside the barque close by her temporary anchorage. Her foresail was set briefly to set her bow on its way before it had descended to the deck and been quickly cleared away from the windlass, and her dolly winch, which was ready for use. 'There are entries in *May Flower*'s cargo book ...' the skipper had whispered ...

Another barge had come alongside the vessel on the other side and both were soon secured and crews were soon clearing the hatches, stacking the sections at the base of the main mast and at the aft end of the main hatch, on the deck in front of the mainsheet horse. The fore hatch followed. The loading of wood soon began in earnest.

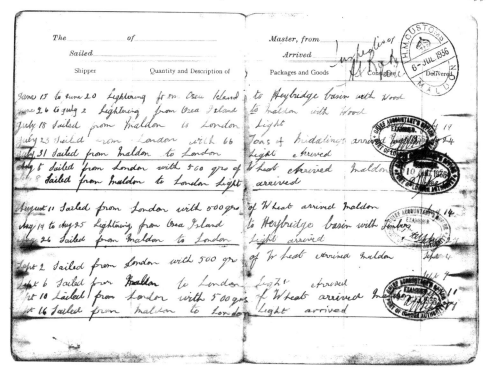

A page from *May Flower*'s cargo book for June to September 1936, showing her working wood from the Osea anchorage. Courtesy of Mrs G. D. Ardley.

Wood was traditionally loaded in what was known as standards. A barge could carry a set number of standards in her hold, provided it was stacked properly. Often, a skipper and his mate would re-stow a cargo when in the London Docks: dockers were renowned for shovelling the wood in, leaving gaps which could cause cargo shift in a seaway, or leaving the barge with a stack on the hatch covers if they wanted their full load: freight was money! The whole was known as a parcel.

The Greenland, Albion and Canada docks were all part of the Surrey Commercial Docks, up the London River, and were the main places of timber import in the south of the country, right up to the closure of the London dock system, by which time ships had outgrown the docks in any case. But the little outposts of waterside commerce sprinkled around the East Coast lived on for many years at places such as Maldon, Brightlingsea, Colchester, and of course where the skipper's mind rested, Chelmsford, via the Chelmer and Blackwater canal. Transhipment was not generally required for Brightlingsea or Colchester.

Up the River Thames, London dockers and lightermen in particular had a hatred for the sailormen. In the docks, lighters were rarely secured and drifted about until needed – this attitude towards seamanship ran against sailormen and their sense of tidiness. The dock's systems eventually led to their demise, never mind containerisation. Neatly secured lighters would have made for a far superior system … Ships, tugs and barges always had to push their way through the floating rafts, further mixing the clanging empty lighters with loaded lighters. Sailormen had a 'right' of passage through the locked basins within the dock system. Sometimes a tow would be given. If not, warping was the only way, unless the tops'l could catch a breeze; however, sailing within the docks was forbidden, although this was not strictly adhered to by barge skippers. Some were known to sail through, tacking if need be, too.

Arthur Bennett, in *Tide Time*, wrote about a period he'd spent on the *P.A.M.* sailing as a barge's third hand working wood in 1947. The barge had taken on a part load from a Canadian ship in the Greenland Dock, which was in the Surrey Commercial Dock group, and they were to move to the Albion Dock. Before moving, though, the cargo was re-stowed. Bennett wrote:

> We cast off at the end of Canada Dock into a reasonably quiet berth to await the arrival of our steamer. Right through the day lighters stacked high with timber drifted slowly down upon us. Sometimes tugs came to sort them out, and once a disgruntled lighterman with more craft to tend than he could manage, moaned bitterly when he arrived to find us hemming him in.
>
> 'You're finished, you b- sailormen,' he ranted. 'If I had my way I'd blow the whole lot of 'em up!'
>
> But Bill [the barge's mate] refused to be drawn. 'Chuck us yer line, old un,' he called, 'and I'll give you a hand.' A sailorman was always in the way. For all that, sailing barges have the right of free entry to the docks and do much of the transhipment work to the smaller outports.

Their shipment of wood, lengths of five by twos (5 inches by 2 inches, or 125 mm x 50 mm section boards), was on a steamer that had arrived late. She'd been held up because her coal bunker had caught on fire while coming across the Baltic from Finland. She had stopped off at Stockholm, in Sweden, to douse it! The barge then had to follow the steamer to her berth and then lay alongside to be ready to accept her shipment of wood, Bennett continued, as the barge's skipper got his barge moving:

> The bridgeman greeted us with a stream of abuse. 'And where d'you – well think you're going?'
>
> 'Alongside our steamer that's just gone through,' we replied.
>
> 'Come on, then. Get a – move on.' Then, just as we started heaving on the dolly winch, he changed his mind and yelled at us to lay off for a tug to come out.
>
> We waited a full twenty minutes. At last the bridge opened and the tug steamed through.
>
> 'Come on if you're coming.'
>
> George (the barge's skipper) could stand no more. 'I've just had enough from you,' he roared. 'Just you shut yer mouth or I'll put in a report that'll shake you up.'
>
> 'What he wants,' Bill muttered, 'is a good smack on the nose.'
>
> But the bridgeman had the last word. He was working late and hated the sight of us. As we hoisted the topsail he said with exaggerated sarcasm, 'Ever read the back o'yer docket?'
>
> 'Drop yer sail!' George shouted, almost livid with rage.

The barge mate had hesitated, feeling piqued! And the barge's skipper, Bennett related, had called sharply:

'Don't argue, Bill. Down tawps'l!'

The mate did as bid, and moments later the bridgeman had locked his hut and the barge's skipper and crew saw him stomp away, no doubt cursing at bargemen and laughing all the way home! The barge made it alongside the ship, but probably not until the following morning: Bennett doesn't relate. He does, though, give an account of timber being loaded into a lighter: they had first in turn. The timber was made up in 'sets', with one end chocked up to allow passing of the sling when ready. There would have been numerous parties of dockers at this work, with foremen calling for the ship's derrick or dockside crane when ready with barely perceptible hand movements ... Tally clerks would be watching to ensure a set would only contain what it should, keeping a running record of what was being discharged, and to where!

The unloading of timber into the lighters just kept trickling along; meanwhile, the barge and her crew just had to wait. Bennett says:

> We watched the deck stack slowly diminish and calculated our chances for the morrow. They [probably the foreman] thought they might be starting on our parcel Friday afternoon, but shortage of craft [lighters] held up the work. The stevedores who had started the day on piece work now automatically reverted to day work, and came after a pack of cards to while away the time.

The *P.A.M.* eventually loaded her parcel of timber on the Monday afternoon, five days after arriving at the docks! She'd loaded twenty-six standards and left the docks late

Timber being loaded into the *Kethole*. Note how the bundles were laid over a temporary beam slung from the barge's hold coaming. There seem to have been two gangs at work below. Courtesy of Patricia O'Driscoll.

that day with a four-foot stack on deck and over the hatches. Reaching Southend the next morning, the skipper was hailed as he'd berthed the barge, probably at the old Gas Works Wharf, east of the pier.

Bennett related that after arriving, George the skipper said he'd been met with, '"Been looking for you for the past week," they told me. "Where have you been hanging about all this time?"'

The skipper of the *P.A.M.* was obviously outraged; however, such were the ways of barging ... Loading from the barque, though, would have been a much more labour-intensive operation, although many had donkey boilers operating small steam winches for cargo work, and sometimes for use with sail working. The barges would have been loaded and been sent away to let another alongside: the barque would herself have wanted to head home for more timber.

The skipper was vaguely aware of a barge looming across the path of the sun: its huge spread of sail created a long shadow – it was late afternoon by then. He'd stirred, feeling uncomfortable. 'Ah ...' he'd murmured; well, it was more of a sigh really. Then he'd thought, why he hadn't a clue, '... That was in the docks ... in the river ... the Blackwater ... the barges wanted to be away upriver ... the barques to square off and get away to sea ... for another cargo. Wood was money ...' At the end he'd yawned, rubbed his eyes and looked blearily around. Indeed a barge had passed close by. There was a low wooden rumble, a splash as a running anchor cable shattered the quiet ... until loops more cable was swung over the windlass barrel, to be set running again. The barge had brought up ...

The skipper had said something. It was unintelligible ... 'What's that ...' the mate had said, as she looked out of the yacht's cabin at the skipper, who was yawning again. 'You awake now?'

'What ... Nothing ... What was that?' he said, as he'd again rubbed his eyes, but more gently, blinking as he took in another arrival in the anchorage. 'Look ...' he said, absently, his head a fuzzy whir: he'd last remembered thinking about his old sailing home – the *May Flower*.

'Been several,' the mate had said, grinning, '... while you were nodding earlier ... No, let's be honest, you were asleep ...' She laughed ... then added, 'Looks to me like the crowd from the Medway and Faversham have come in. Isn't that the *Marjorie* that's just anchored?'

Not choosing to answer her rhetorical question, he'd said, 'You went to sleep too.'

'At least I went somewhere comfortable,' the mate responded with a note of self-congratulation.

The skipper, gazing round, had silently agreed, while thinking, '... A strange dream indeed ... I was surrounded by barges ... There was the rich waft of fresh timber. Sweet, resinous ... pine ... I think.'

The mate had continued to smile as she shook her head slowly.

The skipper had been out for the best part of an hour and the anchorage had filled with craft of all sorts as the tide had finally gone past the top of its cycle. He grinned across at the mate as he'd looked around, taking it all in. Pulling a wry look, he picked up his book from its position of rest on the cockpit table, where it had been placed earlier, unknown to him, by the mate before it had had a chance to fall, and nonchalantly said, in answer to her gentle tease about being asleep, 'I wasn't!'

A Little Corner of Kent

'Over there ... No, there ...' the mate had pointedly remarked as she and the skipper had fetched deep into Half Acre Creek during a meander round the River Medway's creeks during a recent summer ... They were bound for Bartlett, a creek that ran into the marshes and mudflats outside the sea-walled Lower Rainham lowlands, an area of rough grazing, fruit trees and scattered housing and old wharves where a stop for lunch had been planned.

The remark had flown off into the warm, purposeful, westerly breeze as the skipper had hardened up into it. The skipper, too, had begun to muse about their surroundings. Before, though, he'd remembered to look around; satisfied that they'd track clear of the shallows and fetch north of 'the wreck' that had sat, seemingly forever, on the mudflats off the shores of Motney Hill (sometimes Motly or Motley Hill), he'd settled into a light reverie.

'Motney Hill,' the skipper had quietly chuckled. The mate hadn't heard ... 'Ah, yes ... the area's cesspit ... a great big sewage works.' The ruins of a dock that had indented the northern shore still sat, dreaming of its past – 'A load of rubbish probably ...' the skipper had giggled. Much of the land, once marshes, had been a rubbish depository. For many years, it had been a central sewage treatment works for a large part of the Medway towns ...

The skipper's thoughts had then moved back to the wreck – it was of a dockyard lock caisson. It lay over on its side and looked like a beached whale. 'Some say it is of a tug ...' the skipper had remembered. Its shape was obvious to those in the know ... How it had ended up in its lonely spot, he'd never been able find out. It had been partially broken up many years before and now it made a superb navigation mark at the head of the long run of Half Acre's channel, before it split at the entrance into several creeks: Otterham; Bartlett, leading to Rainham; and South Yantlet. Beyond Bartlett, it was possible to sail over the flats, north of an island connected by a causeway, called Horrid Hill, and out into the Medway's Pinup Reach. The expanse had once been Copperhouse Marsh: little remained. Across the marsh a stray way had run out to Nor Marsh and its farm. The skipper had chuckled: that was a passage he'd yet to make. And at the same time, he'd noticed that the mate had been looking at him ... Returning her gaze, he'd grinned at her.

The mate's question had remained unanswered ... Time had ticked on, but only a little. Looking ahead, the skipper had called, as he'd pushed the tiller gently to leeward, 'Coming about ... lee oh ... le'go,' and the little clinker yacht had swept round onto a fresh tack, the mate moving in unison with the skipper's calls. It was early on the tide and all around them the sloping mud banks of the Bishop Oaze and Ham Oaze had hung, teasingly, centimetres beneath the ruffled waters – waters that appeared wide and inviting and were yet ...

'Did you hear my question?' the mate had enquired.

After satisfying himself with their jib's setting, the skipper had chirped, 'What's that?'

Pointing again towards the wooded hills beyond the bluff sea wall they were fast approaching on their present tack, the mate had said, 'That's your Upchurch over there ... isn't it ... your old village?'

The skipper had not responded, though, and looking at his mate, he'd silently thought, 'You know that ... So why ask?' However, he'd nodded in acknowledgement: his thoughts were engrossed; the depth of water; how much further dare I go; and the next tack, of course ... Almost immediately, he'd called for a tack and spun the yacht round. Again, the mate's question was left unanswered.

Yes, it was Upchurch that the mate had been looking at. And, too, it had been the skipper's childhood home; well, one of them anyway. It had been along one of the village's marshy edges. And the sea wall across which they'd both gazed had been a place he'd skinny-dipped after being provoked by girl friends of his sister – the skipper had chuckled at the memory ... his face had coloured, too. The bluff formed the eastern side of the opening into Otterham Creek, the westward boundary of the village. The other place, his childhood home, had been upriver at Frindsbury. It was tucked up a muddy creek, Whitewall, deep in the marshes that had once predominated on an expanse of industrial wasteland, beneath the parish church that sat, as a sentinel, high above on the riven hills: chalk had been cleaved and carved away to be roasted into lime, or with local mud to produce cement. That church was an eighteenth-century sea mark.

The two villages had a shared common connection, other than the skipper's far less important affair; both had had important industries: cement, lime, bricks, and pottery too. Barges had been prevalent at both places as well: building, repair and ownership were both local activities too.

Looking towards those Upchurch hills referred to by the mate, the skipper had said quietly, 'Yes ... It's difficult to believe that among those trees and orchards ...' for he knew fruit was a village business, '... such dirty industries thrived alongside such things as hops, apples and pears ...' Though in the 1980s a golf course had been built on some of the hop fields ... with views westwards up the scenic river.

'Amazing ...' the mate had said, awaiting the skipper's next comments with bated breath: he'd not said a lot!

The skipper hadn't failed her either: he'd added quickly, 'All around the edges of the water we've been tacking up,' he'd turned and waved his arm across the expanse, '... was once a thick conglomeration of marshes ... There wasn't a way through from Sharfleet two hundred years ago either.' The skipper had paused to look around, mindful that they'd been moving swiftly with the tide. Satisfied, he'd continued, 'On the other side, the Bishop, and the areas around Bartlett that run in towards Rainham, were salt marshes too.'

The mate listened as she'd awaited the next tack. 'It's alright for him ...' she'd muttered quietly, almost mutinously, it could have been said, '... but I'm doing all the hard work ... all he does is push the tiller ...'

'Ready about ...' the skipper had called, almost immediately! It was a tack that would take them into the creek where they'd planned to lunch. Much to the mate's relief, her efforts in tending the sheets then ceased. And she'd taken the helm to let the skipper go forward and prepare the anchor ...

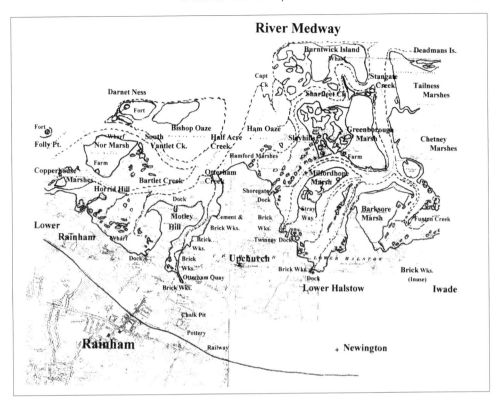

Map of the Upchurch area put together by the author, based on various maps of period 1890–1908, showing land edges, docks, works and places of interest.

During that week, the skipper and mate had been encircling the watery sides of the villages of Upchurch, and Lower Halstow too, poking in here and there on the tide during a particularly fine spell. Both were places deeply engraved on the skipper's heart, and also the mate's: the salty wilderness that made up their greater parts were, for her, the area's brightest jewels. 'Few in those villages realised their extent …' the skipper had oft thought, and wryly murmured, 'To many, it was just dirty, smelly, glutinous mud … covered in disgusting weed!'

Over lunch, the skipper had enlightened the mate about the Roman potteries that had once thrived out on those now non-existent marshes. Many remnants had been found over the years and some pieces resided at the British Museum. The skipper's piece of Samian ware had been found out on that waste too (discussed in *Mudlarking: Thames Estuary Cruising Yarns*). But there had been Upchurch ware and Oxfordian ware too. Pottery making was thought to have gone back into the Bronze Age and before, most likely. Evidence had been found. The Roman potteries were thought to have covered the whole of the Upchurch marsh basin. A Roman villa was known to have existed out on the Slayhills and had been named as such, and during the late 1800s remnants had been found. The villa was thought to have been the centre of the Roman potteries from the first century AD to the third century AD.

Gazing across at the expanse beyond their boat's side, by then a sheet of water across to the Grain peninsula, the skipper had said, waving his arm expansively, 'All that was marshes when a map of the River Medway was drawn in around 1800 ... There wasn't a way through.' He'd indicated, too, with his arm around the Bishop Oaze, north of them, and again wafted it in the general direction of Slayhills marshes, which were mostly blanked by the bluff nose of the sea wall that kept the sea out of Bayford Marsh. That marsh was itself really a remnant of the acres of marsh that had run out to Burntwick Marsh, with no watery breaks. It was the remnants that were now named Slayhills, or sometimes Upchurch Saltings.

'Where's it all gone?' the mate had asked quickly.

'Well ...' the skipper had started to say, but had paused while he'd rubbed his chin, 'it mostly went into bricks and cement ... The rest has been washed away ... I expect ...' He'd looked across at the mate with a wry expression before he had continued, 'Once the bulk was disturbed tides and slowly rising sea levels did their bit, too ...'

The mate had nodded her head gently, thinking quietly to herself, 'The skipper has always asserted that disturbed marsh breaks down quickly ...'

But before she'd uttered any of her thoughts, the skipper had added, 'Although, when I was a boy, the marshes had mostly all gone from those flats ... there remained a thread that ran out to the main remnants of Slayhills. It was largely intact with only a few openings. The biggest opening, and well used, is by Shoregate ...' Sighing, the skipper had added, '... the marsh has been eroded enormously in the last forty years or so ... I've a memory of there being an old way out across it too.' The passage had become wide and deep enough for the safe passage of a spritsail barge too. The skipper

An evocative sight not seen for decades. The spritsail barge *Edith May*, seen during August 2010, is about to gybe in Sharfleet Creek, as she sailed an 'S'-shaped course through, to clear a finger of clay lurking beneath the surface.

had known that a local barge, the *Edith May*, regularly used it and other short cuts.

'Were they roadways?' the mate had enquired.

'Well, not as we call them now, but a way, yes. There were known to be others now long gone too.'

There were still remnants of those two marshland roadways, or stray ways. One had still sort of existed to a greater or lesser extent: over the past forty years, it had degraded much more rapidly than in previous times. It ran out to Milfordhope Marsh and had, until the abandonment of the grazing land, been maintained with rubbish, rough stuff – rubble, broken crockery and such from the Victorian households. That stray way ran from near Twinney Dock out to the marsh in a shallow 'S'-shaped manner. Whether or not it was of Roman origin was not known for sure. The other, thought to date from Roman times, had run out from the land, near the entrance to Shoregate Dock, out across Slayhills Marsh to Burntwick Marsh, and not, as it had later, to Greenborough Marsh.

They had themselves, a few seasons earlier, sailed through that once-impregnable Slayhills barrier. It had been at a point some way east of the current withy-marked

Part of an 1805 map of Upchurch: how different it was 100 years later, after the Victorians set to work. It is similar to David Steel's 1802 map. Note extensive marshland covering what are now mudflats. Sharfleet Creek does not open out to Half Acre Creek: it loops south, near today's Shoregate Dock, and it was shown crossed by a roadway running out to Slayhill and Greenborough marshes. The farm on Greenborough Marsh is seen near the letter 'G'. Also note the tongue of marsh, to the right, in Upchurch. This became Milfordhope Marsh, of reduced size, connected by a stray way to the shore. To the north of Ham Green, a 'roadway' snakes round the edge of Bayford Marsh. A fainter line seen is one of the probable ancient routes out to the potteries that existed earlier in the marshes. Courtesy of Mike Gunnill.

passage that sat close to the entrance to Shoregate Dock and west of the bulk of what remained of the marsh that ran west from Greenborough Marsh. The skipper had chuckled at the memory of finding out, some time before, that Sharfleet, the creek that they were to be sailing through in an hour, had once run south into what had become Milfordhope Creek, a creek that had once run inland to Wetham Green, deep within Upchurch parish. That area had since been enclosed by a sea wall, and had been used for orchards and a piggery in the skipper's youth and since.

The mate had been about to remind the skipper of the maps he'd found in a rather gorgeous book, *Sea Charts of the British Isles* compiled by John Blake. A map of 1688 made by a Captain Greenvile Collins (The National Archives [PRO]: MPHH1/25) of the river from Sheerness to Rochester had shown the run of Sharfleet Creek heading directly south, from around about west of an old beacon that had sat for many years on the Greenborough Marshes, to link up with Milfordhope Creek and the run of a passage inland up to Lower Halstow. There had been no passage through to the present Half Acre Creek, which then hadn't been named. Two creeks, Rainham and Yantlet, were shown to run over an expanse of mud and marsh, Bartlett Flatte. It was thought that a road way – a vicinal way – local or native way – had run out from near where the skipper and mate had anchored. It ran from Upchurch across Bayford Marsh, to the east of Otterham Creek, out to Burntwick Marsh, where pottery and salt were produced, certainly in Roman times, and before most likely (Kent Archaeological Society, *Romano-British Kent – VCH of Kent –* vol. 3 page 142).

By the time of an 1802 map (The National Archives [PRO]: MPH1/518) by David Steel, a nautical publisher, three creeks were shown to run off of the probable course of the present-day Milfordhope Creek, where it had run back east to meet the present foot of Stangate Creek. Those would have been Funton Creek; Lower Halstow; and Milfordhope's run inland to Wetham Green, deep into Upchurch parish. The marshes that then lay on the Ham Oaze (Upchurch Marshes) were shown to be riddled with passages, but no channel. Sharfleet (Sharpfleet) was shown to be in use as an oyster fishery and was shown with depth soundings along its course, indicating its importance. It ran roughly along the line of the present creek bed. The skipper had himself seen that at low water, when he'd sailed deep into it in his lug-sailed dinghy during neaps. Only Bartlett and the South Yantlet creeks were indicated west of those marshes, and the passage through the South Yantlet was as deep and wide as the main run of the Medway at a set of banks that still sat to the east of the Kingsnorth power station coaling jetty. Two hundred years later, that landscape had changed dramatically.

'You know,' the skipper had said, 'the way the Slayhills marshes have been cut through from Sharfleet … there's a deep way … it seems to be following that old route back into Milfordhope …' He'd paused. 'We'll be sailing through there soon!' Then looking at his mate, thoughtfully, he'd added wryly, 'I can't see the marshes on the Oaze regenerating though … The changes wrought by man, eh!'

'No! Yes!' the mate had said emphatically to the two statements: she, too, was all too aware of the sea's gradual rise, and its erosion effect on the remaining salt marshes in the Thames estuary basin.

The skipper's mind, though, was by then on an old Ordnance Survey map he'd seen of the area. It was of 1908, and vast changes had occurred. Only scattered areas of marsh had then still existed all across the Oaze. They had had a number of names:

Hamford Saltings, off the parish's northern point; Slayhills, the only remnant; and Kingsnorth Saltings. The whole though had often been called Upchurch Marshes, which was what they had all been.

The skipper had often said how he admired those old maps: they showed the fringe between land and sea in far greater detail than the nautical charts of today, where there was often just a blurred line ... Chart makers now had little interest beyond what could be navigated by larger vessels and coasters. 'Those charts we used to use ... the pre-1990 ones ... had so much more detail of the creeks and rivers ...' the skipper had often muttered to his mate, when complaining of having thrown out their older charts ... But his mind had strayed again ...

The present remains of the Slayhills roadway or stray way the skipper had earlier mentioned had 'snaked' out across the marshes, where it joined an 'L'-shaped 'wall' that ran north–south and east–west. That 'L'-shaped wall had enclosed the old passage through; it followed no natural route – it was created by man's endeavour alone. The road had also been known as a Sea Road. The eastward leg led to Greenborough marshes, which had appeared at the time to be still in use for sheep grazing. It was no longer as marked and obvious as it had been and was cut with many passages, with gnarled and ancient stakes poking through marsh and fronds of weed. A farmhouse was marked on an enclave of 'high ground' close to the edge of the northern curve of Milfordhope Creek too. The grazing land had been to the east of the farmhouse and had run north and south. The southern bluff had formed the nose at Slaughterhouse Point. The land had had the typical crazed appearance of marsh field patterns formed by drainage ditch-ways. The remnants of one of those drains, where it ran out into Stangate Creek, could still be seen along the creek's west bank, some little way south of the entrance into Sharfleet Creek. Chunks of concrete and remains of rusting pipework sat provocatively in the mud, some distance from the present salting edge. The skipper had often chuckled, wondering, 'How many people recognise those ...?'

'What's that?' the mate had asked inquisitively: the skipper had been silent for some while ...

'Just something that came to mind,' he'd said, grinning impishly, but without elucidating.

Changing tack, the mate had asked, 'What time do you want to go ...?' The skipper had pulled a face as he'd indicated a time, so the mate had set to, to clear away their luncheon things.

Breaking into her thoughts over the tidying up, the skipper had said, 'You know ... You remember where the *May Flower* was moored ...'

The mate had nodded, carrying on ... while absently listening.

'I never took you out onto the stray way that ran out to Milfordhope Marsh, did I?' He'd not expected an answer, and got none, and had continued. 'Well, that ran to the west of what was Twinney Marshes – another Roman pottery site.'

He'd gone quiet, musing about Milfordhope Marsh. It had been used for sheep grazing. It was thought to have succumbed to the Black Monday floods of 1897. There had been the remains of an old vessel, a small barge-like affair that was used to transport the animals, at the landward end of the stray way near to Twinney Dock and opposite Callows Wharf. It had, the skipper knew, also been referred to in a book about the Medway and Swale by Robert Simper. Whether or not any evidence of it had still been visible the skipper hadn't known. 'It's unlikely ...' he'd thought wryly: many years had passed by. There were, though, the remains of at least two other old vessels on the western and southern sides of that island that the skipper knew about too ... A redoubt of land towards the north-eastern end of the marsh had had, the skipper thought, a building within it protected by its own walls. All signs had vanished.

Between Twinney Creek and Lower Halstow Creek had been a finger of marshes running more or less north–south between the rills. Apart from a tiny fragment just beyond the bar across the entrance to all three creeks, at the foot of Stangate, all had vanished. Most, the skipper knew, had been used by the local brick makers up to their cessation of digging in 1966. The skipper had chuckled, remembering, when a child, the steel mud barge and its little crane on deck in Lower Halstow caked in mud – it had replaced digging of the mud by hand ... Before, a spritsail barge could be loaded by a gang of men between the tides. The brick makers had kept one last barge, the *Durham*, with a cut-down rig and latterly as a lighter, to work locally before she too had been laid aside to moulder.

The mate, finishing the chores, had glanced at the skipper from time to time, wondering what had been going on in his mind. All along, while she'd busied herself, he'd that far off look on his face, deep in contemplation ...

'Come on ...' the skipper had suddenly called as he'd marched forward to shorten the anchor cable. That done, he'd hoisted the mains'l and called for the dip bucket ...

Soon they'd been under way with the purposeful south-westerly pushing them along, jib and main goose-winged, their course set directly for the distant beacon that marked (or had) a patch of marsh, by then long gone, east of what was known as Captain's Creek. It was a creek that, essentially, had ceased to exist: when the tide was rising over the flats there was no real discernable channel, but on the 1802 map previously mentioned, a break in the marsh had been shown in that northern end. It was probable that it would have been one of the 'cut-throughs' that had then started to develop in the marshes to the west of Sharfleet. In Lt-Com. John Irving's day, when he'd prepared his Thames estuary pilot book published in 1927, there had been a broken line of marshes, like a tongue, running south-west from Burntwick Marsh (then, still confusingly, named Sharfleet Marsh!).

The skipper had thought, as they passed Bayford's bluff snout, 'Soon the sea will want some of that walled land back below Upchurch ... And it'll have it ... That's for sure.' He'd said nothing to the mate, though. However, he had said, 'I want to go up there, too ...' and had pointed up into Otterham Creek.

'Didn't we go in last year?

'Yes ...' the skipper had answered in a drawn-out fashion, but had quickly added, 'Was only a little way ... Want to go to the top, though!'

'What's up there?'

'An old dock and a boatyard ... and a caravan site that sits alongside a line of old barges buried in a beach ... signs of old industry ... lots.' The mate had pulled one of those faces and sighed ...

'When ...?' the mate had quipped: she liked to be kept informed.

'Tomorrow ... the next day ... this week ... tides are right ... could do it on tomorrow's tide ... a circuit,' the skipper had muttered in a non-committal way while he'd sketched it firmly in his own mind.

The tides had been in their higher cycle and their passage through into Sharfleet was enlivened by the heady scents that arose from the saltings. Purple heads of sea lavender were prevalent, as were clumps of purslane. Their fronds were awash along the edges. Tousled stalks holding their yellow flowers had floated in the tide. It was both charming and beautiful, and also wild and invigorating to the senses. Along those edges, less and less purslane was able to survive. Tide levels were driving the plant species back towards higher marsh levels ... or destroying it where a higher level hadn't existed. Stalks of cord grass had started to predominate. Changes were afoot, the skipper had noted, over many seasons.

The next day, the skipper and mate hadn't gone far ... again. Just a poke up into the approaches to Twinney Dock, Callows Wharf and Shoregate Dock had been discussed. It had been a glorious day, hot and sultry, but with enough of a light westerly breeze to allow for a meander about, while sailing positively. There were only a few miles between those places ... more with the skipper's wanderings, though. The skipper prized those sorts of days ... To him they were of greater value than a forty-mile passage ...

Leaving the foot of Stangate, he'd first tacked westwards into the entrance of Twinney Creek, working up with the tide. The dock at Twinney had been a place the skipper had known as a boy and has been told about in his childhood story, *The May Flower: A Barging Childhood*. It had been 'home' from 1966 to 1968. The dock sat in a maze of marsh and gullies some distance from the inner course of the actual creek, but a gut had run through to a patch of saltings. The original creek had run out from the land in the

Looking into Twinney Dock. The dock served the brickworks on the eastern side of the parish.

'"I remember those lanes ..." the mate had suddenly said: they'd oft traversed them hand in hand ...' Drawn by Mrs G. D. Ardley.

valley that sat between the villages of Upchurch and Lower Halstow. The marshes had long been enclosed from the sea, and now only a trickle had left from a sluice along the sea wall. Twinney Dock was at the foot of high ground that ran out into the marshes in the vicinity of Milfordhope's stray way. The dock had sat to the south of it.

'When we first moved into the dock ...' the skipper had said, 'there was a huge pile of mud or brick-earth just along from our mooring ...' The skipper, helping to dig out the collapsed walls of the old dock while it was being repaired, had found the transom of an old barge boat too ... Since then, the skipper had learnt more of his old home's history. The dock had been built to service a brickworks across the fields towards Wetham Green, a hamlet in the village. They had been the Poot Lane works ... A tram line had run away from the dock and had split into two branches. One branch ran out to Frog Farm, by a group of white buildings that can be clearly seen from the foot of Stangate, where further branches had run into the fields. Another ran directly across Wetham Green's fields, crossing two lanes, lanes the skipper had often walked, and orchards of plum trees. A branch had serviced a large field and it had crossed a path the skipper had used in his childhood to reach the school bus ... The works had been quite extensive, yet there had been no photographic evidence on an Upchurch village website, and the skipper's many sources and contacts had all been dry too. Sadly, though, one had passed away shortly before the skipper had begun his investigations ... The chap had been in his nineties. A friend had said, 'Sadly, dad has passed away ... He remembered the dock, tramways and works ... He'd have helped ...' The gentleman, a respected local builder, had in his retirement ably assisted in the rebuild of the *Edith May* in Lower Halstow's dock, where the skipper had enjoyed many fruitful discussions for nearly a decade ... 'His soul will be out there ... among the marshes he sailed,' the skipper had quietly thought.

The works had ceased around 1930 and the dock had last seen a trading barge around that time, if not before: there had now seemed to be no living memory of the works in operation. The last spritsail barges to use the dock were the *May Flower* and the *Henry* (which departed in about 1980). The skipper had seen that a couple of Dutch-style steel barges were berthed there.

It was interesting, too, the skipper had found, that the tramways that fed the brickworks and docks of the parishes of Upchurch, Lower Halstow and Rainham, west, beyond another dock at Otterham, had not crossed parish boundaries. '... Had there been a local tax ...?' the skipper had thought. All of those places had had tramways running far inland into the fields beyond their shorelines for the extraction of brick-earth.

'I remember those lanes ...' the mate had suddenly said, referring to the ones around Twinney, with more than a little affection: they'd oft traversed them hand in hand ...

In the skipper's childhood days, dilapidated buildings of the old workings had still existed; however, since then all had gone. 'If only ...' the skipper had started to say to the mate, and she'd smiled while grinning in acknowledgement of the unfinished sentence ... Surely, many others had had those thoughts too.

While the skipper had toyed with the boat, the mate had alternated her attention between her book and the passing scenery. It wasn't her type of sailing: she'd have motored. 'Coffee ...' the skipper had suddenly enquired, breaking into her thoughts

A rare illustration of a spritsail barge in the farm dock at Shoregate. Beyond her is the ribbon of marsh that led to, and was part of, Slayhill Marsh. By 2010 this was wasted completely in places and a deep passage out to the Medway has opened up over many decades. Courtesy of Mike Gunnill.

Shoregate Dock in the early 1960s. The way through the marsh is seen above the dinghy to the far right-hand side. Courtesy of Mike Gunnill.

... She'd looked at him, somewhat nonplussed: she couldn't stomach anything other than a cold drink. 'Keeps me cool,' he'd chuckled as the mate had reluctantly risen, shaking her head.

After putting the kettle on, the mate had taken a good look around before demanding, 'Where are we off to next ...?'

The skipper, who was busy nursing the boat round to run out, with a quartering breeze over the flood, had muttered, 'Oh, up the next creek ...'

The mate's eyebrows had risen and dropped as a ghost of a smile washed her face ... She left the skipper to sail up Milfordhope Creek, slipping the odd gentle tack in, until he was able to bear away for an approach to Callows, leaving the marshy entrance to Shoregate beyond them. Callows had been an old farm berth. A wharf of some description had had to have been there: old stakes were found along the shore and it had been the reason why the authorities had granted the skipper's father permission to resurrect it. The old *May Flower* had been moved there from Twinney in 1968. One of the old boys living nearby, a farmhand, had said that there had been a hard too, where barges were loaded from wagons. There had been a patch of mud clear of cord grass and the shore had been strangely shingly – a good indicator.

'Look at all that grass ...' the skipper had said, as he'd sailed along a mirror-like surface towards a lighter that had been converted into a floating home (and marked by chart makers as a hulk – what do they know...).

'Look ...' the mate had chuckled, 'there's a child waving ... Could have been you all those years ago ...!'

The skipper had gone on as far as he'd dared; although the tide was still rising and grounding wasn't a worry, there was more to do on that lazy day. So, letting the boat feel her way round as she'd brushed aside the grasses at her bow, the skipper had loosed the sheets to run back the way they'd come. Passing Shoregate again, the scene of a scrumping incident of years before when the skipper had lacerated his left hand and had been scarred, the skipper mused about the plight of the *Ethel Maud*, a barge built in 1889 by Howard at Maldon. The old girl had been ensconced in an old lighter for nearly a decade, being rebuilt. Some time ago, several seasons earlier, the skipper had conversed with her owner by telephone. 'Doing her bit by bit ...' the owner had said. 'Drop in and find us ...' he'd added. The skipper had still to do that. Shoregate had been purely used as a farm dock: farm produce out and rubbish in, for the fields, probably street sweepings in the age of the horse – hundreds of tons were produced in London, weekly.

'Otterham ...' the skipper had exclaimed, suddenly. 'Let's just pop in there, too.' He'd added, 'We can cut through here ...' and he'd turned through a gap. '... Water's risen since we came past earlier ...' It wasn't the usual route down by Shoregate and they'd touched a few times. The centre plate had scraped and knocked something solid 'Sea wall stones ...' the skipper had smirked as one of the mate's looks had drilled into him ...

Those shallows they'd sailed over were short-lived – well, relatively so at least – for many wouldn't have dreamed of venturing that way! The course took the yacht past the entrance into Otterham, whereupon, tacking, they were able to fetch into the creek. It had still been an hour before high water. 'Plenty of time ...' the skipper had murmured to himself.

The mate was in attendance by then. It was a historic place. It had been a place of industry and commerce. Huge fleets of barges had once sailed in and out, carrying lime, cement, bricks and pottery. Mud, clay and rubbish would have come in too.

The *Olive May*, a motorised spritsail barge, in Conyer's dock head in 1963, when Patricia O'Driscoll was mate. Note the crews' washing airing. Pat said, 'We were able to top up the freshwater tank ... it was nearly dry ...' Houseboats and ex-sailing barges were using the old brickwork wharves at the time. The *Olive May*, built in 1920 at Sittingbourne – up Milton Creek – was of composite construction, framed in steel with wood hull planking (similar to *Cutty Sark*), was large at ninety-eight feet. She was last heard of in Gloucester Docks in about 2000. Courtesy of Patricia O'Driscoll.

'Farm produce would also have been one of the barge cargos shipped out as well,' the skipper had voiced aloud.

'Otterham – it's a strange name,' the mate had murmured. The skipper had nodded and although 'ham' was a common place name ending, neither had known its origin.

Later, the skipper had looked it up. It's thought that 'Otter' was from Old Icelandic for raging or angry, but in Old English it was from *at(+)or*. 'Ham', or 'hamm', was Old English for land hemmed in by water or land ... 'There you go,' the skipper had said.

Near the entrance, they had sailed past a yard. It seemed to be the sort of place that dealt with the refurbishment of house barges. Several arc welders and gas cutters had spewed sparks like Roman candles, and the harsh clash of metal against metal rang out too, piercingly, across the water. The wharves there had been the nub of a brick and cement industry. A huge hole had been cut out of the land beyond, although it had since been largely filled with rubbish. Cement had been manufactured at the Falcon cement works sited there until the early part of the twentieth century, when it had become part of APCM, a cement and brick conglomerate which later became Blue Circle Group. The production of bricks there had only ceased around the 1930s, or a little later. That site was known as the Quarry House works.

Leaving the wharf behind, the scrub-covered hilly shoreline along the creek had soon become more genteel. The hill, Windmill Hill, had had a windmill atop its peak, but it had been burnt down in 1910. Chalets surrounded by well-tended gardens, bright with summer blooms were reached. Some of those gardens seemed to teeter over land-grabbed edges ... the skipper had scowled at that. Staring at the shore, though, the skipper had also seen a row of rotting stumps; he'd been expecting something. They were the remains of a fleet of spritsail barges that sat entombed in the marsh, mud and fragments of clinkered bricks. Long ago, the skipper had known those vessels when they had been poking well out of the beach. And in a book, written by Arthur Bennett, *Us Bargemen*, there was a sad picture of a line of waterlogged vessels that then sat alongside a wharf once known as Woodgers wharf. The skipper had chuckled: the chalets were sitting on the site of another of Upchurch's brickworks.

Reaching deep into the creek, the wind had become more and more fickle, until it had been only the last of the flood carrying them onwards. The yacht continued to drift on with barely any steerage ... The skipper had said, nonchalantly, 'The last brickworks were only closed down in the 1970s ... I think after the first time I took you to Upchurch ... It's a huge housing estate now.' The mate had smiled, but she'd been thinking about the dead end that had been approaching. Around them to the west were the redundant wharves and warehouses once used by London & Rochester, a famous barge conglomerate which had, before its demise, become Crescent Shipping.

Those recent works had been located to the south of the dock, across the Lower Rainham road. The works, though, had once straddled the road. The fields all around were all set well below local road levels and showed where brick-earth had been extracted. The fields had had regimented modern fruit trees set in rows; they were all of the modern, low-growing variety and not the straggly orchards of the skipper's youth. Across the fields, tramways had been built and long dismantled. They had snaked here and there, connecting fields, works and docksides. The tram line had run inland some miles from the dock, southwards, out to yet another chalk pit deep in the middle of the parish. Close by, other pits had been dug in Lower Rainham, but those

Brick workers pose for a group photograph at one of Upchurch's manufacturing sites. Note that the photographer has dated the shot on a brick: 'June–1–1926'. Courtesy of Mike Gunnill.

In the village's chalk pit a loaded line of trucks awaits the off – steam can be seen issuing from the engine's drive cylinder and wisps of smoke rise from its funnel. Note: the men on the pit edge stopped work for the shot too! Courtesy of Mike Gunnill.

had been connected to a works and a wharf on the other side of Motney Hill, the ruins of which still litter the ground. They'd been owned by Goldsmiths, a local shipping, barge, and manufacturing firm. Again, the skipper had found, none of the tramways had crossed parish boundaries.

'Wasn't there a pottery?' the mate had asked quietly ...

'Yes,' the skipper had said, 'I've got a mug at home ...' The pottery had been up near the London road on the edge of the parish, between Rainham and Sittingbourne. The mate had often served the skipper tea in it ...

The pottery had been founded in 1909 by the Wakely Brothers, a farming, barge-owning and brick-making concern in the village. They had made tiles, and drainpipes too: new houses needed both of those! Pottery had seemed a logical progression and the industries had often sat side by side. The Wakely Brothers had had a friend, one Reginald Wells, a Chelsea-based potter. Wells had had a potter, Edward Baker, working for him and he'd moved to Upchurch to take over the running of the Upchurch pottery. Baker's pottery had quickly attracted royal patronage from Queen Mary. Baker became adept at experimenting with glazes too, working with Edward Spencer, an expert in the field. The pottery had been sold by the Wakleys in 1936 and Baker had continued to manage the works through to ownership changes; one of those had been a Miss Winnecott, who had introduced the Claverdon range of tableware and decorative pottery. In 1953 Edward Baker became the owner, and the business passed to his son William in 1955. It had run on to 1963, when it finally closed down. There had been another small pottery and it had closed in 1975.

'Better turn ...' the skipper had said chuckling, '... the water's running out ...' He'd put the helm down and slowly, so very slowly, the boat had inched round. A puff had

Upchurch Pottery in about 1920. The oast houses beyond the chimney are still in existence along Watling Street (A2), the London–Dover road. The pottery has been demolished. Courtesy of Mike Gunnill.

briefly caught the jib, on the wrong side. The skipper had darted to the sheet and let it fly as the mainsail had done her job ... they'd made it: the puff had acted on it, too. The engine had remained silent. The watchers on the wharves and around the waterside chalets had continued to natter away their afternoon as the light air caught the spread sails; the little yacht gathered way and had soon been rustling across still water.

Licking his lips dryly, the skipper had said, 'Tea! Here, you take over, I'll make some ...' The mate had had a soft drink ... And both had enjoyed a succulent slice of cherry cake as the boat had run her passage towards Sharfleet ... The tide had started to ebb soon after their turn and lifted their speed.

Later, approaching their anchorage for the night, the mate had said, 'It's been a lovely few days ...' The skipper had nodded and smiled: he could only agree. The creek had been strangely devoid of craft. They had both commented on that: over many previous seasons, even weekdays meant a few riding lights could often be seen at night ... Now, though ... 'Where are they all ...?' the mate had chuckled, enquiringly. The skipper had only shrugged, his thoughts tightly bottled within his breast.

They'd brought up in one of their favourite anchorages, in a shallow bay in a few metres of water at low tide, along the edge along Greenborough ... The breeze seemed to almost die as they'd reached the spot and as the anchor splashed overboard, its chain running after it, the boat had stopped sailing and had snubbed, as if to say, 'Thanks ... but enough for today ...'

Sitting over a glass of wine, after a simple pasta supper, the mate had said, 'That book you read recently ...' and pausing, as if in thought, she'd asked, '... did it mention any of Upchurch's industry?'

'No, it didn't.' The skipper had stated emphatically. 'It only touched on Upnor and Hoo below the bridges at Rochester ... The book seemed to be only interested in the industry above ... Though I found it interesting, sure.' The skipper had paused, 'Oh yes, my old home at Whitewall Creek got in too ... The people who followed in the path of those dead industries weren't mentioned, though ...' The book had brought to life the Medway Valley industries ... but, sadly, it had left out those of the lower end, where it widened to fold into its bosom the expanse of open marshes and mudflats that lay between the same, more distant, valley sides. It had also been the second book that the skipper had read that seemed to find it difficult to say that 'houseboats' had come into that creek, the home of his early years ... but that story had been told elsewhere ...

You'd never have thought,' the mate had said, reaching for her glass, 'that this little corner would have had so much ...'

'Did I tell you ...' the skipper had started to say, '... Stangate used be used as a quarantine station ... up to the early 1900s ...'

'Yes, yes, I'm sure ...' the mate had cut in, adding quickly, '... Let's just enjoy it ... quietly. Can't we ...?'

A Creek's Sad Lament

All former life had died, yet she was not dead. As time ran its course, she became a haven for wildlife only. As she'd waned, marsh plants had taken root among her banks of rising silt, deposited along the line of many neap high waters. Those silted, plant-colonised banks grew, perpetually, unhindered. They rose, year by year, as successive spring tides inundated them. The wildlife, birds in the main, fed from her clear running spine and silvery mud banks that ran, long-limbed, between her filigree skirts of budding marsh. Her environs had become a birds' paradise. She, of course, had once been a working waterway. A waterway that time forgot, that man forgot, apart from the few. Eventually, in time, the waterway was betrayed, its usefulness destroyed.

As time rolled on, memories of her past excitements faded; elements of her glorious heritage were lost; and the memories of many old souls who had worked her became ever more jaded – though many of those souls would, by then, sadly have passed quietly away. Along her edges plant life had multiplied, and in time became established salt marsh. The marsh had spread inexorably among the decaying remains of her many abandoned wharves and discarded, tired old spritsail barge hulls – barges that were left to rot, either in sisterly groups, or alone along one of her solitary, once busy shores. All became engulfed as the waterway's industry had drifted into a terminal decline. The shores crept inexorably outwards from their man-made confines. The creek narrowed. The natural world predominated, reclaiming the waterway for itself and its few users.

The waterway had once been a powerhouse among its many similar-sized sisters. It had once hummed with industrial output and the frenetic activity of water-borne trade. Cement, bricks, paper and rubbish had been her industry; that was, apart from a period of prolific barge building. The rubbish from London's housing included ashes, which were used in the manufacture of bricks. The ash, when collected, was mixed up with all the other rubbish and it had to be sifted – this was done by women, children and the old. The ash, when added to the traditional brick ingredients, resulted in a stronger brick with a greater tensile strength and was something in great demand as buildings rose ever higher. The area's trademark yellow brick came from the addition of a small quantity of chalk into the baking mixture. Lime used in mortar had been produced around the chalk hills of Kent and south Essex since earliest times, and upon the discovery of Portland cement at the time of a huge increase in property building, the industry flourished side by side with bricks. It helped, too, that the area fringing the Thames, Medway and Swale was also found to have substantial deposits of brick-earth, so with chalk and huge quantities of mud and clay, the Swale and its creeks were ideally situated.

Now, a visitor could only marvel if 'he' only knew. It all happened along those banks; banks that had largely returned to nature; banks that still showed, to a knowing eye, the hand of man. The hinterland hereabouts was of a generally low nature too, the more so where brick-earth and clay had been extracted. Down near the waterway's juncture with the main body of the estuary that fed it, shallow lakes had formed from the worked-out land. Its bounty had disappeared into those countless bags of cement, barrels for export, and barge loads of bricks. That new watery world had become the reserve of bird life. Away from the creek's edges, the land that had been covered in a swathe of orchards, once replanted after the brick-earth had been extracted, was now largely used for wheat and other cereals. Sheep still dominated the low grasslands to the east along the banks of the east–west body of water known as the Swale, though here only a high wall kept the re-encroachment of the sea at bay. Along the waterway's edges, where man's barriers had been broken, her banks and old wharves displayed his detritus. Glass shards, cracked and broken pots and clinkers from his brick furnaces could be seen. Cement production had ended by 1970 and the works were demolished. Brick making had continued along the creek's banks in what was known as the Lower Field, downstream of the Brickmaker's Arms (which became a private house), until early 1979, ending the cycle that had begun in the 1820s.

Man, the environment's foremost shaper (well, he thought he was then and continues to think so!), had first reclaimed the low surrounding marshes that once soaked up the flood tides; then, he'd channelled the waterway to suit himself: it ran mainly in a north and south direction, allowing sail transits to be accomplished with less trouble and need for 'poking' or punting (working a vessel up on the tide with sweeps, i.e. oars), or towing. Its run used to advantage the prevailing westerly winds, or the easterlies that were sometimes a feature of that coastal area. It was ideal for the comings and goings of the tan-sailed spritsail barges that traversed the creek for some 200 years. Its death was a fairly recent phenomenon: even in 1927, Lt-Com. John Irvine, RN, in an East Coast pilot book (the first aimed at the Corinthian pleasure sailor), had written, 'This creek [Milton Creek], gained from the Swale by a tortuous channel passing to northward of a broad patch of saltings, dries at LW. [low water] but is navigable at HW. [high water] springs to vessels drawing 8 ft … and is principally used by local barge traffic.' That sail trade had ceased by the early years following the end of the Second World War, and her successor, the motor barge, had gone by the late 1970s too.

Not all of man had turned their backs upon the flow of the twice-daily tides, though. Fishermen using rods were often to be seen, sitting contemplating the languid flow of the silt-laden water as they waited for a fish to bite … Others allowed their rubbish to be blown into the waterway. Man's tidal detritus – discarded drums, used plastic sacks, traffic cones (found in many strange places …) and much other dross – found its way onto the marshy banks, whereupon most was quickly absorbed. A collection of sailing folk loved that stretch of water too. The club (well, a member) acquired one of the old Murston wharves – Smead Dean's cement works wharf – and had installed a floating pontoon, and had also taken the trouble to mark the lower reaches of the waterway with withies – a waterway once kept scoured by the passage of loaded craft. Those withies were unique too; they had little coloured floats attached to their tops – buoys, for when the withies were submerged. The gallant band of sailors had cleared the creek too, removing a large quantity of tidal detritus that sat in the navigable band. Of course, none in authority had appreciated that … or so it had seemed. And also, up near the waterway's head a museum had opened – back in the psychedelic days of the late 1960s flower power era, when well-meaning men and women, not floating in

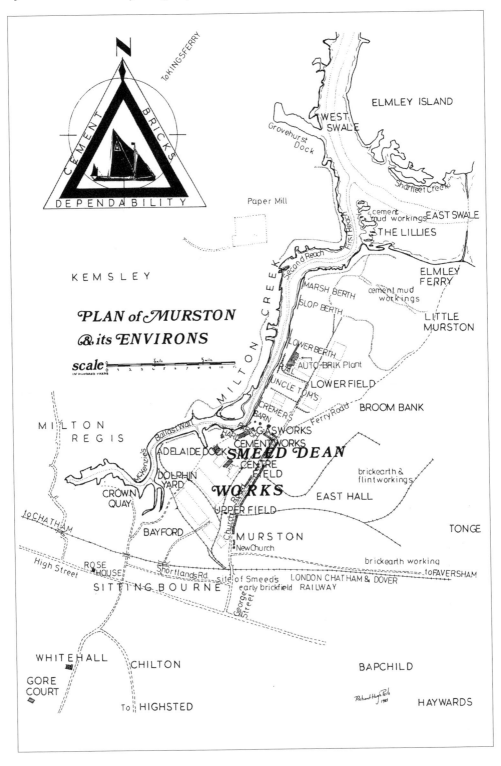

Milton Creek, showing areas of habitation and the works that thrived along its banks. Latterly, newer berths were built along the west bank above Second Reach – they're no longer in use. The bridge crosses the creek in the vicinity of the Lower Berth. Map from *George Bargebrick Esquire* by Richard-Hugh Perks, published by Meresborough Books, Rainham, Kent, 1981. Courtesy of Richard-Hugh Perks.

The top end of
Milton Creek,
as seen about
1980. Drawn by
Mrs G. D. Ardley
from an original
painting by
Andrew Ardley.

a haze, had taken direct action and rescued an old barge yard. The yard had closed, though; the barges had had to quit: authority failed in a duty to preserve. There were forces stronger than the comforting 'infantile' efforts of the archivists endeavouring to maintain the status quo – they could not withstand the pressures crushing them. Those pressures came in all directions. It was very sad, it hit all, but to some it was expected. So eventually, try as they might, the museum, like the club, was frozen out, erased. The yacht club's little band of sailors, who'd gamely endeavoured to stem the tide, who'd made little headway among the towering elite in their golden spires of officialdom, closed up and sailed away. Why, you may ask, should all that have happened? Well, from those towers, glory, glory, a bridge was announced. Its building would effectively sever the waterway from its seaborne connections.

Someone had pulled the wool over the glazed eyes of many: the skipper saw, in a glossy publicity document for the waterway's regeneration a bold claim. It spoke of providing a lively creek setting with boats (power and sailing craft?), cafés, and a green corridor to open up its heritage. That was alongside a host of other advantages ... The document talked of reconnecting the old port of Sittingbourne to the Swale estuary ... 'Small craft could have been encouraged to visit ... small numbers ... a visitors' berth ... near the town ... museums ... shops ... parkland ... raise the merit of this place ...' the skipper had muttered. 'But how ...' he'd asked, silently, 'would that be ... with a bridge across the waterway ...?' Calling loudly, he had added, 'The heritage is being disconnected from its feeder.' He'd paused, thinking. 'Ah, now ... Beautiful, evocative, tan-sailed spritsail barges berthed up at rejuvenated Crown Quay again ... Now that would be something. That would be Living Heritage ... but no!'

For a short while, the skipper had remained silent. He saw in his mind words, language and pictures. 'That vision was just that, a vision, and no more,' he'd said. But, it must be said, the skipper supported the idea of green corridors, though: the land edges were to be returned to the people, with due regard for the intrinsic value of the habitat and its non-human world. The loss of water access, the waterway's real heritage, No!

Later, talking to his mate, the skipper had soon jumped on his soapbox again. 'But ...' he'd muttered, '... a continued non-use of the waterway will only lead to one eventual ending: its silting up. It's silted over the last two decades anyway.'

Another time, too, a listener in his yacht club bar would have heard the skipper going on among a little group. 'It's happening ...'

'What! A bridge ...! Are you sure?'

'Yes, a bridge ...' he'd said.

'Not a bad idea, perhaps ...' one wag, butting in, had said before adding, 'But where ...?' He was looking at the skipper intently.

'Up past the first bend ...'

'I agree, but ...' the wag had cut in again, but was cruelly cut short by his fellows. And he'd remained silent thereafter, soon wandering off. All he'd wanted to say was, '... Perhaps it'll be a high level bridge ...'

'... With a mere four-metre clearance ...' the skipper had finally said. His voice was emphatic. It had left all of those around him knowing that he'd looked into it.

'What good is that?'

'Err, my point ... My point exactly!'

'Frozen out, we are ... Sailors, that is,' someone else had chipped in, as the conversation came to an end. All had nodded sagely. They'd all had long experience of officialdom, its wiles and its ways, in the name of progress.

It went to 'trial' at a public inquiry. Yachting's elite ('That's right, them in their ivory tower down south,' guffawed the skipper) tried to help, they said, but had had to accept their limitations ... The inquiry inspector concluded that the bridge would prevent navigation by some craft ... only. 'That's most except a rowing boat,' the skipper said upon seeing the inspector's words. The inspector said, too, '... in view of the wider benefits the Sittingbourne Northern Relief Road would bring' (to the town), he concluded that the exclusion of craft with masts acceptable.

'What of the balance of man and nature? At the very least, can't a wharf be resurrected ... a pontoon ... below the bridge ... What of the town's maritime heritage?' the skipper had shouted in anger: local organisations should have kicked harder.

For a while, both the skipper and mate had returned to their own worlds, hidden within their respective books.

It wasn't long, however, for his concentration was so disaffected, before the skipper had suddenly said, looking up, 'Be different if it were to cross below Cowes ... severing that honey pot from the Solent, or if it cut across Bembridge Creek,' the skipper said, grinning. He'd added for good measure, laughing wickedly, 'Can you imagine a bridge across the Beauleigh River ... Well that's a jolly good idea!' He'd laughed deeply, but he was angry. Then he said, thinking of something he'd previously touched on, '... into a cord-grass-infested gut. Just like the upper reaches of Faversham Creek within that town's midst.' Then, after a pause, he'd said, 'It took time ... Only a short time, too.' And loudly, for good measure, he'd added, 'Go and see!'

'You're being too sensible ...' the mate had said, and then with greater exhortation, 'It's not our patch ... Don't get het up ... Drop it ... now ... please!'

'I like to sail up it – it's a free waterway – has been for ever – they're taking it away. I feel betrayed!' He'd choked. The mate had smiled at him, thinly.

That was as all as may be. Once in a while, a yacht or a dinghy had nosed their bows into the creek, just the intrepid few. The skipper had seen craft leaving the waterway over the years. Spritsail barges had made their way up to the working museum near the waterway's head. Though it must be said, more barges had merely found their final berths there: only the few made an escape, rebuilt or otherwise. The place attracted the decaying ... a lower wharf would have been better suited. There was another old dock, Adelaide Dock, below it. And, as said, the yacht club came and attached to that site was a magnificent slipway, too. 'Those lower wharves would have made a wonderful spritsail barge centre ...' the skipper thought.

A year before the dreadful deed was enacted, the skipper and mate had motored gently up the waterway on the early flood. They'd admired the splendid open scenery, the marshes, wildlife and bankside decay. The skipper had lamented the wasted opportunities that seemed to shout for attention. He'd seen the little yacht club's fledgling facilities, endeavouring to breathe new life into the waterway. He'd seen perfectly good wharves. He'd seen a concrete fabrication company. All of that light industry inhabited the remnants of old brickfields, and fresh ground too. Most of that new industry had their backs to the waterway, ignoring the possibilities of water-borne trade. 'Shouldn't aggregates and such come by water?' the skipper had thought, and also, 'It's what other sensible people should ask.' The skipper and his mate had taken their boat up until they'd run out of water, somewhere above the entrance to the old barge yard. There, they'd turned, hoisted sail and sailed away ... It was described in *Mudlarking: Thames Estuary Cruising Yarns*.

It was the year after their last visit and in view of the waterway's demise, the skipper had suggested to his mate that it might be their last opportunity to creep up to the top of the creek in their yacht. 'I'll still be able to ... to poke up in the dinghy ...' he

Barges seen at Crown Quay in about 1930, with a barge under sail in the background off Burley's cement works, near the entrance to the Dolphin Barge Yard. The barge boat out on the water, being rowed, would now be in the middle of the cord grass and glasswort seen in the previous illustration. This view looks towards the position of the skipper's boat. Taken from a postcard owned by Peter Gillard.

A sea of cord grass and glasswort infests what was a large open basin below Crown Quay and was once Sittingbourne's access to the sea. It was kept clear by dredging. The quay's remains are seen below the water tower. Viewed from *Whimbrel*, late August 2009, possibly the last yacht that sailed up to the creek's head.

had said with more than a little hesitation. 'But ...' he'd paused, 'just one last time ... can't we?' They were on passage to Queenborough, towards the end of August 2010. The wind was on their aft quarter. '... It's a fair breeze ...' the skipper had remarked, desperately wanting to – waiting for comment – yet his mind was made up ...

The pleading, childlike look on her skipper's face and his doleful eyes had melted her heart ... Smiling sweetly, she'd gazed across the wide open waterway to the colourful, hilly, backdrops that wrapped their beloved Swale within those bosoms: 'It's as pretty as any of Suffolk's rivers', and looking at him she'd said, 'Yes, go on, why not,' while thinking, '... it's more open ... more wildlife, too.

They sailed to the top of the waterway, taking it all in. It was a different view to their last visit. The tide was near the top of its run rather than half full, down below the banks. The marshes were full; fingers of water crept this way and that, like a maze. Sailing close to Churchfields Marsh, they'd gazed across to the squat tower of Milton Regis church to see that its walls of Kentish rag stone were coloured by the sun. The view was appealing indeed. It was lush and green. The open countryside was in full view. 'This is beautiful,' said the mate, thinking, 'Wouldn't it be nice to moor up for a day, sit on the mud overnight, and walk into the town ... shopping ... see the sights ... visit the museum. It's all going to go ... no more yachtsmen up here.' She'd paused, turned, looked at her skipper, and thought, 'He is right ...' before adding, and continuing to look at the skipper, 'Sadly, park visitors will never see the panorama as we've done today ...' She'd paused, then stuttered '... I've enjoyed seeing it ... this last time ...'

The skipper had turned to face his mate; his face had had a wry look. 'Motor boats could ...' He'd previously told her about the coming of a park along the western bank

The open land seen beneath *Whimbrel*'s boom was the site of Burley's huge Dolphin Cement Works. Out of view to the right is the entrance to the destroyed Dolphin Barge Yard (Museum).

of the waterway and the waterside developments planned out by the town. The park was going to run up near the town, encompassing those marshes they'd been passing, Churchfields, along the western bank. He'd grinned. Looking about, he'd said, 'Yes, I'm savouring this,' and turned back to navigate the boat ... keeping generally to the middle of the waterway. He knew the run – it lay virtually in the middle, with nicely dished banks rising into those marshy edges. His knowledge had come from many visits, creeping up on the tide. His first visit to the creek had been around thirty or so years before.

The sail was glorious, perhaps a swansong for the waterway. The *Nellie Parker*, an old spritsail barge, sat as if deeply loaded. Awash, her exhausted hull looked whole. The skipper had remembered the last time he'd seen her. Then, she'd been perched up in the cord-grass-covered mud banks. Her hull, he knew, was shattered and gaped open. Leaving the old *Nellie* astern, he'd remembered a post – well, it was part of another hull, actually the outer end of a wreck (an old lighter) – that had been the home of some of the skipper's childhood friends. By then, the opening into a little gutway that led to the old barge yard had come into view and the skipper had peered in at a vessel, a big steel barge. The barge was the *Celtic*. She'd floated high above her surroundings, looking quite forlorn. Her hull was streaked with orange-red rust. It seemed that the poor old barge had been abandoned ... she'd been used as a sail loft for some years. Some of her spars lay askew and others were broken. Her rudder hung at a crazy angle, a rusted transom gudgeon visibly torn. The yard's old workshop had gone, though – burnt down in mysterious circumstances, it had been said. (The skipper's mother had lost items on loan to the museum in the blaze.)

Leaving the entrance to the sad-looking barge yard behind, they'd sailed round a shallow bend and confronted the waterway's end, Crown Quay. Between them and the quay was an expanse of marsh. It was flooded by the spring tide; it was a tide that had once gone on, further inland, before man intervened. And, it was said, it had formed an ancient barrier to the town. Crown Quay sat within a whisker of the heart of Sittingbourne, a moderately bustling Kent town, a town that had known a rich past. In the town's high street was a beautiful statue in honour of bargemen. Uniquely, it connected the town to her waterway – how many knew?

The yacht's crew saw that the water gently lapped the edges of 'the natural land', against old quays and man-made frontages. Most looked abandoned. Recent clearances showed that new life was on its way ... To their port side, some men were seen working in a yard, moving concrete pipes and other items on pallets. Edging over, towards a line of immersed plant life that the skipper recognised as sea asters (which have stalks of almost a metre at that time of year), he'd watched the depth, nodding to the mate as he'd put the helm over to tack round.

A cheer had grabbed their attention as their manoeuvre was completed: the men working in the yard close by had stopped work. The driver of the huge forklift had got out of his cab and wandered over to join his mates as well. All stood gawping. They'd cheered loudly ... had clapped too. The skipper had turned to his mate. Both were grinning broadly. Behind their smiles, though, their thoughts were tinged with sadness. The skipper had called back, 'You'll not see this sight again ... after the bridge comes.' The men had turned to one another, as if to confirm the skipper's words, before they'd heartedly waved again ...

The mate had said, 'I think they enjoyed this ...' The skipper merely nodded. His thoughts had gone back to Irving's words about amounts of water up the creek in 1927.

A spritsail barge passing the bend seen to the left-hand side of the previous illustration. She is well loaded, probably with bagged cement for the London Docks. Following the great earthquake in San Francisco of April 1906, huge shipments of Kent-produced cement went out to rebuild the city. Note the beehive cement kilns; they were obsolete by the time the picture was taken around the 1920s. Courtesy of Richard-Hugh Perks.

He thought, 'All that depth at the top of the tide, what an asset it could have continued to be.' He grimaced wryly, thinking of a previous thought, '... A barge centre ...'

They sailed away. The skipper said, emphatically, '... Doubt if we'll be back,' adding with a little hesitation, '... not even in the dinghy ...' The mate nodded.

Deep in thought, and passing the remnants of the spritsail barge *Gladstone*, all but enveloped in her jacket of mud infested with cord grass, the skipper had grimaced: it was around that point that the great road scheme and bridge was to cross. He said nothing. They were known as the Marsh Berth and Slop Berth. The slops unloaded there would have been mainly London's street waste. Spritsail barges had ceased bringing refuse into the creek by the late 1930s, but it continued coming by lighter until 1960.

The two old wharves hereabouts could have been part of a grander venture, perhaps. With some imagination, those wharves could have been brought alive: the town was no more than a stone's throw away ... A 'What if ...?' had bubbled in the skipper's thoughts: spritsail barges had continued to use the creek when visiting the barge yard near the waterway's head, and one barge had sailed in regularly during the 1970s. The barge was the *Mirosa*, during a time when she'd been sponsored by the Blue Circle Group. The *Mirosa* during that era had had a huge emblem in her topsail, reminiscent of the age of coastal sail when companies advertised their trade in their barges sails. The skipper had later been told a tale about one visit the *Mirosa* had made to the cement company's wharf at Murston by a respected historian. The *Mirosa* was engineless and had had to turn up the creek, tack that is, but found that the tide had turned against her ... 'The barge's bow hit the mud just down from the quay ... she was wedged,' the story-teller had said. 'She wouldn't poke round ... A line was got across to her ...' he said. 'It were attached to a lorry ... the lorry took the strain ... the barge moved ... then it set off...' he said laughing,

Adelaide Dock in about 1930. It was full of spritsail barges waiting to load or discharge. Coal and chalk would have come in, bricks and cement out. Beyond is the tower of Milton Regis parish church and the chimney to the left-hand side is the same chimney seen to the left of the illustration of Burley's Dolphin works. By the time of this picture, the old works were clearly being demolished. From a Pamplin Prints postcard, courtesy of John N. Mount.

A sad sight: below the site of Burley's cement works, before the wharves at Murston, is the silted Adelaide Dock. It was once a busy place. On a high tide, water still makes its way to the dock's head, where a few boats were seen.

before adding, 'The barge came off that mud bank and a foaming wash built up as the lorry ran up the quay … men were shouting … The line was slipped and the skipper used the barge's way to work across the creek and ranged alongside the wall.'

The skipper had added, 'He probably used his leeboard as a brake … Seen him do that at the Iron Wharf, down in Faversham.'

The historian had chuckled at that, and had finished his yarn by saying, 'The *Mirosa*'s connection to Blue Circle finished in 1979, when the brickworks were closed down.'

However, back to the skipper's trip. Later that day, having gibed round to creep slowly against the tide towards a mooring buoy off the sleepy and quaint Sheppey town of Queenborough, the skipper spotted two huge, rust-coated barges laden with giant steel tubes. The barges lay in the quiet waters, attached to rusted, weed infested moorings that had been in use for aeons. A tug, he saw, was inbound too. A mass of froth preceded her battered stem. A laden lighter was close up to her transom. It had turned past the gnarled remains of the old Flushing steamer pier. It was coming towards them; its funnel exhaust hummed.

As the skipper had edged close onto their chosen mooring, the skipper had heard a noise that had cut the atmosphere deeply. He saw the mate hook their line onto the buoy; he'd loosed the sheets; the mate dropped the jib, but none of that mattered. The noise was loud, resonant; it came again. A deep bong rang out from those echoing barge hulls as the tug's wash had slapped around them, hammering them together. It came again, and again. They sounded like a set of muffled base bells from a church tower. 'Hell!' he'd said, viciously, realising what had been the cause for the noise: he was looking at … He'd grimaced. 'Could only be one place for that lot …' he sniffed indignantly and added, haltingly, 'Those pipes … they're piles … August, now … work starts soon.

Coming back aft, the mate had enquired, 'What's the matter …?' and added, 'I've left the other line to you … You deal with the mains'l, too.'

The curving run of Murston Wharf as seen during 2008. This was early on the tide and the possibilities for this facility, then, were many.

Murston Wharf, the same curve as before, seen from the opposite direction (from downstream) with a host of spritsail barges; chimneys, for the gas works, and for cement and brick making; and beyond, in the distance, a barge yard. The yard's redundant slip still reaches out into the creek. The barge with the sweet-looking sheer, with her gear down, is the *Alpha*, 41nrt, built at Rochester in 1896. Her remains rest along the edge of Skipper's Island in the Walton Backwaters. The picture is from 1928, shortly after *Alpha* joined the fleet of Smeed Dean, owner of all those works. Courtesy of Richard-Hugh Perks.

Pointing, he'd murmured, 'Look, listen ...' then clearly and ardently, as a deeper bong ... bong had floated across the water, 'The bells ... They toll for that tranquil creek ... we were up earlier.'

'Err, what?' had been the mate's bemused utterance, as she'd stepped back into the cockpit, heading for the galley stove.

'For the creek ...' he'd murmured again.

Time froze. The pipe-laden barges had continued to boom in lesser tones as the wash waves themselves subsided, leaving the tide edge along the mud bank dirtied and topped with froth. The water calmed and once again became almost flat, apart from a gentle ruffle generated by the light breeze. The barges became silent. A silence pervaded the clinker yacht's cockpit too.

It had been merely a few moments, but the march of time crept back into the skipper's consciousness. He was aware that the mate was still looking at him. 'Those pipes ... They're for that damned bridge ...' he'd said, emphatically.

'Right!' the mate had said, adding, 'Tea, then ...?' Not getting or expecting a response, she'd gone below to put the kettle on. 'Stay low. It's best,' she'd thought.

The skipper had continued to gape ... He'd stood shaking his head: the beginning of the end was timed for the following month, he'd known. From the corner of an eye, a tear rolled. The skipper had thought that it had gone unnoticed by the mate; however, she'd been watching, surreptitiously, from down in the cabin and had smiled as he'd felt its warmth softly roll onto his cheek. Then as he'd resolutely flicked away that saline drop, he thought, '... Like they're brushing away that creek ...'

He'd stood and gazed a while longer before finally turning away, his attention drawn to the mains'l that gently slatted and shivered above his head ...

The skipper and mate sailed back ... Steel and concrete have severed a natural and perfectly useable waterway at a position that can be seen at the edge of the top illustration on page 164, just downstream of a house, originally the Brickmaker's Arms. It was an extremely sad sight ... The workmen, briefly, stopped and stared!

The Jolly Boys

'Didn't you have a new prop last year …?' the chap at the helm had said as he'd looked inquisitively towards the skipper. His craggy face, a face that had already shown the shadow of a weekend's beard, had creased into a grin.

'Err, yes,' the skipper had said.

They were about to head out of the creek where the little clinker sloop was berthed. A fresh north-westerly would soon be hurrying them along. Soon, the mainsail had been hoisted by the skipper while his crew, a quiet, unassuming chap and a good shipmate to boot, had turned the boat through the wind before blessedly silencing the engine. 'That's great …' the skipper had called, 'I'll run the jib up.'

'Why was that?' the crew had asked, adding, 'What happened, then …?' He was referring back to the propeller, of course.

'Well, I was taking my eldest brother for an overnighter last autumn and …' Pausing and looking sheepish, the skipper had continued, '… and it was my fault. I hadn't noticed he'd left the dinghy painter too long … I'd gone astern to clear the berth … there was a whoosh as the dinghy leapt towards us … I disengaged rapidly …' The skipper had grimaced as he'd added, 'The dinghy painter had gone round the propeller …'

'Oh yes,' the crew had said, keenly awaiting the rest of the story.

'My brother – the one who lives in Newfoundland – was mortified.'

'What did you do?'

'Well, I dragged my clothing off, to my thin cotton boxers, and leapt overboard and untangled it…' The skipper had laughed because the mud had still been showing at the side of the boat, and afterwards he'd hosed himself down on the jetty before jumping back into his clothes. 'It was quite warm … the sea water, that is.' Grinning widely, he'd added, 'The fresh tap was darn chilly, though!'

'What about the propeller …?'

'Ah …' The skipper had then told the crew about two of the blades being damaged … one had had a chunk out of it. And because it had suffered from dezincification, it hadn't helped matters. 'Didn't stop us, though,' the skipper had added, grinning avidly again.

'Don't suppose it would've,' the crew had said, laughing. 'You hardly use it …' He'd been referring to the engine … By then they had swept out of the creek and were bounding over the wind over tide lop over the shallows as they'd crossed the Ray Sands.

At that moment the kettle had sung out and the skipper had said, 'Just keep her around our present course – east of the chimney,' and he'd pointed ahead through the shrouds before ducking below to make some coffee.

Returning, the skipper had said, 'It was quite a couple of days we had.' He'd then added, 'It was a cracking sail and I left my brother to it, across the Thames and we

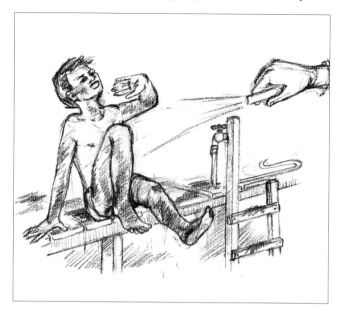

'The fresh tap was darn
chilly though!' Drawn by
Mrs G. D. Ardley.

took turns up the Medway. We'd sailed up to Upnor. There was some tacking up the
reaches, as expected, but we made good time.' The crew had grinned: he knew about
having to tack up that river ...

The skipper had stopped briefly to offer a touch of advice to his crew: a ship had
been seen – well, there'd been two actually – coming down sea reach from the west ...
bearing down at speed. Another two were away to the east, with a dredger working
the channel too. They'd gilled around for the closest, and then scampered across to
open out the southern side of the river, where they'd had the waterway to themselves.
No ships would trouble them there!

'Anyway,' the skipper had said, 'We'd had a good evening in the local hostelry ...
and a nightcap ...' He'd paused, for the crew had been grinning like the Cheshire Cat
... 'The next day was breezy. It was a south-westerly. The boat tramped down from
Upnor with only half her mains'l at just about full speed ... I don't think she'd have
gone any faster.'

'Lovely ...' the crew had intoned in a drawn-out fashion while grinning more
broadly than before! The crew, although he'd learnt to respect the wind and the sea
conditions, had never minded a bit of a blow. The crew had been known to the skipper
for nearly three decades, but it had taken a home move on the skipper and mate's
part to find out that the chap had had a natural bent for sailing after he'd surprisingly
asked to try it out. The Royal Yachting Association had had a campaign for members
to encourage 'virgins' to have a go and that year the skipper had given several people
the opportunity, out on the water.

'We only had that sail up all the way back, until off the entrance to the creek, where
we'd picked up a buoy. It was a cracking passage ...' The skipper's brother had then
enjoyed a spot of mudlarking, running across the sands and paddling his feet to make
'quicksand', like he'd done as a lad! Chuckling, the skipper had then added, 'The mate
called my phone just as we'd moored up ... She was checking up on us ... The weather
in the morning had been concerning her ...' Then the skipper had chuckled louder still!

'Err, yes, my mum said something along those lines yesterday ... I told her it was fine and you didn't go if ...' The skipper had been nodding, so the crew's sentence had been left truncated. He'd added, though, '... Her indoors was happy ... Well, she knows you look after me – trusts you!' The skipper had laughed ...

Then, as the boat had continued to leap through the water, jumping about in the short sharp crests as they'd approached the Nore Swatch, they'd both joked like little boys ... and thought how 'foolish' the crew's sweet-natured good lady was. Both had chuckled too: how often had they called in, late, after too many nightcaps, to their respective mates? Of course, they'd always been secured in a harbour ... The crew had grinned at the skipper and said, 'We're expected to call her later ... After we've been ashore.' He was referring to his mate. 'She said, "Enjoy your Jolly Boys' cruise" as I left ...' Both had been thinking of that welcome beer at the end of their present passage, too ... The two men's women had long before coined the phrase that seemed to characterise their menfolk's regression back to being a couple of young teenagers when off on their own. Other crew members who'd sailed with the skipper hadn't quite reached the same peaks, yet!

The skipper had soon moved into the relative shallows of the Grain Flats, where it had been much quieter, and with less of the foul tide the boat had surged forward. The wind, too, had appeared to have freshened a little and the clinker sloop was beginning to tug at the helm; easing the sheet, the skipper had concluded that less sail was needed. 'It'll make life easier when we're harder on the wind ... inside the Medway,' the skipper had said, grinning, so at the end of the run down the Nore, or

They know who they are! Some of the 'motley' crew that have made up the 'Jolly Boys' – the original is on the top right-hand side, helming the boat as he and the skipper departed from Faversham under jib.

Jenkin Swatch as it used to be known, the crew had rounded up while the skipper had pulled the reef into the mains'l.

'We did the same last year … Didn't we?'

'May have been the previous,' the skipper had replied. 'A squall was bearing down on us and I clipped on and just got it done before a furious tempest hit us … Then it was gone!' he'd added, laughing.

'I got wet …' the crew had said.

'Ah, well … You should have put your oilies on when I suggested …!'

Trenching for the Brit-Ned power cable had been in operation at that time and the skipper had directed the crew on a course round the edge of the marker buoys: a call to a guard vessel had failed to elicit any other instructions … Earlier that year, a pile of spoil had been seen running out across the Grain Flats. It had sat some four metres above the sands and ran in a diminishing line out across the very area that the skipper had usually sailed … It had been flattened by the time of their present passage.

It hadn't been long before the open mouth of the Medway was spread before them and with the keen nor'westerly pushing them over the tidal tumbles along the edge of the Grain Hard, they'd fairly romped along. The boat had loved it. It banged into the short waves and froth and laced spume trailed astern.

Clearing the entrance of the river, they'd angled across the stream towards the West Swale. The skipper had said, 'Heck … There's still fifteen minutes to high water …'

'Crikey …' the crew had spluttered, 'that's a fast …' Then he'd added, 'Is this still okay?'

The skipper had nodded, after the merest of a look around. It had been approaching dead water and any tide was assisting them forwards, alone. Then he'd said, 'When I did that television stunt last September … a bloke said to me when I was ashore afterwards … weren't you with me?' The skipper paused, 'Of course you were … Oh, yes. He'd said that there were still humps out on the flats over there … They're the remains of burials on the marshes from the prison ship days – mostly French prisoners from the Napoleonic wars.' The skipper had pointed across the water. The flats, however, had been covered by the tide. But the crew knew the long spit that ran out from the marshes of Deadmans Island and the mudflats that stretched away to the west along the island's tide-eroded marsh edges.

'Ever seen any?' the crew asked keenly.

'No. Though I've not actually looked … But I probably will … one day.' Pausing, the skipper had added, 'We're nearly there …' The crew had nodded. The skipper had then discussed their approach and passage end with his friend.

Going forward, the skipper had called to the crew, 'Round up …' and he'd quickly dispensed with the mainsail and secured it as the crew had ably looked after the boat, letting her jog along under jib alone. 'We'll run on down to a buoy close up to the floating pontoon,' the skipper had said, grinning and looking his crew's way. 'There's one or two spare …'

The skipper's crew had carried out that operation a number of times, at both ends of the boat, but never under sail when at the helm. He'd looked up, enquiringly. The skipper had said quietly, and firmly, 'Just keep her onto the buoy … slightly on our port … Ease the jib sheet out … then back in … a little. You'll get a feel of the power in the breeze … ease in and out as you need …' The crew had given the briefest of nods. Then concentrating, hard, as the buoy had neared, he'd feathered the jib and played it as the buoy came onto the boat's head.

As he'd hooked onto the buoy's cocked shackle the skipper, with his head turned aft, had called, 'Got it.' He'd quickly added, 'Let the jib sheet fly.' The dedicated mooring line had soon been set and the jib doused and tidied along the guard rail. The buoys in that mooring trot had never been the easiest to get a line onto and moments of hilarity were often observed – and experienced. The skipper called back, 'Well done!'

'Beer …?' the crew had called in return. 'I think we deserve it …' He'd grinned. 'I'll get the chips and dips out too …' had floated to the skipper's ears as the man had disappeared below to rummage in the stores lockers. No sooner than the refreshments had appeared, the skipper had had the cockpit table set … 'Good passage?' the crew had said setting down the glasses and two bilge-chilled tins.

The skipper, cracking his beer, had nodded, grinned broadly and said, 'Yes, cheers – the sun's shinning too!'

Chatting over their beer, before a wash and brush up to prepare for the 'town', the skipper had chatted about the old Queenborough steamer pier, the nearby historic dockyard at Sheerness and other things.

The pier had been built for the Flushing ferry service to Holland and had been served by a branch from the Sittingbourne & Sheerness Railway. The steamers had been run by the Zeeland Steamship Company between 1876 until 1927, when the pier had been too badly damaged by fire to be used. It had since been partially cleared but the area had continued to be a hazard … 'That's why those two beacons are down there,' and the skipper had pointed across the water.

The crew had nodded, regularly, sipped at his beer, pushed the skipper's towards him, provocatively, as his own had lowered to refill point … and maintained a rapt interest too … 'Drink up …' he'd said, from time to time.

The bells of the parish church had suddenly rung out. 'That's a quarter to …' the skipper had chirped. 'Time we were ashore …' The bells had rung again as they rowed ashore. The bells had rung seven, and both had grinned, thinking of their dinner and the promise of jugs of foaming ale. The bells, too, were as if to welcome the two sailors within the town's bosom … The church had had a long history of welcoming sailors. Nelson, it was said, had been a communicant there while serving as Admiral of the Nore.

Later, the crew had said, 'Where else have you sailed then?' They were ashore by then, enjoying a jar at the Old House at Home, a waterside pub at the top of the old town hard.

'Well, where do I start?' the skipper had murmured. Taking a pull from his pint, the skipper had launched into his tales: 'Well, there's Mombasa on the Kenyan coast,' the skipper had said, grinning impishly, remembering. 'I had many sails on a little gaffer. Think she was either a Blackwater Sloop or a Deben four-tonner … can't remember which. She was a lovely little thing, though.' The skipper had paused to explain a little about the two boats and their rig … 'The boat was owned by the padre of the seafarers' mission. My first sail was after a cocktail party on the ship I was on … We'd met and chatted and he'd found out about me having a boat (so far away …) and said, "Come sailing tomorrow … Be after the morning services … Meet at the yacht club …" and I was in!'

'Blimey … You lucky old …' the crew had chuckled.

'I got aboard with a motley selection of people (there were two others from the ship) and the padre said, "She's all yours …" and pulling a cold bottle from his haversack, he cracked a beer. I'd never set a gaffer. I knew how, more or less, though … and remembered to raise the throat and peak together.' Pausing, the skipper had added, '… The gaff comes up parallel with the boom until the throat is up – the bit by the mast. Then the gaff is peaked up …' Chuckling, the skipper had then said, 'He had this bloody great headsail set out on the bowsprit end … As soon as that was up, it flogged and slatted about … Then when I called for the mooring to be let go, we went off like a train … with me spilling the afternoon's breeze from the mainsail. I'd had to let that sheet out pretty damn quick too, almost on a run.' The skipper had then grinned. 'She took me by surprise … then I'd got her… Well, fairly safely anyway!'

That first sail was not the skipper's last. 'On the following weekend …' Pausing, the skipper had filled in a little detail. 'The ship had six weeks in that port … I remember vividly how working below was murder … The humidity and heat were stifling … We started early, around five, and finished at one …' The skipper had then added, 'I had a longer sail around the inner harbour and out towards the entrance … We stayed inside the coastal reef. The padre virtually left me to it … again.'

'Was that it?' the crew had asked cautiously, feeling that it wasn't …

'Well, not exactly. I had quite a few outings. Actually, I can't remember how many … Six weeks, remember …' the skipper had said, before continuing, 'There was a beach party outside the harbour – on the way out to sea. It took place on a gorgeous secluded beach inside the coastal reef. What I remember most is seeing so many dhows sailing in and out – it was a wonderful sight. The dhows berthed up Tudor Creek. It's round the "landward" side of the island … it was a fantastic …' the skipper had bubbled and

A melee of working sail loading and discharging in Colombo Harbour in 1983, when the skipper was there. Mombasa's Tudor Creek was little different. The huge sail on a dhow is lashed to the long yards seen on its deck. Note also the way the yards are built up from lengths of timber lashed together.

enthused. 'The dhows used the old port, very Arabic too … There's an old fort up there too … Fort Jesus, I think.' Chuckling, the skipper had added, 'There were scantily clad women running about on that do … Wives and girlfriends of yacht club members … They always seemed to be like that … scantily clad! I had the boat, though …'

The crew had pulled one of his faces – the face of 'Cor blimey, I wish I'd been there …'

'Dirty old man …' the skipper had thought, knowing his crew's penchant for a pretty face! The skipper was reminded of another sailing buddy that had had, harmlessly, a way with the lasses usually found behind the beer counter, but that was found during a club cruise to Faversham at another time … While in Mombasa, the skipper's ship had been berthed in Kilindini Harbour, a purpose-built deep-water haven for modern ships. The name was a Swahili word for 'deep'. It, too, was essentially a ria in the same manner as Fowey and Falmouth (in Cornwall): all flooded river valleys.

The skipper had also taken part in a dinghy race at the Mombasa club. He'd sailed on an old Star-class boat owned by a venerable old gentleman, a remnant of Britain's colonial days and domiciled in Kenya. The boat seemed huge for an open vessel, but they had had a proven Olympic track record, and still had. The gentleman's crew was seemingly older and was a native to the coast and he'd diligently instructed the skipper on all he'd needed to know: the gentleman's usual crew wasn't coming along … Oh yes, the skipper had been chided and barked at many times before that day's racing was over … 'But, ah, what a sail …' the skipper related to his crew, laughing at the memory of his old helmsman's rebukes!

The skipper had become aware of his crew tapping a glass – well, the skipper's was being tapped. 'Come on, drink up … I'm for another … before we eat, don't you think?' Nodding to the rhetorical question asked, the skipper had obliged, quickly quaffing the last of his tasty pint

The crew had quickly returned with two foaming pints of Kent ale; smacking his lips, the skipper had taken a long intense pull before setting off again. 'Of course,' he'd said, 'Mombasa wasn't the only place I've seen dhows under sail.' The skipper had stopped, and looking across at his crew had remembered something, but saying nothing then, he'd continued, 'When I was up the Gulf (that's the Persian Gulf) I use to see them regularly … There was the time I was on a ship patrolling those waters checking up on the passing ships.' Pausing, the skipper had said, 'Iraq and Iran were at each other's throats that time.' Taking a sip of his ale, the skipper had continued, 'Then, of course, there was the other time …' and he'd paused briefly, '… during Saddam's Kuwaiti adventure.' The crew had known about that part of the skipper's sea life. Grinning, the skipper had then said, 'Dhows were just about the only vessels carrying cargo around then!' On that later Gulf visit, the skipper had ultimately been part of a convoy of invasion ships that had worked up through the Iraqi minefields sprinkled in the shallow Gulf waters. It had been a ruse, but, quietly, the skipper remembered things that had remained untold and, also, the two mined navy ships of the United States. Both ships had survived, fortunately with few casualties, and remarkably with no fatalities. A large missile cruiser had later been scrapped, though. They themselves had had a narrow escape deep within the advance area, passing mines close by on the surface. Those had been blown up!

'Where else, then?' the crew had said, instinctively realising that all had not been told.

'Well, there was Colombo,' the skipper had chuckled, slopping his beer as he'd done so. 'I had a week in Colombo many years ago. I ended up taking part in a dinghy racing match.'

'Oh yes, more freebies from a do, was it then …?'

'Well, yes, I suppose so …' The skipper paused and had looked up towards the ceiling of the public house, as if for inspiration, then looking across at a group opposite them, a bunch of fellow sailors, chattering in a mix of tongues, German, Dutch and English – the two former flags had been seen in the harbour earlier – he'd added, 'It always amazed me how people, of so many nationalities, went out of their way to look after so many of us when in a port abroad.' The skipper had then run quickly through a list of places where he'd been royally treated … However, he'd soon returned to the proper subject.

'Colombo,' he'd said. 'The harbour was full of dhows and other local but similar vessels.'

'What about the sailing?' the crew had earnestly asked, his stomach beginning to rumble and wanting his solids.

'Yes, well, I ended up in a team taking on the Royal Navy [one of their ships was attached to – in charge of – the skipper's] and the Sri Lankan Navy. It was some distance away from the city and harbour. I went to Lake Bolgoda … to the Ceylon Motor Boat Club.'

The skipper had later learnt that Lake Bolgoda had had a long history with the Ceylon Motor Boat Club, dating back to colonial days. It was a time when men spent lazy days up-country trying out newfangled motor boating, while, it was presumed, their wives relaxed about the club, drinking tea and catching up on gossip. The lake had also suffered

Close racing on Lake Bolgoda, some miles outside Colombo, Sri Lanka. The dinghies are a mix of GP14s and Enterprises. A Laser can be seen too – there weren't any of those on the lake in 1983. The picture was taken in 2010 by a local sailor. Courtesy of Rohan Pett (now residing in Sydney, Australia).

from pollution caused from effluent discharges from chemical and logging enterprises, badly damaging the lake's ecology. 'Man never learns ...' the skipper had thought. The lake had had the good fortune to have been targeted with a conservation project designed to rejuvenate its water quality to encourage fishing and tourism. This, the skipper found, had been aimed at the local population, especially fishing. 'That lake was huge, it was like an inland sea,' the skipper had said, chuckling. He was then chatting to his mate about the event, at a much later time. The lake was actually some 370 square kilometres in area.

'What happened in the race?' the crew had patiently enquired.

'Ah, yes, well, we lost!'

'Who won?'

'The Royal Navy did! We sailed in Enterprise dinghies, I think, but could have been GP14s – I think the former, though.' Laughing, the skipper had said, 'My helm was my boss ... A bit of a dinghy man down in Poole Harbour ... Didn't think I'd been taking it seriously and got a bit ragged around the edges because I wasn't that au fait with racing rules,' and laughing again he had added, 'Especially team stuff ...'

'Come on,' the crew had said, 'I think we should order ... Barmaid said the cook had some good stuff on ...' The skipper had detected the twinkle in his crew's eyes, so they'd stayed put.

The watering hole right at the top of the old town hard in Queenborough had had an interesting few years. It had seemingly been in the doldrums a few seasons back but had of late been on the up with a change of ownership. The publican had been keen to make changes and the skipper had had many exchanges on visits with his mate. The publican at the time of the skipper's tale gladly took sailors up to a garage for fuel and had been known to make a run into a larger supermarket. Queenborough had suffered from a fair amount of bad press and sourness among some visitors and to the skipper it amounted to nothing more than sheer snobbishness on the part of those sailors, and as for the press he'd never cared tuppence: 'What do they really know ...' he'd long thought. The place had history: situated down on the south coast, it would have been a honey pot ...

Wandering down the floating hard at West Mersea earlier that season, the skipper's view had been firmly cemented. He'd overheard a conversation, spoken with mouths full of plums, from among two sets of sailors, couples. One set had been heading down, the other shoreward.

'Oh ... back are you?' had drifted clearly to the skipper, for he and his two crew had had to stand aside and wait for a clear passage.

'Oh yah, been down to the Medwaay ... not been bifore ... We went into Chatharm ... not a lot there ...' had come from a man – the boat's owner, it had been assumed.

The man's wife had giggled, and had said something about the outlet shops ...

'Oh yah ...' the other lady had said, 'I just lurve them ... Don't you?' Then both had clutched each other's arms and with lowered voices had exchanged confidences while the two men had continued to mutter about the Medway ...

The skipper and his crew were still waiting, patiently, to get past ... and they then heard, from one, 'Go anywhere else ...?'

The skipper hadn't helped hearing the sting ... 'No, err, well, yes ... actually ... We moored at Queenborough larst night ...' the boat's owner had uttered, hesitantly, before adding, mockingly, 'Yah ... What a bloody dump ...' The skipper was mortified. It hurt. He'd felt mortally wounded.

The skipper had wanted to say, as he'd eventually moved clear, 'You bloody snob ... You don't really know the place ... its history, as old and more interesting than yours here ... its fine buildings and plain honesty ... or the Medway for that matter ... its sheer beauty either ...' but hadn't. It had played on his mind for some time, too. 'Should stand up for what you believe in ...' he'd later told himself and his mate when in discussion about the episode. The skipper hoped that he'd one day be atoned for not saying, 'Excuse me ...'

The skipper had at that time been sailing up to Pin Mill with his youngest brother and a cousin crewing, both good shipmates and strong contenders for inclusion into the 'Jolly Boys' club. They'd had an enjoyable and good sail up from Canvey Island that day and were returning after enjoying a gorgeous dinner at an Indian restaurant in the village. The places along the front had been closed ... The skipper's brother had said, 'Bit nasty, weren't they?'

'That was good,' the crew had said, mopping up the last of his steak's juices ... and breaking up the skipper's private reverie.

'Oh, err, yes,' the skipper had said, awaking from his thoughts. 'Let's have a wander up the road, shall we?'

On the way up the road, the skipper had briefly told the crew about sailing from the Florida Yacht Club in Jacksonville, when he'd crewed on a Carter 34 centre board yacht. It had been during a regatta race. He'd been put in charge of the 'Cunninghaam' (the drawl had totally lost the poor skipper) but soon realised it was the kicker, in Brit-speak! At one point the owner, at the helm, had called urgently for the Cunningham to be tensioned, as they'd come round on a close reach. The skipper had almost been elbowed aside by two young men, hunks with huge biceps, but had at least tailed the line. The skipper and his crew had had a good laugh about that ... 'There was something else about that sail,' the skipper had bubbled. 'We started off on a balmy hot day and this line of deep, dark and menacing clouds rose up. We were hit by an amazing period of rain ... it didn't last long,' and chuckling he'd added, 'There was a squall ... a ferocious and short spell of wind!' It had been after the squall that attention to the Cunningham had been needed ...

Sitting over their last beer – enough was enough and a sensible approach to the homeward journey was needed – the skipper had said, 'There's one other place that I remember sailing in when I was at sea ...'

'Where's that then?' The crew had asked, grinning over the rim of his jug of ale.

'Nova Scotia,' the skipper had said, adding, '... in Canada. I was on a ship. We were on naval exercises ... all the way across the Atlantic and up north ... The Iceland Gap, it's called ...' the skipper had said cautiously, but it had long been history, before adding, 'And we went into Halifax for a maintenance period.' While the skipper had supped at his glass, not wanting to lag behind, he'd become aware of the moving hands of the pub's wall clock. 'Time ...' he'd thought. All along the crew had looked at him, expectantly, waiting.

'It was on a yacht owned by the liaison officer from the Royal Canadian Navy – he was looking after the shoreside affairs and needs of the ship. I got to know the chap because I was in charge of most of the shoreside work being done ... big deck pipes ... it was an old tanker. Most of our ships were old then!'

The crew had nodded.

'I don't know where the yacht was moored. It had been left some way from the chap's usual mooring – something to do with some racing he'd been doing. Anyway, another of my staff came too.' The skipper explained that the other chap had had his own little boat,

The yacht *Apocalypse*, which the skipper helped sail round the Nova Scotian coast in 1985. She was left at her mooring near the world-famous lighthouse at Peggy's Cove.

a Silhouette, berthed in Plymouth. Then he'd continued, 'The naval officer's wife and a few friends made up the rest of the crew. It wasn't the biggest boat I've been on, but I had an absolutely fabulous day.' Chuckling, he'd added, 'The winds were quite light and motoring took up a chunk of the passage, but hey, sailing round the rocky shoreline was something I've always remembered ... It was so different to what I was used to here.'

'Mud and marsh are softer,' the crew had intoned, 'but I'd love that too ...' The skipper had murmured something about hiring a boat ... the crew had guffawed and almost choked into his glass before he'd added, 'The old girl wouldn't have that ...'

The skipper had grinned at chaffing his crew a little, and continued, 'The rocks were so smooth in places.' The rock was from molten lava spewed from beneath the Earth's crust and dated back some 400 million years. They had been carved by glaciers before being washed by the Atlantic's waters. 'They're the same rocks as those in Northern Ireland and on the west coast of Scotland,' the skipper had drawled. Getting back to the subject, the skipper had said, 'We went round this picturesque lighthouse at a place called Peggy's Point ... The boat was left moored somewhere nearby, in a cove. It was so secluded.' The skipper had remembered that the cove mooring had been surrounded by wooded slopes, and also, around the point area many of the waterside buildings sat on stilts along the edge of the water. They'd reminded him of Newfoundland, where he'd also spent time. 'The lighthouse ...' the skipper had then said, 'is said to be one of Canada's most famous and most photographed.' The first lighthouse had been instituted in 1868. It was a wood building and was replaced by the present structure in 1914, the skipper had at some stage found. Finally, the skipper had concluded with, 'We were out on the water for some eight hours ...'

Later, back aboard, the crew had made a coffee to enjoy: the night was moderately balmy for the time of year; the breeze of earlier had dropped away too. 'A little something in it ...?' the crew had called.

'I'd say ...' the skipper had uttered and it had soon appeared, passed out by his crew who'd grinned, cherub-like!

Over the years, depending upon the weather forecasted, the skipper and his crew had managed to reach either Faversham or Upnor on one of their September weekends away from their respective ladies: both places had always been enjoyed. Their present trip had been planned a little differently. The 'women' were meeting them for lunch at Faversham: the crew's wife had never been to the town and the mate had said she'd do the run over ... They had planned it months before. So, too, had a departure on the same tide to drop back out of Faversham's Creek to sit off Harty for the night. A visit to the hostelry on the hill had been planned as well.

After awaking and poking his tousled head out of the fore hatch, the skipper had quickly come to the conclusion that their sail to Faversham was going to be a little more than casual. A fresh breeze was coming at them from the south-west and the reefed main would still be needed. Clouds had skittered across the sky, a deep blue of late summer as if some darkness had remained, lightening and darkening the water around the boat. The clouds had had an inky hue to their undersides, but the skipper smiled: the forecast hadn't mentioned showers ... The skipper had lightly shivered, though: air was fresh.

Pulling on a clean shirt and ... The skipper had rattled the cabin door and called, 'Coffee ...?' to his crew, who'd appeared sound asleep. Moving around the main cabin, the skipper watched as a bedraggled, stubble-infested face peer out from its owner's sleeping bag. The lips on the face moved in that morning-after way before they emitted murmurings of approval.

Coffee, ablutions and breakfast over and cleared away, they'd quickly departed to catch the bridge at Kingsferry at around the usual time, on an hour. They'd sailed off of the mooring cleanly before tacking southwards, round the bend into the reach where the ramshackle old jetty sat on Long Point.

'Lovely!' the crew had said as they'd heeled to a gust coming around the low hill that sat south of Queenborough. The gust had allowed the skipper to harden up and save a tack before he'd been able to bear away up Loden Hope. The wind direction had made it necessary to put a tack in to round Long Point and from then on it had been plain sailing to the bridge.

The tides were in the spring cycle and had been exceptionally high for a number of days. A strong saline whiff drifted across the water from the saltings. The crew had breathed in, savouring the flavour of it on his senses. The skipper had too – it was something special, heady and glorious!

'Tide's going to be low through the east Swale,' the skipper had said, chuckling, 'A bit of touch 'n' go, no doubt ...' He'd added, 'It's about on the turn – well shortly, anyway.'

'I'll see the banks, then?' the crew had enquired. The skipper had nodded and pointed to the chart, where it sat in its plastic wallet at the forward end of the cockpit. The crew had picked it up and pored over it for a while ... 'Have I been through when it's low? he'd asked.

The skipper had nodded from his position at the helm, tiller tucked in between the cheeks of his bottom, and said, 'Yes, but not as low as we're likely to find it!' The skipper had always enjoyed such activities ... ditch-crawling ... They'd wanted to make it into Faversham creek as soon as possible and take the young flood up to Iron Wharf, where the girls were to meet them. Lunch had been planned at a local hostelry.

Closing the bridge, the skipper, who had been monitoring the radio, called the keeper. He'd heard another yacht ask for directions. The skipper had said that they would be in time for the stated lift ... 'She's going our way,' the skipper had said. 'Must have been waiting a while – we haven't had anyone in front of us...' Sure enough, rounding the last shallow bend, the boat had come into view. 'We'll leave the sails up and gill around ...'

Their sail from the bridge through the Swale was tremendous. Leaving the entrance to Milton Creek behind, the sheets were eased away fairly free and the sloop had picked up her skirts, leaving a 'motor boat's' wash. The yacht ahead of them, moving under power, had pulled up shortly after clearing Elmley Ferry and the skipper watched as they were preparing to drop anchor. He'd chuckled ...

'We going to get through ...?' the crew had asked, pensively.

'Never not been able to ...' the skipper had said chuckling. At that moment the centre plate, down a few turns, had caught the shell and mud bottom, sending its slivering and scraping noises up through the boat, clear to all. The skipper had moved quickly to lift it a turn. Soon he'd had to do it again and again; finally he'd said, 'Right, it's right up!' The crew had half grimaced before grinning. The boat seemed to be riding the humps of the Swale's undulating bottom. She lifted slightly, then surged. At one point the skipper thought that they would stop, but no, on they'd gone. At around the midpoint of the narrow low-tide passage, the skipper had said, 'Here you take over ... just keep her so ... a little over to the south of the water ...' The bumping and scraping had lessened to only now and then. 'I'll put the kettle on – fancy one ...?'

'Ooh ...' he'd retorted, flicking his eyebrows up and down ... and pulling a Page Three face. The skipper had imagined that his crew had been thinking of his 'girl' in the next port – which was just so!

Poking his head out of the hatch, the skipper had pointed ahead and said, 'Mind that bit ... keep her over to the south a bit more ... looks wide, yet it isn't. The mate put us on that many years ago ... hadn't heeded my warning ... we gave the bank her name!' He'd added, 'The old chart has gone now, though. They were good, the older charts – far more detail ...' and disappeared at the sound of the kettle's comforting whistle.

The tide had been running in and lifting the boat further from the shallows for most of that passage, and upon reaching the area off Harty, two spritsail barges were seen coming in from the mouth of the waterway. One, the closest, was instantly recognised by the skipper as the *Mirosa*. 'The other,' he'd said on being asked, 'is probably the *Greta*.' She seemed to the skipper to be on her last leg across from the Whitstable areas, where she was known to operate during the season. The skipper had directed the crew to sail on past the entrance into Faversham creek for a look. 'Another half hour ...' he'd said, contented in his summation. 'We'll sail about ... Should be up there just after twelve ...' he'd added. The crew had flicked his eyebrows again. The skipper had privately wondered if his crew wanted a bit of peace and quiet upon arrival ... He hadn't said anything, but thought, chuckling, '... I'll mention it at lunch with the girls!'

Finally, the skipper had said, 'Right, we'll sail up into the entrance to the creek and I'll stow the sails as soon as we're headed ...' They'd made the first inward leg before the skipper had doused the canvass and harbour stowed. Ropes and fenders were then passed out and rigged, ready. The tide had then basically carried them sweetly up the bed of the creek. They'd touched from time to time but the boatyard at Iron Wharf had soon come into view. It had not been a view of the creek that the crew had seen

The *Mirosa* seen on a squally day, with leaden skies, off the entrance to Faversham Creek in the East Swale. She was built by Howard of Maldon as the *Ready* in 1892. Her original name was bought by Trinity House in 1947 for a new tender. The skipper knows her well, and went aboard several times around 1968–69, soon after her re-rigging from use as a timber lighter, but hasn't been aboard since. She has been extensively rebuilt by the present owner since his acquisition of her in 1977 – now probably the longest private ownership of an active spritsail barge. She is a credit to all concerned.

before. 'Be able to sail out ... if this wind stays put,' the skipper had said, grinning. The crew had nodded approvingly: he too had learnt the joy of using the wind and not diesel ...

A call rang out, a chorus in fact: 'What kept you ...?' It was the women!

The skipper had taken over on the last leg and he'd swept round, nosing the bow into the creek's bank, and allowed the tide to take the stern round ... Coming away, they had nosed up alongside a spritsail barge, the *Orinoco*.

Later, just as the tide was about to begin its ebb at Faversham, the boat was ready to leave. It had been a sailing departure, under the jib until harder on the wind further down the channel. The girls had watched, fluttering handkerchiefs ... and anything else was pure conjecture!

It had been a strange and unfamiliar part of their cruise, the yacht's crew both thought later. It was surreal even, yet nice. It was something not done before. They'd been having a cup of tea before getting a little eye rest. They'd chatted about the latter half of the day's passage. 'Blimey,' the crew had said, 'I enjoyed that sail out ... All those people taking pictures of us near that pub ...'

The pub had been the Shipwright's Arms at the entrance to Oare Creek. The people, walkers, had been on the sea wall, essentially, to its east. The yacht had had to be tacked around that last bend, a troublesome bend. The engine had remained silent ... The mate would have been thoroughly impressed. The yacht's crew were! The skipper hadn't taken too much notice: helming and depth were his only concerns, as several tacks had been needed to clear that narrow and curving stretch of water.

The crew had grown to love the Swale and couldn't understand those that besmirched the waterway – the Medway too, for that matter. That love had been further cemented on their last evening at the Ferry Boat Inn. It was a delightful place to have a meal and look out upon the water … Their supper visit ashore though had, it seemed, gatecrashed a wedding party … women in a mixture of low-cut flouncy or ultra-short frocks wobbled and frolicked with their men, or otherwise. Children ran hither and thither, excitedly chasing their tails, enjoying the occasion, rightly. It had been noisy and after their food and a couple of jars, the collective opinion was, 'Let's go!' And they'd left the revellers to enjoy themselves … A quiet nightcap under a sky lit by stars with a few puffy clouds floating by would suffice for the two old boys that night.

Apart from seeing a painting, dated 1954, of a 'G'-Class flying boat, the *Golden Hind*, taking off from the waterway where they themselves lay at anchor (the harbour had provided a fairly convenient place for such activities in those early days of passenger aviation), the skipper and crew had had the luxurious experience of pushing their dinghy out over an expanse of mud and broken shell. It had been one of those East Coast moments: reaching the dinghy, it was obvious that the tide had gone out a very long way.

'I'd leave those on if I were you …' the skipper had muttered as he'd seen his crew about to bend down to remove his shoes … Lacerations to his feet would have resulted. Removal of their socks would have been a good move … but they hadn't thought of that … Once the dinghy had reached the water, after an eternal age, the water hadn't deepened any quicker. The foreshore thereabouts was flat. 'Springs …' the skipper had said, '… Tide's gone out further … Keep pushing.'

The crew had chuckled, 'Lovely …' and said, '… We should have stayed put for another beer …' But it was a bit late by then!

Rowing back to the boat, both had enjoyed the magnificent spectacle of a star-laden sky: at that end of the Swale, light pollution was low (as low as it possibly could be …). The skipper had whispered quietly, 'The mate and I love this anchorage for what's above us.' The crew had gazed in awe. Reaching the boat, the mood changed back to hilarity as a saga of shoe rinsing had taken place … never mind the mud-sodden socks. In the dark, the mess had been largely hidden and, as all East Coasters know, mud had a tendency to stink. It hadn't let them down!

Over a nightcap, the skipper had finished talking about other places he'd sailed. There had been several lakes around England. One had been in Wiltshire, where the skipper had enjoyed sailing on water heavily shrouded by woodland. It made interesting sailing in a Topper-class dinghy, little bigger than a sail board, and a Mirror dinghy. Another had been in Gloucestershire, in an old gravel pit. Those had been experienced courtesy of his sister. Graffon Water had been another experience too, sailing in his youngest brother's Albacore – a cold moulded wooden dinghy dating from the early 1950s.

'I have done a coastal trip…' the skipper had said. 'It was on a 34' Westerly, my pal's yacht.'

'I know the boat,' the crew had said admiringly, remembering a meet-up some years before.

'It was ages ago now,' the skipper had continued. 'I crewed the boat back to Burnham-on-Crouch from Gosport to Portsmouth. It was from the marina next to the place you and the family visited when I was on a ship once …'

'Oh, yes ...' the crew murmured.

'We sailed to a lovely little harbour across on the Isle of Wight – Bembridge harbour it was. I remember sailing in close up to a shingle bank – it was a bit like Stone Point, going into the Walton Channel ... Remember we've tacked right up to the shore there ...' The skipper saw the crew nod knowingly. It was a place he knew. 'The next day we sailed as far as Shoreham. Going in there was exciting – straight in from the sea ... Then the next day we had a marvellous run up to Ramsgate. It was great seeing the coast from the sea ... but it wasn't like the estuary. I knew I was "home" as we had crossed from the North Foreland towards the Crouch.'

'Did you enjoy it?'

'Yes, well, yes mostly. I'd do it again!'

'Another coffee?' the crew had said: the skipper had had enough of recounting ... 'Flavoured ...?' he'd added. It had been a silly question, really!

By the end of their weekend, they had achieved all that they'd planned. It had been an exhilarating sail back on their last day too. On the final leg, they'd turned, tack after tack, up the Ray Channel to a vacant buoy off the end of Smallgains Creek to await the tide.

Sometime later, after putting the dinghy to bed, the skipper had had a last few words with his doughty crew. As he'd waved him goodbye, the skipper had grinned: the crew rarely shaved for the duration of his time afloat and he'd always looked tramp-like by the end! 'I like arriving home like an ol' salty sea dog ...' he'd always said, while grinning like a hyena.

It had also been the case when they'd been up on the Deben and Walton Backwaters earlier that season, the skipper had remembered. Then he'd laughed: the end of their present trip hadn't been any different either ... Rubbing his own chin as he'd driven away he'd thought, 'He's was always like that at the end of our trips ... at least I shaved yesterday ...'

'I like arriving home like an ol' salty sea dog ...' he'd always said. Drawn by Mrs G. D. Ardley.

A Soupçon

It was autumn. Late summer had been a time of mists and mellow fruitfulness. It had run into what is euphemistically known as an Indian summer. Would autumn continue in that fashion? The previous few seasons had been glorious and the skipper had hoped for the status quo to continue. But, of course, it hadn't. Lazy sails out on the tide and the last weekend away with the mate had soon become mere memories …

The skipper though, it must be admitted, had had a busy time what with one thing and another and his sailing had been curtailed a little as a result. There had been a number of those special days, which all sailors revere, when tides and weather were in union. The skipper had uncharacteristically given them up. Later, though, he realised meekly and with humility, he'd have been wiser to have dropped his pen in favour of a breeze caressing his cheeks and for his eyes to have drunk in the luscious curve of his boat's sail, pulling well and heeling the comfy girl in a pleasant manner, the gurgle along the clinker lands and muffled murmurings as the wake left the stern … Ah, yes!

The dear little clinker sloop had spent two weeks out on the club's hard standing for a little work. A new propeller, a new rudder pintle made and fitted, and a new centre plate wire too. These trifles, though, had been largely, and cleverly, tied in with a holiday away, while the propeller was being machined. Good planning … or what?

Following her short sojourn ashore, the boat had breathed an audible sigh as she'd kissed the salt again, but time and tide had not allowed a sail that day. A few days later, the skipper got out though on a glorious early afternoon tide. Boats were coming out up at the slipway, but he'd quickly discarded any feeling of guilt: he'd assisted around his club, jetty repairing, all morning. It was a tide and day that beckoned. He had to savour that sail for it was the last for several weeks, a lengthy wait by his standards.

The wait seemed to go on and on. It rained. That itself was an unusual feature: locally along the southern shores of the Thames estuary, it was a renowned dry spot – the country's driest. With the rain, or when it wasn't raining too, the wind blew. Boy, had it blown. Sailing was out of the equation. The skipper's life seemed to dull His mate chivvied and cajoled. He was glum and had become a nuisance, his mate had asserted.

Sometime after his sail, a week, two weeks perhaps, the skipper couldn't remember, he was prattling over the dinner table at home, a romantic one, with candles too, beaming at the mate. It was on a Saturday evening – he'd cooked one of her favourite dishes. She'd had a hustled week at her school. But she was as stoical as ever. They'd talked about this and that; however, at a moan from the skipper, she'd quipped, with some passion, 'Life doesn't revolve around sailing!' while maintaining a hold on the skipper's gaze.

'Life doesn't revolve around sailing!' Drawn by Mrs G. D. Ardley.

It had stopped the skipper in mid-sentence and what was being said was rapidly left astern ... During his enforced pause, he'd peered across at her. Initially he'd pursed his lips, thinking, 'I'd better be careful here ...' His thought, 'Doesn't it!?', very nearly spoken too, would have spelt trouble ... But quickly casting caution to wind, as swiftly as he'd been known to tack on many occasions when creeping up a creek, he'd grinned broadly, he'd raised his glass and said, '... After you it does!' He continued to grin.

The mate, with a pained look, imprisoned even, had murmured, 'Hmm – I'd love to go ... but ...' The 'but', though, wasn't completed and picking up her glass and toying with it for a moment, she'd added quietly, 'I propose a toast, to *Whimbrel* – my good ship too!' She smiled softly, with affection. Her look had had a longing too.

The skipper had quietly concurred. The mate's unfinished 'but' lay on his mind: he knew ... just occasionally his fairly unconstrained work–life balance chaffed, just a bit, right where it hurt most.

The wait continued for another week.

On the morning of the day in question, the skipper had listened to the forecast. 'No sailing today,' he'd said over his toast and Seville marmalade (at least that had been nice!). The mate had not even blinked. Her mind was clearly and correctly on whatever was happening later at work …

Looking his way, she suddenly said, 'What you doing today?'

'Oh, college and the creek,' he'd said quickly, to which the mate had nodded. 'I'll help out with a few jobs …'

The skipper's place of work was not far from the water and the surrounding land around was quite open, with a just a few tall trees. Getting up from explaining how to do some fraction work, he'd absently gazed out of a window. Watching the visibly slight movement among the branches of a little cluster of trees that still had leaves clinging on for dear life, the skipper's heart suddenly pumped. The movement was gentle, too gentle for too much wind; he was thinking of the morning's torrid forecast. 'The wind's not come,' he'd said instinctively. The sky, too, as he'd looked upwards from the window, had had a look of summer. It was like the Indian summer that they'd enjoyed a while ago, when the boat had been out of the water …

A student had looked up and said, 'What's that …?' his look inquisitive and non-understanding.

The skipper had stopped with a start, realising that he must have spoken aloud. Turning and grinning, he'd said, 'I was thinking … I might get out for a sail … Wind's not come up.'

The student had then laughed. He knew of the skipper's hobby. 'You need a sail!' he'd said, laughing.

Later, reaching the creek and guiltily making for his boat as quickly as his legs would carry him, he'd set to, to ready his craft for sailing. The covers were off in a trice and stowed with the cabin washboards. 'The jib …' the skipper had said to himself, thinking '… Caution, boy …' as he'd thrust the bagged sail up through the fo'c'sle hatch. The kettle was set on the stove and a mug with the makings for tea set ready before he'd headed out on deck again. Moving forward, the unnecessary mooring lines were cleared, and the fenders too. Releasing the halyard frapping lines, he'd bent the burgee onto its hoist. It was soon fluttering aloft, tugging, its stick tapping the mast in that tinny way. The wind was a little heavier up at the mast head. 'Not too much, though …' the skipper thought, pensively.

The tide was well on its way towards its peak as the mooring was cleared. The jib was quickly hoisted and the boat came alive – her eagerness quivered at the tiller. The engine fell silent as the stop was swiftly pulled. The kettle whistled right on cue … his mug of tea was soon made. A watcher would have seen a contented old soul, mug in hand, as the boat brushed the tide aside.

The tide was still rushing into the creek. It was close to the marsh tops that were edged with sea purslane, whose seed heads displayed their autumn tinge of russet, orange or brown, depending on the light, or where the sun was. Those fronds waved in the tide's run. Cord grass – which was usually visible too, had the skipper got to the boat earlier, to be ready to slide away as she'd floated – was all but immersed. The grasses too were dressed in their seasonal suits, less green, more yellow, and their tops were bent to the flow. A gaggle of geese, bobbing about upon the gentle wavelets that fetched across the creek, hadn't known which way to turn, unsure of the 'island' bearing down upon them. Eventually they'd lifted off to settle where there was food. Succulent weeds were their want. These were to be found in among the fingers of water that filled the gullies that ran willy-nilly through the saltings along the creek's northern bank. They'd honked noisily as they joined many other geese, as if to say, 'That boat's out here again ...'

Clearing the end of the moorings and a bobbing, mud-splattered green buoy, the skipper left the deep-water channel and cut across the flats, setting a course more or less broad on the wind, westwards. He'd then gone forward to set the mainsail. The boat felt its effect immediately and her speed increased rapidly, carving a curling wash that ran away in the ever-widening arc of an arrow head. Casually coiling and hanging off the halyard, the skipper cast his eyes to the west. The sun sparkled on the water's surface, casting about mirrored flashes of light. The hills in the distance seemed a bright golden yellow, contrasting with a deeper hue, greener, perhaps even a bronze patina in the expanse of marshes that ran, unobstructed, in that direction. It was the sun that did it: it had shone brightly since being unleashed earlier that morning from the cataract that had hidden it for many days. It coloured nature's bounty serenely.

After what seemed a long time, but was a mere moment, the skipper's concentration had quickly returned: a puff had changed his direction – the boat, that is – towards that enchanting marsh. Waving fronds of cord grass seemed to beckon. 'Time to take the tiller!' the skipper had thought, and a watcher would have seen him skip back aft and make a corrective action. No hands were involved – a gentle push with a thigh was all that had occurred before he'd tightened in the jib sheet and eased the mains'l a little. His shave, a year or two back, with the saltings described in his book, *Mudlarking*, was still fresh!

That reach took the game little sloop deeply up the narrowing neck of water that ran between the marshes to the south and sea-walled shore to the north. The northern shore was, due to a constant battering by wash waves and a rising tide levels, losing its marshy fringe. The battering, mostly, came from motor vessels disobeying the speed regulations within the area as they traversed back and forth, seeking the open water in an attempt to get a 'run in' before needing to turn for home and their shallow mud berths. The skipper sympathised – just a little – but the damage was terminal. He'd often holler, 'SLOW DOWN!'

In the distance, a little gaff cutter was carving the same course. The skipper's yacht was reducing the range between them at a steady rate. The skipper knew that he'd probably not overhaul her: further inland the wind would drop significantly, and the gaffer's shallower draft would allow her to fetch even where the skipper would be dissuaded from going!

Walkers along the sea wall had stopped and stared. What a sight it must have been. Two tan-sailed vessels coming in from the sea, it would have seemed, careering into the bosom of a safe haven. But by the time the skipper had reached the upper limit of the navigable water, the wind had become fluky. It had wavered in strength, sometimes attacking the sails then leaving them limp and slack, making tacking difficult. The skipper had thought, 'Pinching isn't an option up here.' He was often able to keep the boat going under her mainsail's drive alone, while the jib fluttered as he steered through a long change of tack. 'Better to keep her full and tack more often ...' he added. It was fine and dandy to do as he'd wanted in steady conditions, but a sudden wind shift could force him the wrong way. 'Something to be avoided in confined waters ...' the skipper had continued to mutter – while not even considering the option of his engine!

The sad sight of the abandoned spritsail barge *Scone* resting in a gut off Benfleet Creek, just above the road bridge onto Canvey Island. She was built as late as 1919 at Rochester and was dumped here after a stranding in Barking Creek twisted her hull in 2003. She floated for a short while, but by 2004 flooded each tide. By the time of the picture, taken in 2010, her planking had begun to come away from her stem. On deck sits all the gear needed to rig a barge. Slowly, various items have been removed ... to be recycled, it is hoped.

Reaching the venerable headquarters of the Benfleet Yacht Club, the skipper put the helm over, loosed off the main sheet and allowed the backed jib to pull the boat's bow hard round across the tide. Eyes, the skipper knew, were fastened on his manoeuvre. It was something he'd done on numerous occasions and he hadn't been fazed by it. 'Let them watch!' he'd thought and murmured, 'You should be out here too ...' He'd then laughed, while thinking of the two boats he'd already seen: ditch-crawlers like himself.

After completing his manoeuvre, the skipper thought of the creek beyond the barrier. He'd had a desire to sail up the creek with his little tender in tow and to anchor up below the tidal barrier that blocked normal navigation. His aspiration was to row above the barrier and a bridge that crossed the creek beyond, to have a closer look at an old barge that had been laid to rest in a gulley within the marshes a little further on. The barge, the *Scone*, was just ninety years old, young in comparison to some of her surviving sailing sisters, and many old yachts for that matter, too.

The *Scone* had initially been brought into that backwater as a temporary measure, but the world had overtaken her: her time was up, it seemed. Some years before this the *Scone* had suffered a stranding on an uneven bottom at a berth up Barking Creek and she sank. After refloating she was towed down the River Thames by a local tow boat, awaiting onward transit to Hoo on the River Medway where, it was reputed, she was to be repaired ... She had lifted on the tides, slowly filling each time, and settled on her bottom. This had happened for no more than a week or two. Each tide did its work, slowly and assuredly, doing more damage to her tired joints, creating a growing number of openings, until the old girl failed to pick up.

The skipper had said, upon first seeing the vessel from the road on the mainland shore, 'That's the end of her ...'

'Well ...' the mate had added, 'it's happened to your old home.' Yes, indeed.

'The barge world considers her to be laid up,' the skipper had later said, grinning, when he'd read a report about her. It was sad, yes. However, few vessels, especially of her size, ever enjoy a resurrection and the skipper had watched her week by week, month by month and now year by year. Over that time, the skipper had seen – with keen, knowing eyes – items around her decks had been gradually disappearing. Winches on the whole, but then one day he had seen that her entire windlass had been removed, including the thick oak bitt heads to which the windlass was attached – probably hacked off with a chainsaw. That had astounded him! His only thought was, 'Let's hope they're bound for another vessel that needs the old ironwork.' A nice thought, romantic even: most barges of today had obtained their gear in such ways. The skipper had himself, as a youngster, carried away cleats from old hulks for reuse on his sailing home. That was described in his book about his childhood and was always close to his heart. The skipper had seen, though, something more sinister: he thought that a dark line had appeared to one side of her stem. It was the unmistakable sign that the fastenings of her hull planking were rotted and were giving way. 'It's not long now ...' he'd thought, 'before more obvious distress becomes visible.' Remembering that, the skipper looked about – a wry look clouded his face.

The skipper was by then running back down the creek towards the wider waters, clear of the profusion of moorings that infested the upper stretches. He made himself a hot drink ... nipping below to place the kettle on a flame, fetch out a mug, spoon out his coffee ... finally, as the kettle sang out, to pour in boiling water. Those steps were completed one at a time, nipping out to ensure the boat remained on course. It had, in a very zigzag fashion which must have looked comical indeed from the sea wall.

Standing with his mug in hand, the skipper's thoughts wandered to a collection of craft that sat in marshy rills just beyond the bridge – Benfleet Bridge. He grimaced, slightly, and said, 'That lot wants clearing up ...' It was a motley cluster of vessels; many had sprouted huts and were obviously being used as houseboats. That in itself had never bothered the skipper, but the general untidiness and unkempt aspect it presented had. He felt that it gave the area a poor image, however picturesque it looked on the day of a high tide, brilliant sunshine, and blue sky that coloured the water and marshes in their gorgeous hues.

His semi-conscious eyes were alerted by a dot of red that had come up quickly on the bow. 'Must keep close to that one ... mud bank beyond it ...' were his thoughts as he nudged the tiller with his thigh. A white-sailed yacht was approaching; the two skippers saluted one another – kindred spirits, assuredly!

The afternoon sun was by then colouring the marshes deeply with tinges of its orange glow. The water looked to be bronze where he was able to look down gullies unruffled by the breeze. 'Ah, this is grand,' he'd whispered reverentially.

The skipper had dowsed the mains'l off the old wharf, General Booth's Wharf, and continued under jib to the entrance to his creek. There, he had started the little diesel that lurked beneath the cockpit sole and stowed the jib.

Looking up from tying off his fenders, the skipper saw that the seasonal swarms were back. Knot gyrated across the sky, thickly, almost black, fluid in movement. Then, as if thousands of grains poured from a jug, they'd seemed to disappear into the low marshy land at the island's point. They had, of course, alighted. It was for but a brief moment. A disturbance among them, or a wave from a passing ship out on the London River, had set them off again. The skipper left them swirling around. His concentration and eyes were needed elsewhere!

Shortly after berthing, while the jib was cleared away and the mainsail covered, the skipper had seen that the boat was taking the ground. 'Good timing!' he murmured, his eye brows momentarily flicking skywards as he moved aft with the burgee to collect the ensign.

The kettle, placed on the stove before covering the mainsail, began to whistle again too. 'Tea!' he said loudly. Clutching his mug firmly, he'd relaxed, smiling. He looked around his wonderful local environment. The faint, satisfied smile became a grin. He reflected, sipping contentedly at his tea.

He'd stood like that for a while and those thoughts were only disturbed as the mud, by then rapidly appearing around the boat, popped as the tide fell away. The water had left the mud's surface shimmering; it reflected the hues of the sky, by then a soft yellow. It tinged the gloop that was neither grey nor brown in appearance. 'Ah, that popping … just little creatures adjusting to life in their burrows … mud's musical melodies,' thought the skipper. The creatures were surely glad to be relieved of another of their twice-daily inundations. Other noises, the gentle gurgles of small trickles of water, lifted to his ears, and the air was also thick with a heavy saline scent from the receding tide. The skipper exhaled, then slowly inhaled, deeply. It was heady.

He glowed. '… It was so lovely …' It had been unplanned. It was a gift and he was a thankful man indeed.

Winter

A weak sun had been shinning. It had been a little later than mid-December, after a bout of heavier than usual snow. The skipper was sweeping the semi-frozen white stuff from the boat's decks and cabin top while intermittently watching the progress of the tide as it made its sluggish way up the creek. It had run through the many rivulets in the creek's bottom, flooding them before drowning them beneath the onward flow. The stream had carried its usual cargo of scum and foam that darted about in the swirl of a surface breeze. It was a breeze that held the promise of a grand full-sail sail. The skipper had felt truly alive and tingled with excitement.

Finally, as the skipper had reached the aft end he had seen the tide run up the scoured gulley of the boat's mooring and lick round the rudder. The rudder was buried in the embrace of the gloop that cushioned the clinker sloop and moments later it had seemingly climbed halfway up the rudder's blade … Resting awhile, he'd stood gazing, mesmerised almost, at the way the tide continued to creep inexorably, constantly moving. It never stopped … As it had swept across a flat area close by, it had gurgled as it filled a hole, pausing momentarily in its rush before sweeping onwards, until finally that piece of mud had been drowned too.

Returning his attention to his current job, the last of the hundred millimetres of snow had finally been swept overboard. Putting the broom in a safe place, he'd gone below. 'Hmm, sail bag out … Jib, I think …' he'd murmured, lifting the forward hatch and pushing it out. Pausing below a few moments to light the gas beneath his kettle, he'd noted its outer surface, usually bright and shiny, dulled by frosted condensation. The inside of the boat, surprisingly, had been relatively dry around the deck head. Grinning, he'd gathered up the burgee, ensign staff and boat hook and headed deck-wards. On deck, his thoughts were on any ice left after his sweep: the mate's voice about being careful had always come back to him clearly in such conditions, or any other for that matter.

Moving about the decks, the skipper had got on with his sailing preparations. It had helped to keep the cold at bay – not that he'd been cold. For that winter, the mate had insisted that the skipper obtained a pair of thick trousers … double-skinned. The insistence had been such that on a hop around the shops before the approaching Christmas, he'd been led firmly by the hand to a rail of garments in a fashionable high street store. All protestations of cost had been met with, 'Here's your size …', and it had been a case of acquiesce or suffer his mate's colour choice. Little choice, really! So, cocooned in his double-layer trousers, two club jumpers and a heavy-duty outside coat in an eye-watering fluorescent yellow, he worked away. It was not his usual boating attire … He'd soon begun to steam inside it all.

Suddenly the kettle had begun to whistle. It had been well timed, too: the burgee had just risen to the mast head and, tying it off, the skipper had gone below to save his gas. The burgee had flicked to the less than moderate, generally southerly wind, a good direction for a gentle sail under the high hills of Hadleigh Downs.

Shortly after, sipping at a steaming mug of a proprietary packet soup, the tide had lifted the boat. The bow had picked up, and then the old girl had rocked gently as the aft end lifted too. The engine was on in a trice. The last line, the aft, was hooked up on the wooden walkway and they were away, through a silty gruel of creek mud and churned creek water. Out in the stream, the engine was slowed to tick over. In a trice the skipper had loosed the main sheet and removed the last ties. The mainsail had risen rapidly and he'd sweated in the last centimetres before it had gathered the breeze.

A practised trundle aft had been needed to adjust their heading before the skipper had shuffled forward again to hoist the jib. 'Ah …' he'd thought, '… that'll balance the boat …' Then he'd briefly looked about as the halyard had been coiled and hung off on its cleat … looking aft, checking the boat's wake, he'd quickly dealt with the mainsail's halyard and control lines before regaining the helm where a mere caress, as soft as a feather's flick, was needed to correct her course as she'd forged against the flood, virtually on her own.

Some mallard and brent were working the mud along the marsh edges. First the ducks and then the geese had lifted off to alight in the saltings proper to continue grazing the shallows. The skipper had watched, mesmerised, his mind filled with the noises from the birds as they'd chattered. It had sounded friendly and unconcerned: birds were used to the comings and goings in that creek.

Gently sailing out of Smallgains Creek with a little snow remaining on deck …

Continuing to grin, the skipper had again returned his gaze upon the boat's passage, thinking too that it wasn't the time to daydream. Not another soul had been on the move, except far out in the run of the Thames' main ship highway where a veritable fleet of dredgers were at work, deepening the channel. Dredging had been needed to facilitate the coming of a fleet of sea giants: huge container ships that were being built to service the world's insatiable need to make things in lands far off and transport them halfway round the globe in an exchange of goods. It was a to and fro trade that was generally balanced – well, most of the time ...

Sucking on the last of his soup, the skipper had stared in awe at the panorama that opened up as the confines of the moorings were cleared. Patches of marsh were covered in snow. It had had a greyish look due to being tinged with sea salt. Over on the Downs it was white, a white that dazzled in its brightness. The wooded glades and denser swathes of thorn looked starkly black in contrast. It was a view not often seen. The faded greens of the saltings in the foreground also had a more robustness of colour, too. It was a grand sight.

Following his earlier intuition, the skipper shaped a course towards Two Tree Island, part of the Hadleigh Downs Country Park. A tack or two had to be slipped in: the wind, bent westwards by the hills, wouldn't allow a straight drive up the channel that lay between mud and sandbanks as it ran near to a westerly direction past the island.

'Ah ...' the skipper had thought, gazing out over the eastern marsh, 'Some would say that Two Tree Island belongs to Southend ...' Well, those eastern marshes known as Leigh Marshes did. Few newspaper reports, magazine articles, or books for that matter, allowed the bulk of the island to belong elsewhere. The skipper had always found that strange indeed ... 'It comes down to bloody local snobbery ... Castle Point doesn't have such a ring to it ...' and he'd laughed: surrounding areas were 'endeavouring' to suck up to Castle Point's Hadleigh 2012 Olympic all-terrain biking event – marketing it as 'theirs too'!

The island had once had a farm upon it and had long been known as Leigh Marsh, even though the bulk had lain outside Leigh's boundaries. It had once been part of the domain of Rochford Manor, as had, largely, that entire corner of Essex. The farm was one of the enterprises that became part of General Booth's Salvation Army Colony, centred on Hadleigh Downs. It was bought during the 1890s and the scope of ownership ran along the front at Leigh-on-Sea, where the cockle sheds presided over what was a public strand. Belton Hills and its farm were included too. And since, like the skipper's own home nearby, many householders have found that because their land had once been under Salvation Army ownership, a stipulation in the deeds continued to forbid the sale of liquor or any activities of a licentious nature ... At the memory of his reading of that in his deeds, the skipper had chuckled, vigorously, but without any feeling of disrespect towards his land's past owner, or anything else for that matter that had flicked across his mind!

Along the sea wall of the island only a few hardy dog walkers were seen, and later along the wall that protected the sunken marshes under Hadleigh hills, only the odd walker or runner was seen enjoying the fresh air ... quite the day for it. No cyclists were seen that day, however: the ground was frozen and covered in snow patches – it had still been barely zero degrees. Tacking that lovely stretch of water, which ultimately led to the island's other yacht club, the Benfleet, had kept the skipper's

Hadleigh Downs covered in snow – a rare event – in December 2010. Beyond the jib sheet's knot, upon the hill and valley in the distance, the 2012 Olympic all-terrain cycle track was being prepared – a dark line shows part of a twisting hill section. The down rises around 85 metres from sea level.

blood circulating, and subsequently his hands were warm too. Even with gloves, the cold had been bitingly raw. Regular mugs of hot chocolate had also helped. Not another soul was encountered on the water. 'It's such a lovely day ... the best for quite some time ... in terms of sunshine and light breezes ...' the skipper had thought, knowing that many considered him quite mad!

Eventually and reluctantly, the skipper had turned for home. It fetched the wind on the boat's starboard quarter and at times he'd run, goose-winged, to the fluctuating shifts caused by the Downs. Further down, back towards the island, passing Booth's old wharf, the wind had had a 'truer' southerly edge. 'Perhaps I'll be able to sail into the mooring ... Maybe it's just the hills ...' the skipper had mused before grinning wickedly.

Sometime later, having earlier come up into the wind outside his creek's entrance and disposed of the mainsail, the boat was gliding serenely along the creek's almost mirrored surface, scarcely leaving a ripple in her wake. The skipper had briefly gazed up at the burgee, where barely a flicker had disturbed its drooped appearance, and made the decision to leave the headsail up: dropping it would leave too little way on the approach into the mooring. He'd not even given the engine, silent beneath his feet, one thought. The only other movement, sound even, was the roar of the club's workboat, operating somewhere close by but out of view. The skipper knew the regular operator and could visualise his stubbly face, with a barely lit roll-up hanging from a bottom lip, as he stared fixedly through the workboat's wheelhouse as he'd worked the boat's controls ... The chap, a sailor, and a gentleman too – he'd waited for the skipper to pass by, or slowly sail into his mooring on numerous occasions – was a club stalwart.

'Regular mugs of hot
chocolate had also
helped' Drawn by
Mrs G. D. Ardley.

Judging his moment, the skipper had loosed the jib's sheet and steered across tide to his mooring. The boat's way carried her into her slot. It had only needed a gently push from the skipper as he'd flicked the aft mooring onto its cleat to bring the boat up ...

That sail had been one of only three that the skipper had achieved that December. It had been his least recorded for many a year. 'Can't do anything about the weather ...' the mate had warbled weakly over Christmas, adding, 'I'd like to go out too ... but not with this cold,' stopping to cough violently. 'Take your Mother out on Boxing Day ... When's the tide?' she'd added, her cheeks reddened by her throat's exertions.

The skipper's mother was close at hand too and her ears had pricked up. 'Ooh yes please,' she'd said, without hesitation ... 'I've got my warm trousers ...'

The skipper had nodded and made a remark about it being dependent on the forecast: his mother, for all her years of sailing experience, was less than a year away from eighty ... Later that week, the skipper had indeed got his mother afloat for a serene Boxing Day afternoon potter. It had been more of a drift: the breeze had been very light, but the sun had shone bravely for them. Both had gazed long at massed swirling clouds of knot as time and time again they lifted off from the marshes fringing the eastern point of the island. Other birds fought for space too, often mixing on the fringes with the knot before being left behind. It had been something the skipper's mother had not witnessed so closely at hand before – a winter's present indeed!

December was dutifully dropping off the calendar and the New Year beckoned. The evening's forecast had been listened to, ruminated over and thought about. It was for a light northerly ... 'We going for a sail, then ...?' the mate had enquired, a little after the forecast had finished. She'd added, 'I've looked at the tide tables ... We can take our breakfast with us ... bacon and fried egg sandwiches ...'

It had sounded worth it for that alone. The skipper had turned towards the mate, though, and said, 'Sounds wonderful ... But let's listen in the morning to the local ...'

The skipper hadn't finished: the mate had cut in, and grinning wickedly had said, 'Of course ...' The skipper knew his mate's propensity for checking the weather ... Then, with a twinkle in her eye, she'd said, 'Come on; let's have a nightcap ...'

In the Wake of Others

'What am I doing … A simple question … surely,' the skipper murmured softly, reflecting briefly: the day had changed markedly. Gazing out of a window, he'd seen that a gentle breeze had begun to swish several trees within his line of sight. The sun had erupted and shone too. It dazzled in its intensity.

It had been in that deep, dark time of the year when the daylight was short and the hours of darkness long. It was when the chance for a sail, if able, should have been wrapped within one's arms, cuddled and enjoyed. For some time it had been cold, wet and windy. It was towards the end of the twelve days of Christmas. At last, though, the sun had broken through what had seemed a permanent shroud of cloud. The skipper had been at his desk. He murmured, '… And the tide … it's on its way in … but I'm busy …' He grimaced slightly in thought, dismissing the incoming tide.

After a short while, the skipper had grinned and said, his voice seemingly hesitant, 'But I enjoy writing, too.' He sat smiling and added quietly, 'Especially reminiscing about things I love …' Then more clearly, he'd said, 'Sailing from place to place.' He paused as a thought tacked back and forth on the chart within his mind. It hadn't been, 'I should be out there now' – even though such thoughts were always close to the surface. Smiling, he'd murmured, 'Yes …' but hadn't immediately finished his sentence … He sat, frowning.

For a while he'd sat immobile, except for a noticeable nodding of his head. Sighing loudly, he picked up from where he'd left off a little earlier. 'Yes,' he called more firmly than his previous murmur, his face deadpan, 'yes, pottering around … all those odd places I've found … over the years.' His mind was racing – he was many leagues away.

Moments later, a gentle, fragile smile had begun to lighten his face as he'd reached forward to tuck his folder away. Thinking of his mate – she also partook of most of those adventures – he said, quietly to himself, 'We go where others have gone before.' His face became radiant as he'd chuckled, '… In their …' but hadn't finished. He'd burst into laughter and then, leaning back in his chair, had reflected for a moment or two while gazing with a fixed stare at the ceiling. Still smiling, he'd murmured, 'There's something …' and he paused. It was as if he was looking at some distant object or peering at a swathe of marsh, puzzling at what looked at first sight a dark smudgy line, yet knowing full well that there was an opening … somewhere. Then he'd said, '… It's … It's the very atmosphere of a place, a moment perhaps. It's in my soul. I feel immersed – at one with the salt, sand and mud …' The skipper shivered: he felt all of this intensely, and involuntarily his body had shuddered again, vigorously. 'It's not only what's going on … it's what's gone … before …' His thoughts were racing; he felt many seeds germinating. His thoughts were cruelly cut short: the mate was calling. But he'd lingered, momentarily – enough to dream – just a little. They were stored away … jotted down for safe keeping.

It was some days later. The skipper had picked up a book that his mate had just finished. Looking at her, the skipper had the answer to a question of a few days before. Well, one part anyway: moments earlier, the skipper had seen his mate's delight. Her demeanour and disposition had showed more than mere satisfaction. She'd looked across the short space that separated them with eyes starry bright. It was as if she were far off, in a different world. It had been a look he'd often witnessed: that book had transported her. 'It's … It's what it's all about …' he'd uttered absently: knowingly, too!

The mate had looked at him; her face was patterned by an enquiring look. Then, as if she'd known his thoughts, she'd said, 'You should read this …' indicating the book, adding with seriousness, '… Might find it interesting.' The skipper's eyebrows quivered slightly and then, as the mate's final comment jolted his consciousness, they flicked sharply upwards, '… Writer once lived in Bradwell …'

The skipper had, over a period of time, read through the book. It fascinated and interested him immensely. The book entwined snippets from the writer's early life in the waterside village of Bradwell. The village sat alongside the River Blackwater, on the eastern fringes of Essex's Dengie peninsula. The writer, Michael Morpurgo, had encapsulated within how his childhood and later experiences had been drawn upon. 'It's his personal cruise through life,' the skipper mused knowingly.

Michael Morpurgo had created the position of Children's Laureate jointly with Ted Hughes in 1998. He was appointed third Children's Laureate in 2003 and was the author of many works aimed at children. 'But a book is a book … for all to enjoy …' the mate had intoned to the skipper many times. In the book the mate had 'thrust' his way, *Singing for Mrs Pettigrew*, published by Walker Books, the skipper had found an interesting insight into another man's writing. Morpurgo had talked about having an empty page in front of him. He described his feelings when thinking about what to say … what he wanted to write … and how he'd get started. The skipper had empathised: he had often felt the same, too … Morpurgo's writing had left the skipper deep in thought.

It had been days later when the skipper had returned to his jottings. Looking at his notes, he'd thought back to Morpurgo's words as he'd re-established his course and murmured, 'Well … I agree …' He'd then paused. His pause had lasted for probably mere moments, yet it had seemed an indeterminable age, but suddenly the skipper had bubbled with excitement, 'Yes, yes, and too … It's the discovering and writing about those discoveries, all those experiences and pleasures, that I am called to.' His mind had been a whirl. He'd added, seriously and with feeling, 'I love to explore … potter and sail … in the wake of others … in the boat … but there are books too … all waiting to be discovered … to be explored … to be enjoyed. I've many that I love, but there's more, many, many more.'

Those last thoughts of the skipper's had awoken in him a deep desire. But what was it? The skipper had risen from his chair. He'd wandered around. Stopping suddenly before his bookcase, where there was a wealth of much-loved maritime literature, he'd pulled a volume from a shelf. It was a book by Frank Mulville, but, 'Why that one?' He'd not known.

The skipper was off on a cruise, of course. 'Ah! But where …?' you may ask! Well, the skipper's voyage would take him from the Blackwater into the other Essex rivers, deep into Suffolk, down to Kent with its intricate maze, and finally to his home waters: the Southend-on-Sea shore. The skipper's passage would meander along an unknown path within those bounds. It would ultimately have many long reaches, a good few tacks, for sure, before the run for home was before him. It would happen through the writings of a host of other authors' books that lined his shelves entwined with his own musings. He'd thought too about many more books he knew about, but hadn't copies of. His taste buds were titillated. He salivated and swallowed. His thoughts ran wild. Books, row after row, a colourful array of spines, all beckoned. Pages fluttered ... the cruise was under way.

Morpurgo had lived in Bradwell. It was, perhaps, the reason why his eyes had alighted upon a volume by Frank Mulville: 'Mulville had lived close by and sailed from Bradwell too ...' the skipper had thought, never mind that it had been on the shelf closest to him. Anyway, he'd enjoyed Mulville's books – a whole range of them.

'Yes,' the skipper said, 'my old sailing home, the spritsail barge *May Flower*, had been in and out of Bradwell too.' The barge, from around 1898 to 1932, had been owned by the Parker family, who had interests in local farming and barges. So, the skipper had always had a close affinity with the quaint little place. His heart had often fluttered when passing the ramshackle and disused Half Tide Quay on his way up to the marina. The marina had been carved out of the marshes during the late 1960s, making Bradwell 'a port', many years after it could have been: 'the old quay should have been developed ...' he'd oft mused, '... had the railway been run out from Southminster,' which lay a little inland to the south. 'But ...' he said, 'many are glad it hadn't been,' adding loudly, 'Bloody shame the quay has been allowed to wither and die, though.'

He'd chuckled: the mate had always said, 'You shouldn't say such things ...'

'Bah!' he'd always thought.

Bradwell Waterside, in many respects an underdeveloped place, had remained unspoilt, even with its redundant nuclear power station. The station's dismantled core was being encased in concrete. Its building sat, and loomed large, among a stand of trees across the shallow, sloping fields that ran away from the waterside hamlet down

The spritsail barge *May Flower*, alongside the Half Tide Quay at Bradwell, *c.* 1920. The *May Flower* was built in 1888, in Frindsbury, Kent, and was owned by the Parker family at Bradwell between 1898 and 1932. She was the skipper's childhood home some years later. Photograph from Ron Green's collection.

towards the sea wall and the River Blackwater. For all of that, the place had retained a rural backwater air. Fields sat behind hedgerows and on the way into the village, from the waterside, clapboard dwellings sprinkled the road edges. Those roads, narrow and no more than macadam tracks, which on a blistering hot day felt as you were floating as if on a soft-iced cupcake, all helped to maintain the aura. It was a place dearly loved by the skipper and his mate.

Morpurgo hated the power station, though, but the skipper was a pragmatic 'green' at heart. Nuclear power was green, wasn't it? 'Stuff's dug out of the ground ... Sits on top, in some parts of the world ... Granite's radioactive ... Much better than sulphurous fumes and carbon dioxide,' he would boringly intonate to his mate.

The mate's eyes would roll around their sockets and glaze over, as if to say, 'No reason to build another here ...'

'But why not?' the skipper would quickly quip, thinking, 'It's usually, "Not in my back yard" ...' Well in the skipper's case, in geographical reality, it was. He lived but a few miles away, as the crow would fly. Bradwell was well within the disaster damage contours. 'I remember when the station was being built – well, it was all but completed and operational then,' he'd once told his mate. The skipper had sailed on the Blackwater on his parents' barge in 1964, on the way up to, and later away from, Maldon, where the barge had undergone repairs.

The skipper wondered what Lewis Jones, Cowper, Baring-Gould, Copping, Alker Tripp, Griffiths, or Ransome even, would have made of it. All had lived through an amazing age of invention, new industry and rapid technological progress. Three of those men had lived into the nuclear power age too, and Jones was a pioneer of electrical treatment at The London Hospital – this treatment became radiography. 'They'd have accepted it,' the skipper felt: seamen utilised technology to enhance their skills and abilities. They had an affinity with the advancement of science. It was all, mainly, for the good of man. Modern sailors had embraced the Bermudan sail, the comfort and dependability of the modern diesel engine, and of course, they had in recent times discarded the centuries-old sextant for a 'you are here to the nearest few metres' electronic gizmo! The skipper had nodded: even his little clinker yacht had a little satnav now. 'Practicality – it's a seaman's number one asset,' thinking of his former life as a professional mariner. 'Whoops! I've digressed, somewhat,' he said, chuckling.

Getting back to Bradwell, the skipper had said, 'Frank Mulville spent a lifetime sailing out of Bradwell Creek. For a cruising base, or as a point of departure, the creek is superbly protected from heavy winds ... especially from the northern quarters.' The creek sat behind Pewit Island. The land mass equally provided protection from the southern quarters too. 'Once inside the marina you're cocooned,' he'd added, thinking of a recent enforced stay he and the mate had enjoyed: they'd used the time intelligently and gone exploring.

Leaving on a cruise he was making across the North Sea, Mulville said, in the opening chapter of *Terschelling Sands*:

As we slipped quietly through Bradwell Creek on the ebb tide a light westerly breeze came ruffling across the Blackwater to cool the hot sun and to hasten us on our way. We hoisted the mainsail, the foresail and the big headsail and bore away towards the Bench Head ... Mulville, his mate and young son were on their way to Holland and the German coast. [Quote used with permission of Wendy Mulville.]

'But,' the skipper had said, 'it could have been anywhere. Harwich Haven, the Backwaters, the Deben, the Crouch, the East Swale or the Medway.' Then the skipper murmured, 'All of those places call for a leaving, sometime on the ebb ...'

The skipper's thoughts, though, had departed for Maldon. It was passage made often, whenever he'd cruised on that coast. His thoughts went to the arrival of others in the river too ...

In *Swin, Swale and Swatchway*, written by the man who probably spawned the cruising yarn, H. Lewis Jones M.A., the skipper found a fleeting glimpse at the man's jaunty laissez-faire attitude to such trifles – 'There'll be more cruising to come', which paralleled the skipper's, 'Never mind ... It'll still be there to savour another time ...' Jones said, '... and the wind freshening we shifted jibs and just lay a course up the Blackwater; we kept a close look-out for the entrance to Bradwell Quay, but there was no time to go back and look at it ...' Later, on the way out of the river, Bradwell and Pewit Island are mentioned as being passed by. The reader, though, is left 'quite certain' that the place would have been explored during another cruise. The skipper chuckled as he followed Jones' passage up the wide open Blackwater before moving into the more confining stretches at Stone Point and Osea Island.

Frank Cowper had anchored off Osea Island while on a trip to Maldon when preparing his book, *Sailing Tours Part 1*. Over the following one hundred years, the anchorage had remained a popular and lovely place to drop the hook, providing the right conditions pervaded. 'Yet ...' the skipper said, '... with my mate, I have for many years preferred the quieter anchorage within Lawling Creek.' Their favoured place was just above the entrance to Maylandsea Creek. It was quiet, remote, and further from other human beings, but that's as may be ...

Aboard Cowper's yacht, the crew had turned in after a good supper, probably after a merry chinwag and a dram or two. Cowper said, referring to the night, 'We make all snug ... and sleep the sleep of repletion ...' Of the morning, he'd continued, 'The air was fresh and salt. We felt vigorous enough for anything; especially breakfast. How good was the smell of the frying bacon and the frizzling eggs, the toast that was warming, and the tea that was making.'

'Ah, yes, how pleasing ...' the skipper beamed: he often described such joys afloat too. And so, like the skipper, Cowper made into Maldon.

Of Maldon, Cowper wrote (they stayed awhile and explored the countryside thereabouts):

> Maldon would be an excellent place for yachts of from 10 to 100 tons if the town authorities would build a dock wall and gates across the creek, just below The Hythe. It is narrow enough there, and would provide splendid accommodation, besides affording Maldon the advantage of having the sea always there, for the contrast between Maldon at high water and Maldon at low water is striking.

The skipper had some thoughts too. 'What if those plans had come to fruition? It would have made Maldon quite a little port.' The approach to the proposed dam and locks would have been from the channel along the Heybridge Basin shore. 'It's interesting, too ...' the skipper noted. 'Jones made a similarly bold proposal for down on the River Medway. It must have had a lot to do with the 'can-do' spirit of the late

Victorians ...' A little pause followed as the skipper was thinking of lost opportunities in his present time, '... Let's not forget: these men were well-educated Corinthian sailors, who often set their minds to thinking,' he said, adding, 'Perhaps it was because they had little else to worry about!'

Musing to himself, the skipper had a thought. There was an attempt to build a dock at Maldon. It opened out onto Heybridge Creek, or would have done. It was built when the railway came to that end of town. It wasn't used, other than for a log pond. A quiet night in the Mersea Quarters beckoned the skipper before taking an ebb tide up to the Walton Backwaters, deep in the bosom of the Tendring peninsula, leaving Cowper to his explorations. Cowper had awoken the skipper's thoughts; they went back a little further in history as he metaphorically sailed down the River Blackwater. 'Cowper may have known this,' he thought, 'but I'm sure a dock had been planned.' The skipper was quite right, too. In 1848, when the Eastern Counties Railway had arrived on the Heybridge side of the Blackwater, a dock had in fact been dug for shipping. The opening to the river had not taken place because the project was abandoned. The resulting 'pond' was used by Sadd's, the timber importers, for seasoning hardwoods awaiting milling at a works erected upon its banks. 'Ah well ...' he'd murmured, rounding well inside the beacon that marked the extensive shingle and sand spit that ran out from the Tollesbury marshland. The beacon, known as the Nass, was a Norse name dating to Britain's Viking past. The skipper had always reflected on the thick morass of anchored yachts that always clouded his view – his present visit was no different, but it hadn't always been like that ...

In 1880, the Reverend Sabine Baring-Gould (the vicar of East Mersea from 1870 to 1881) had had a novel published about a local girl. It was an evocative yet sad tale of Mehalah, her trials and tribulations. The book's title echoed her name ... It, like the land thereabouts, could have been called savage: that land, if indeed land it was, needed to be respected. Baring-Gould said:

> Between the mouths of the Blackwater and the Colne, on the east coast of Essex, lies an extremely marshy tract veined and freckled with water. At high tide the appearance is that of a vast surface of Sargasso weed floating on the sea, with rents and patches of shining water traversing and dappling it in all directions.

'It hasn't changed a jot' ... the skipper had exclaimed, his thoughts far off: he was fastening to a vacant buoy between Cob Marsh and Packing Marsh islands. He could have been referring to the last time he'd been in the anchorage ... but no. He was thinking, past the conglomeration of yachts, back to Baring-Gould's time again. Baring-Gould said:

> A more desolate region can scarce be conceived, and yet it is not without beauty. In summer, the thrift mantles the marshes with shot satin, passing through all graduations of tint from maiden's blush to lily white. Thereafter a purple glow steals over the waste, as the sea lavender bursts into flower, and suddenly every creek and pool is royally fringed with sea aster. A little later the glasswort shoot up, first green and transparent as emerald glass in early spring, then turning to every tinge of carmine.
>
> At the fringes of the land, where all vegetation ceases to live, the marshes are alive and wakeful with countless wildfowl. At all times they are haunted by gulls, called sea mews and roysten crows.

A converted ship's lifeboat (known as a 'ris-on') heading past the old Nass beacon into the Mersea Quarters during the late 1940s. Note: the length of the pram dinghy is around half the length of its mother ship! Photograph from Jack H. Coote's archive, courtesy of Janet Harber.

Placing that book back in its comfortable place among its friends, the skipper remembered sitting back one evening in the cockpit of his yacht moored in the Quarters. His mate was still at work, doing a necessary spell in her school after the end of term. They were due to meet over at Bradwell the next day, or day after, he couldn't remember which. His thoughts ran to a feeling he'd had out in the rills between the islands of mud and marsh, deep below at the bottom of the ebb. He remembered shivering, and an intense feeling of loneliness had pervaded. Was it just that ... or was it more: dreadful deeds had occurred in those waters. Thoughts ran through the skipper's mind: Baring-Gould is said to have found Mersea Island and its environs 'bleak and inhospitable', preferring his native Devon, to which he returned in 1881. The skipper had thought it strange: Baring-Gould had written so movingly and accurately about the area, encapsulating the marshland aura perfectly. The man had a profound understanding of the environment and the goings on in which he lived and wrote about. Strangely, the skipper had found later, John Betjeman failed to mention Baring-Gould's story from the saltings when talking about the man in a radio broadcast of Friday 21 September 1945 (from John Betjeman, *Trains and Buttered Toast*, edited by Stephen Games). Apparently, Baring-Gould had not liked the place or the people!

The skipper was soon flicking through Cowper's *Sailing Tours Part 1*; he read:

The rich brown oaze of the old Hall Marsh is gleaming in the glow. The sea birds call from flat to flat, and the world is as it must have been when the Vikings came to harry the land. There is scarcely a sign of human life around us. Sunken Island looms ahead. It was there, they say, that grisly boat's crew of murdered coastguardmen was found. Lonely as these mazy creeks seem now, the tragedy of life and death has been played here in all its acts ... Did they sell their lives dearly, or did death come swift and sudden out of the dim darkness around?

That, surely, was why the skipper had shivered ... sitting alone ... a sudden eerie and haunting call from a curlew ...

The skipper's eyes had again roamed the array before him and he had a wistful sail. (This had happened on many occasions that he'd sailed that way with his mate and as always on such voyages, they'd often take it in turns to sit quietly reading, though in the skipper's case that meant periods of musing ... numerous interruptions of his mate's time out ...) He moved slowly along the shores of the Tendring peninsula, largely with the tide, until an easterly picked up in the late afternoon had whisked him across Pennyhole Bay. Reaching the Hamford Channel he'd bustled into the Walton Backwaters, the dinghy galloping behind, expectantly, frolicking in the knowledge that a quiet explore deep into the purslane-fringed world was soon on the cards.

Reaching the Walton Backwaters, the skipper breathed deeply. This, like the swathe of marsh in his beloved Medway and Swale, a deeply marshy and watery world, was bliss. 'Gracious,' he said, 'Ransome must have felt the same, I'm sure.' The skipper sighed, 'Nothing really changes ...'

In her biographical work, *Arthur Ransome and Capt. Flint's Trunk*, Christina Hardyment included a jotting from Ransome's diary of August 1937. Ransome was dabbling over a new book, provisionally called *The Mastodon's Lair*, and his diary note said, 'Muddy creeks ... tidal ... an island ... like Walton Backwaters ... a hut ... a house ...'

The skipper sighed again ... 'It hasn't ... changed,' he whispered. The book, of course, became that classic, *Secret Water*. And many have continued to use Ransome's name for the place: many outside Essex know of it, however many within know it not.

The skipper thought of others too who'd gone there. And too, in his thoughts, he was pottering in his dinghy. It was some while after ensuring the anchor was well snubbed and decks had been tidied. He let the dinghy go, free on the wind, a beam reach in an easy direction. It had felt as if he was following ... Then he'd remembered that Maurice Griffiths had written in *The Magic of the Swatchways* – something about looking for a quiet night. Griffiths eschewed a collection of yachts around Stone Point, the twinkling lights of Walton and other anchorages. He'd wanted solitude ... and he'd said:

No. To-night I had a lot of writing to do, and it was one of those pitiful rare occasions when the so-called 'urge to write' did not require to be dragged forth ... each board brought us nearer to the narrow opening that would suddenly appear in the mud to starboard and lead between two islets into the shallow mere beyond ... It was too dark to see the quay at the head of the creek, but one or two lights told where the cottages that looked over the water at high tide stood near the wharf ... I saw one stray withy apparently out in the middle ... I looked at the wake ... a line of bubbles was rising to the surface from under the rudder ... Then she stopped. [Copyright: Maurice Griffiths, *The Magic of the Swatchways*, Adlard Coles Nautical, an imprint of A&C Black Publishers, Ltd]

The skipper, waking from his reverie, had thought perhaps he'd be wise to head back to the clinker yacht, remembering all too clearly the dressing down he'd had some years before ... He'd stopped at a yacht and gone aboard for a coffee ... dusk had fallen ... it was late. In the gloaming that lit the creek – it was Pyfleet, by the way – the skipper had enjoyed a rare gem of a mystical glide home under a star-studded sky ... It was quiet. The dinghy's forefoot had barely made a ruffle on the placid surface that shimmered under the early night sky. The mate, who had, she'd implied later, been dancing on the cabin top looking out for him until darkness came, was still looking out as he'd come alongside. She'd become worried. 'That was a bit funny,' he said, smirking, and then thinking, '... Well, perhaps I was a little naughty ...' He'd grimaced and then he'd chuckled, remembering the mate's finger wagging admonishment again!

Resting awhile, the skipper had briefly closed his eyes as he'd sighed contentedly. Then he'd murmured, 'Ah yes ...' as his thoughts had returned to the Backwaters. Suddenly grinning he'd added, 'That was a pleasant jaunt ...' And he was back down to earth.

His thoughts, though, had been about to track elsewhere, but before they had, he'd remembered that Maurice Griffiths once waxed lyrical about a spritsail barge creeping away on the tide in those parts. The barge had come away from a wharf deep in the marshes. The skipper had often mused about which wharf it had been: there were several that Griffiths could have been close too. The skipper, though, had recently been in the area and had chuckled about a sail he'd had up to the wharf up at the head of Oakley Creek. He'd been sailing in with just a soft zephyr to help him along with the tide. From another boat motoring out, he'd heard, '... He won't get very far ...'

'... had enjoyed a rare gem of a mystical glide home under a star-studded sky ...' Drawn by Mrs G. D. Ardley.

'Just watch me ...' the skipper had wanted to call out as he lifted an arm, smiled, and called, 'Morning ...' The tide had indeed helped his clinker yacht up to the top, where a freighter was unloading, perhaps raw materials for fertilisers or munitions ... for that was the reason for the place's solitude. The land thereabout was closed to the public and no landing was permitted. The breeze had picked up during the morning and by the time of his turn he'd been able to tack round a particularly deep bend on the way out before beating up to Landermere Quay, finally to drop anchor between the steep banks of the shallow upper end of Landermere Creek, surrounded by the heady scents from the saltings close by. Few other yachts ever came, he'd found over the years. He remembered, too, the sound of a cuckoo that had risen up from over Skippers Island. He'd thought, 'Now what bird has lost its eggs?' and with an absent mind he'd replaced his book, adding, 'Its presence has a dark side, too ...' He was referring to the cuckoo, of course!

Reaching towards his books, the skipper had said, 'And where next ... wind's still kind ... somewhere in the south-south-easterly quarter.' Then, stridently, 'It's the Stour,' he commanded. 'The mate loves it ... Good enough reason as any ...' He chuckled.

It was the very same book he'd just moments before put away – *The Magic of the Swatchways*. Maurice Griffiths wrote about coming up to an anchorage, in the rain, off Wrabness one time (as the skipper had too, it being related in *Mudlarking: Thames Estuary Cruising Yarns*). Griffiths wrote:

> A flash of lightning rent the heavens and for a moment dazzled me. It was followed by a mighty crash of thunder that racketed across the sky and rumbled away of the sodden fields to the south ... the skies were filled with a blinding glare, and for an instant revealed the high cliff off the port bow ... while the resulting thunder-clap gave vent to its terrific majesty ... I stowed the dripping canvas and let go the anchor ... when three hours later, I went out on deck to look at the night before turning in, I found a still, starlit scene ... [Copyright: Maurice Griffiths, *The Magic of the Swatchways*, Adlard Coles Nautical, an imprint of A&C Black Publishers, Ltd]

The skipper's thoughts ran to his own arrival at that anchorage off Wrabness. Another yacht had come into a mooring ahead of him and the man, also sailing alone, had called out, 'Be alright on that one,' as he'd pointed at a weed-infested buoy, 'Owner's away.' It was while sailing alone: his mate had jumped ship for a few days. The anchorage of Griffiths' time had all but gone. Private moorings had been laid under the cliffs, probably because it was the best protected anchorage on the river, with water to float at low tide. The skipper had hung his soaked oilies from the boom, where they'd dripped beneath the cockpit awning. He'd sat, after mopping up, with a warming mug of tea and gazed in awe at rods of rain diving into the water, leaving it pock-marked, breaking the oily-looking surface into a myriad of radiating rings. All around, the water had soon seethed. A low-level mist had developed. Through the opening aft, past the boom tent, the skipper had caught intermittent views of Holbrook school, high on the hills of the Suffolk shore, as it had been lit by shafts of lightning that darted about.

Usually, while sailing on the Stour, the skipper and mate had sailed up to Manningtree with a fresh flood: shops lay close by the Stour Sailing Club's clean hard, and the larder would be restocked. They'd always found it a friendly place to visit, too. The Stour was once a bargemen's river. There were builders down at Harwich (before moving to

The skipper's yacht, *Whimbrel*, anchored off Mistley Quay on the River Stour during 2010. Astern on the mudflat are the remains of the spritsail barge *Bijou*, abandoned there after being hit by an incendiary bomb in July 1940. Beyond her is Manningtree.

Ipswich): the Wrinch farming and barge-owning family at Ewarton Ness, on the Suffolk shore, and Horlock's at Mistley, barge builder and owner of many fine vessels.

The skipper was then off on another tack, thinking of barges. 'Ah yes …' he'd said to no one in particular, '… a 1930s gentleman, Martin, I think, spent a period of time aboard a sailing barge. She was the *Vigilant*, I'm sure.' Following a foray as a bargeman, Martin had written about it in *Sailorman*, published by Oxford University Press, 1933. It was to this that the skipper's eyes had then alighted. The man, E. G. Martin, had set about learning the ropes to become a barge mate. The intrepid gentleman devised all sorts of improvements, too, to make the barge go faster and sail better. On the page that the skipper's eyes had come to rest on, Martin, like the skipper's thoughts, was on his way to Pin Mill …

The *Vigilant* had left Mistley and was under orders to lighter wheat from a barque in Butterman's Bay, up into Ipswich Dock. Leaving the Stour, Martin had been given the wheel by the skipper of the *Vigilant* while he'd popped below … Martin tells of his insecurity and oversteering, yet the skipper hadn't batted and eyelid – he'd quietly watched from the aft cabin hatchway, pulling on a cigarette. Martin said:

I caught hold of the wheel and the skipper [not our skipper, reader] went below. This was a strange moment, for *Vigilant* was the largest as well as being the strangest sailing-craft which I had ever steered. She seemed to be going to pay off, so I eased the helm a little. For a moment nothing happened, and then came a sheer to windward. I met her – too late – and had to put the helm far over before she steadied – or rather, I should say, came back to her course and fell right off, far beyond it. It was some minutes before I could get her to settle down. Presently I noticed the skipper standing on the ladder with his head in the companion-way just behind me … keeping handy just in case.

The skipper had enjoyed that read and continued to travel with Martin and his trusting barge skipper. Martin then related:

At Shotley Spit we flattened in the mainsheet for the turn to windward up the Orwell. Now my only job was to tend the bowline on the foresail. When she winded for the first time I kept the sail aback too long.

'Just let it across steadily,' called the skipper, 'so that it doesn't kick – don't back it, or her head blows off.'

So I eased it across carefully each time, and we worked our way up river in short tacks with the flood beneath us.

Presently the skipper called to me to come and take the helm – and he went forward to the bowline.

The skipper, sitting back in his chair, was grinning: Martin recounted, at length, how he'd fancied that he'd not done very well. Finally the passage was nearing its end. They passed a barque that they were to load from on the morrow in Butterman's Bay and Pin Mill had hove in sight. Martin said, 'We were going up very fast with a good tide under us, and soon we came to Pin Mill.'

The skipper had looked up from that book murmuring gently, 'That was lovely. A classically simple description about a passage during the days of trading sail – no waffle

Jack Coote's *Iwunda* anchored close into Mistley Quay in around 1950. Jack is rowing his children ashore. There is a motor barge and a rigged spritsail barge alongside. The warehouse, in the centre, hiding the church, is the same building on the left-hand side of the previous illustration. Photograph from Jack H. Coote's archive, courtesy of Janet Harber.

about waving sedge, dappled colours and ...' he'd stopped: it was a different sort of writing. He closed the book, thinking of the times he'd witnessed barges beating up against a stiff breeze. 'There was the *May*,' he said, 'I think my youngest brother was with me, crewing for a few days. Yes, the barge, she was a grand sight galloping back and forth up past all those shiny yachts tethered to their buoys, her mains'l brailed to her sprit ... chines, alternately rising to kiss the sun ...' The skipper was himself transported to Pin Mill and his thoughts raced. He wondered what Ransome would have made of the sight of well-kept and gaily painted charter barges carrying their human cargoes. Those craft in Ransome's time were grafting work horses. Continuing to wonder, the skipper's eyes danced across book spines, spines painted in multifarious colours, a rainbow, before finally alighting on one.

Pin Mill has remained an evocative place. The front, under the woodland which belonged to the National Trust, had become a little scruffy, but some progress had recently been made to correct that, especially by the inhabitants of the houseboat moorings that thronged the upper mudflats. For that, the skipper was pleased. While on a recent visit there, the skipper had seen that the old barge hard, beloved by Ransome, was being regenerated. The walkway was being heightened; lengthened, he'd been told; and too, the barge blocks were being renewed: those tan-sailed craft were welcome once again for maintenance ...

Houseboats had been in the anchorage since before the time of people such as Martin, Carr and Ransome. All of those though were here often in the 1930s and their paths must have crossed. Under Ransome's pen, the place became immortalised in *We Didn't Mean to Go to Sea*. Pin Mill was the home of a little gaff cutter, the *Goblin*. She, with a group of children, became the yarn's eternal stars in a wonderful tale of the children being left on the boat, it going adrift off Harwich in a fog and their subsequent adventures sailing across to Holland ... and back home. It was on this book that the skipper's eyes had alighted. Opening it to the first chapter, he was immediately transported ...

Ransome wrote:

Everything on the river was new to them. Only the evening before they had come down the steep green lane that ended in the river itself, with its crowds of yachts, and its big brown-sailed barges, and steamers going up to Ipswich or down to the sea. Last night they had slept for the first time at Alma Cottage, and this morning had waked for the first time to look through Miss Powell's climbing roses at this happy place where almost everyone wore sea-boots and land, in comparison with water, seemed hardly to matter at all.

They spent the morning watching the tide come up round the barges on the hard, and envying the people who kept putting off to the anchored yachts or coming ashore from them. Then, in the afternoon, an old dinghy had been found for them, and now they were afloat themselves, paddling about admiring the yachts in the anchorage.

'Ah yes,' the skipper thought, 'how often have I sat and stared or sailed silently by under a fickle breeze in the dinghy and gazed ...'

The skipper read on:

Pin Mill in the time of Arthur Ransome and Frank Carr. Apart from the cars, little has changed. Photograph from Jack H. Coote's archive, courtesy of Janet Harber.

It was getting on for low water. They had watched the falling tide leave boat after boat high, but, as Roger said, not exactly dry, on the shining mud. On the hard, men were walking round a barge that had been afloat in the middle of the day, and were busy with scrappers and tar-brushes. A clock chimed six from amongst the trees on the farther side of the river. The river, wide as it was, seemed almost narrow between the bare mudflats …

The skipper read a little more. The children had quite a conversation about which of the boats they would choose for themselves, he thought: 'they mentioned all these things … proper capstans … has she got an engine … types of sterns, because, "Daddy says …" and sail types …' Pausing, the skipper said, 'In his [Ransome's] world it was just so!' (Excerpts from *We Didn't Mean to go to Sea*, by Arthur Ransome, published by Jonathan Cape, reprinted by permission of the Random House Group Ltd.)

The skipper was also reminded of something he'd read in a book, *The Yachtsman's England*, by Frank Carr, a man who later became key to the development of the National Maritime Museum as its second director. Carr berthed his yacht at Pin Mill; it was the end of his season and he was aboard the yacht with his wife, reminiscing over their sailing exploits of that year. Carr said:

The season was over, and, in early October, the ship lay on her mooring at Pin Mill, waiting to be put to bed for her winter's sleep. We had cruised far around the coasts, revisiting old haunts and exploring fresh places. We had, of course, done less than half of what we had set out to accomplish, because always we over-estimate what we can perform in the time at our disposal; and, instead of hurrying on with our intended programme, we are apt to dawdle by the way, spending a extra day here, a couple there, making expeditions in the dinghy for which no time has been allotted in our plans. But now the cruise was finished. On the morrow we would begin the sad business – for me it was always a sad business – of unrigging the ship and laying her up. Tonight was ours to talk over the memories of the cruise, and to remember with gratitude all the pleasant things that had happened, and for friends that we had met.

Carr's wife commented on all those people they had met cruising that season too: the skipper, reading, wholeheartedly agreed. He said, absently, 'It's indeed wonderfully fascinating to meet all those people we do – from all walks of life – all friendly – the children too, especially seeing them enjoying little boats, building their knowledge of a life, all being well, they might follow in years to come ... they've always been the future ...'

Thinking of the Carrs' comments about places they'd been to, the skipper was away. His next thought was the Deben, a lovely little river and easily reachable from Pin Mill. It lay to the north, beyond the soft Suffolk hills that the skipper was so fond of. 'Shall we go,' he'd said, adding, 'Let's!' but before he'd done so, he'd remembered his own setting off downriver, earlier that year, bound for the Backwaters to pick up a fresh crew for a few days – with a plan for a sail into the Deben, hatched many months before, as it happened ...

He'd sailed away from his anchorage in Fox's Bottom, just below Pin Mill hard and beneath the National Trust's thickly wooded hillside, where the call of woodpeckers vied with that of the oystercatcher! Clearing his anchorage and sailing down towards Cotton Creek, a barge was seen to get away too. He'd watched as she'd heaved up her anchor, lying head to wind with a bargeman's breeze blowing ... but late on the ebb. 'No sails being set ...' the skipper had mouthed silently, but thinking much more. It was a north-westerly; it would have made for grand sailing. The barge had motored off, like a dog with its tail between its legs ... keeping not far ahead of the skipper in his own yacht. The skipper had thought then, 'What would the bargemen of old thought ...' The skipper's own were along the lines of, 'What a waste of fuel ...' Martin and his skipper would surely have agreed. Later, as he'd met the fresh flood tide in the harbour off Harwich hard, the skipper watched as the barge had punched the tide, throwing up mounds of white froth around her bluff bow. As he had regained nature's help into the Backwaters, the barge had been seen far out towards the Stone heaps, bound down the Wallet, where some sail had at last been broken out ...

The River Deben was reached by sailing out of Harwich Haven and turning to port ... round Languard Point and up the coast a few miles. To penetrate that river, the sailor had to cross the river's fabled bar. The skipper, it must be said, had never experienced any trouble there: it was prudent not too! But he knew others had, and it was to one of these tales that his thoughts quickly ran – albeit it was about leaving.

The skipper's hand had soon alighted on another of Maurice Griffiths' books. The book, *Sailing on a Modest Income*, recounted a story about leaving the River Deben in the early 1920s. Griffiths had just taken delivery of his first self-owned boat, a little clinker seventeen-foot sloop, an old Broads cruiser. With a friend as crew, they'd set off from Woodbridge in January to sail the boat round to Ostrich Creek, below Ipswich. It was blowing hard. Griffiths wrote:

The anchorage at Ramsholt shortly after the Second World War. The quay has since been renovated, as has the hard, seen as a line of timbers where many dinghies are drawn up. Photograph from Jack H. Coote's archive, courtesy of Janet Harber.

The mate looked keenly at the snow-laden sky and sniffed. 'Rotten prospect,' he ventured, 'wind sou'west, dead beat to the Orwell ...' ... As soon as we got out of the lee of the land the wind laid us down to the lee rail, and the sight that met our eyes as we opened out the bar caused my heart to miss a few beats. Big seas were breaking on the scattered banks of shingle and throwing up fountains of white spray that was driven far by the wind. One could not detect a break in the line of white anywhere. ... The little boat dived into the heart of the steep, breaking seas ... A minute later she stopped suddenly with a grinding scrunch, while the tide swirled round her stern and carried the dinghy past to leeward.

They got off because the mate had stripped and gone overboard. He'd put his shoulder to the boat's hind quarter ... they lived to tell the tale. 'Ah,' thought the skipper, 'there by the Grace of God ...' adding, 'There's a better way, of course: wait for softer conditions ...' Even in calm conditions the sea sucks and wheezes at the shingle banks and at the turn of a fresh flood, spume can be thrown up by the sea's sheer devilment. The skipper has described the crossing of a bar with characteristic colour elsewhere.

Coming into the entrance of the Deben, H. Lewis Jones explained in *Swin, Swale and Swatchway* the trials experienced by him and his crew. They'd had calm conditions, just enough to sail. He describes the moving shingle knolls that shift around from year to year, especially after storms. Lewis Jones wrote:

Woodbridge Tide Mill and Granary in the early 1950s. Photograph from Jack H. Coote's archive, courtesy of Janet Harber.

Woodbridge as seen in 2010. The Granary and Tide Mill looking as if new ...

... and it never does to trust to one's recollection of what the entrance was like last year; and as to charts, they are an absolute delusion. That will do. Now then, pinch her all you can; we have got an ingoing flood with us; and I will get the pole overboard. [It was long before the advent of echo sounders!] There is the top of the big knoll just awash. At low water it is all dry beach right up to the cliffs.

The skipper thought, 'Even that's something that changes, too ...' He read on.

With little wind and not being able to reach their intended destination of Woodbridge that afternoon, the crew had popped ashore to talk to a coast-guardsman who was working in a patch of garden and sold them some potatoes. Lewis Jones said, '... Anyway; so we pull on board again, make sail, and get up the mudhook [anchor], and work by short boards past the half-mile long island of sand and shingle, which lies right in the middle of the river below King's Fleet.'

They sailed up to Ramsholt Dock to anchor – then all went ashore in the dinghy to explore ashore – very much the ethos of the skipper and the mate when cruising.

The skipper thought then of his own mate. She was probably exploring too – it would be letters and sounds with her class of 'tiddly tots', though. Time had travelled on ... it was time for him to prepare the essence of their supper. That job, supper and such, was part of what he'd done for years since their life swap – she, working full time, and his, well ... 'a life of riley' some said!

Some while later, coming back to his cruise, the skipper had pondered. 'The windy river or not ...?' His eyelids fluttered in the wake of his roving eyes as they traversed the array of literature in front of him ... 'Oh come on,' he'd chuckled, 'let's go there too ...' leaving any thoughts of Woodbridge behind.

'Ah, yes ... Sailing without an engine, as Jones and his contemporaries had ...' the skipper said, picking up his thread again. 'With the mate, I sailed our first boat without an engine for a season. It gave us a valuable year of education ...' It had more so for the mate, for skipper had only then recently dragged her out of her Midlands environment to the East Coast ... the land of salt marsh and mud. Why those thoughts had occurred to him, the skipper was completely mystified, however. While away cruising, oft as not, the skipper would chirp away, with a holier-than-thou attitude, about first-class modern yachts zipping past them, under power, carrying a fair tide and a fair breeze ... 'You've all seen it ...' he'd muttered, adding, 'I've never understood – and never will ...' His voice trailed away as his eyes had arrested; he'd quickly plucked the object of his desire from the shelf.

The book, *Suffolk Sea-Borders*, by H. Alker Tripp was a much different animal to others in the stable – more of a 'boys' own'-type composition and very typical of the period. He sailed, of course, without an engine, hence the skipper's affinity. Tripp, though, apart from being a competent early twentieth-century sailor, was a pioneering traffic management expert and his prowess at understanding and dealing with the complexities of what the internal combustion engine-powered vehicle was doing to the road system of London and across the country led him, ultimately, to advising many authorities around the world. Eventually, the man received a knighthood, but that's by and by.

Tripp was on a voyage with a couple of friends. They were making for the Ore entrance and he wrote:

In a few minutes we should be in the haven.

'Where's the wind gone?'

My voice was one of protest and even consternation, for the wind had left us. All in a single instant it had decamped; not a breath remained. We were powerless, at the mercy of the tide …

The kedge was put over the side and they'd waited. A puff or 'squall', Tripp termed the changes in the weather as they came upon them from time to time as they'd made up to the river's entrance, to wait off the bar. He'd written about how it had then rained, hard, and he described it as 'the fantastic perpendicular fury of it …' The wind, though, had remained dead.

'Ha, haven't we all been there?' the skipper had thought!

Finally, Tripp wrote:

At long last, as the rain tailed off into a subdued patter, a vital touch quickened from the eastward. This was the real thing; swiftly we gathered way and swept towards the haven. Then, before it had time to flatten, we had taken the pilot on board and the in-going current had us; almost out of control, we were swept, sent coursing like a cork in a rain-brimmed gutter round the sharp bend. Answering her helm in another draught of wind, the yacht was sailing in the river.

'Ah,' the skipper had murmured and nodding his head vigorously said, 'Yes I remember numerous fights to get into and out of rivers against the tide … with an engine too … But not this one, though … yet.'

On his way around the East Coast in the path of Cowper, another sailor, Dick Durham, also arrived in the Ore and Alde rivers, and, like Tripp and Cowper for that matter, had chums crewing with him. Durham had taken up a challenge by a publisher, Ashford Press Publishing, to recreate Cowper's voyages in the writing of his *Sailing Tours Part 1*. Dick's charming and lovely *On and Offshore* was the result. The skipper's thoughts had run to it earlier, thinking at the time, 'There's a bit in there … for later …' He'd looked it up.

Durham and his crew had accepted a challenge to take part in the Aldeburgh regatta. They even careened the boat to clean her bottom. His boat, *Almita*, was an engineless wooden centre-board cutter which Dick then kept along the shore at Leigh-on-Sea. *Almita* had a look of a deep-keeled boat to the unknowing and was known locally for being slippery through the water. Shortly after the start of the race, and Dick wrote:

Like the Aussies, though, we had some tricks under the water. Pete coaxed *Almita* over the start line just ten seconds after the gun and soon we were cutting inside our competitors. They keep deep yachts on this river and, if you don't know the truth, *Almita* too looks like what she once was (before alterations and a plate had been fitted) a deep keeled boat. So eyebrows were fluttering as we clipped off corners of the river and lured other boats to do the same.

'What do you draw?' asked one indignant sailor as we passed between him and a cud-chewing cow standing nonchalantly on a ditch outfall.

Jack Coote's
Iwunda anchored
off Iken Cliff on the
River Alde above
Aldeburgh, *c.* 1950.
Photograph from Jack
H. Coote's archive,
courtesy of Janet
Harber.

'Six foot,' said Pete, 'but we can cut it back to five through the mud,' he added ambiguously. The inquisitive yachtsman then followed our wake and promptly ran aground.

The skipper loved that! He laughed, remembering: it was something he'd watched other craft do when following his own boat ... Lack of a close attention to depth – a let's follow and be damned attitude – meant they ploughed the mud ... nearly sticking to the putty. The skipper's yacht had a draft that ranged from a little less than a metre to a little less than two. Many times he'd confused the unknowing!

The skipper, after putting Durham's book back in its place, thought, 'It's time to be moving towards home waters ...' But before he'd done so, he remembered something anecdotal. Aldeburgh was a spiritual home for Benjamin Britten and his friend Peter Pears. It was here too that E. M. Forster met the pair on the beach while working on one of his books. The sea air refreshed him and the town had intellectuals, like him, living close by. 'It's funny,' the skipper had thought, 'how so many people find inspiration from the sea ... even if they have no real love for it.' Britten, of course, had loved the sea.

Leaving the Ore and Alde, the skipper thought of the Colne as a good place to head for. 'A quiet night in Pyfleet, perhaps,' he'd thought, as if departing with his mate ... 'Ah, yes, that would be nice ... But a shower at the yacht club would be good.' The skipper grinned as he'd sniffed unconsciously!

Another charming book that the skipper alighted on was Herbert Thompkins' *Companion into Essex*, which was, incidentally, dedicated to a John W Burrows J.P., F.S.A., a south Essex benefactor who had donated tracts of woodland, including playing fields, to the local populace. The man had once lived close by the skipper's own home, too. Although not essentially a sailing book – though its genre exists in a few titles known to the skipper – it had a wealth of incidentals and anecdotes of Thompkins' travels around the hinterland of Essex. A number of his journeys were indeed along the rivers and coastline, and after departing from Harwich in a friend's yacht for the Colne, he wrote:

I have many happy memories of the Colne, the adjacent creeks and the marshlands thereabouts. One morning, aboard the *Panther* with my friends ... I left Harwich

Barges and picnickers on Brightlingsea hard in about 1930. Note the style of hats being worn. The nearest barge is the *Pacific*. She was an iron barge built in 1884 and was later motorised by London & Rochester Trading Co., and was still working after the Second World War. Courtesy of Alice Everard.

betimes, after poring upon maps and gossiping about the weather. We left Shotland [Shotley] Spit Buoy well to starboard, in a stiff breeze from the nor'west that drenched our bows with spray. Two strings of wild duck flew high overhead as if to lead the way. The *Panther* spanked along merrily; we were soon abreast of Walton once again. Off St Osyth we passed the Priory Spit Buoy. Cold rain fell about us as we turned into the Colne for the difficult approach to Brightlingsea ... Once in Brightlingsea Creek, we were in a thin drizzling rain; all around was a forest of little masts; many gulls, somewhere between the creek and St Osyth wailed dismally in the deepening gloom. [Excerpt from chapter 15, 'Beside the tidal Colne', page 178, of *Companion into Essex* by Herbert W. Thompkins, second edition, 1947, published by Methuen and reproduced by permission of Taylor & Francis Books UK.]

'Yes,' said the skipper, grinning deeply. And laughing knowingly, added, 'Why! Haven't we all enjoyed such a passage?'

The skipper had recently enjoyed a week on the rivers Crouch and Roach. So it wasn't a surprise that it was to that area his thoughts fell. It was to this river, apart from the local Medway and Swale, that the skipper had sailed with his mate on their dark blue-hulled 'People's Boat' during her first year of sailing, decades beforehand. Lifting a book from the shelf in front of him, he'd soon found what he wanted. 'Ah,' he said, '*Sailing on a Modest Income* ... a compilation by Maurice Griffiths ... there's something in there ...' And so there was. Griffiths had included a delightful piece written by W. Edward Wigful about the River Crouch. Wigful was a man of many talents and wide coastal cruising experience; he was an able artist, too. His description of the quiet and quaintness (the skipper's words: Wigful said 'old-fashioned place') found on a run ashore for stores was as much as the skipper had himself described in *Mudlarking: Thames Estuary Cruising Yarns* ninety years later. Wigful had 'cruised' the Roach too, extolling the virtues of Barling and Yolksfleet creeks, sailing round Potton Island and Paglesham as a place to visit. 'Yes,' the skipper said, 'ah, yes, I agree. For me they're still the gems – unless a racing man.'

At the end of Wigful's article is a letter transcribed by Griffiths. It was from Frank Cowper. After thanking Wigful for his approving words about *Sailing Tours Part 1*, Cowper comments on the fact that by 1901 the anchorage off the Burnham waterfront was crowded, yet only as far back as 1891 barely a yacht was seen along the waterfront. 'Ah,' the skipper murmured.

For a short time the skipper had sat with a perplexed look. He had been trying to remember something. 'Ah,' he'd suddenly said again, diving for another book, 'here it is ...' He chuckled, flicking the pages. The skipper had found a clear reference to the Royal Corinthian's presence on the River Medway long after their supposed move to their Burnham-on-Crouch berth: in John Irving's *Rivers and Creeks of the Thames Estuary*, published in 1927, the clubhouse was clearly shown just to the west of the Port Victoria quay, opposite the entrance to Stangate Creek. 'I wonder,' he'd thought, closing the book. Then thinking back to Cowper's comments of 1901, the skipper muttered, 'In the mean time the Royal Corinthian had moved from Port Victoria ... but when had they?'

Later on that same day, while the skipper was still somewhat vexed by 'his' Corinthian problem, he'd tackled the mate over their dinner table when catching up on their respective day's activities. 'I need to find out ...' he'd wailed.

'Look at the club's web site,' she'd quipped, wondering why he hadn't already done so, pushing aside the 'zinging' that washed around her mind from her recently finished jobs for school the next day and thinking, 'Ah yes ... there is a real world out there ... somewhere ...'

The skipper had, of course, investigated the Corinthian's web site at some stage or other. He gained a contact too, a former flag officer of the club; both sources provided a bucketful of interesting information. The Royal Corinthian was instituted in 1872 by a group of small craft (gentlemen) sailors who sailed without the help of paid hands. That aspect was an important point, enshrining an amateur distinction. Initially, they met at various locations in London. In 1879 (on 12 June, incidentally the skipper's birthday) a clubhouse at Erith was opened. Men such as Erskine Childers and, earlier, McMullen had sailed from Greenhithe, a little downriver, but Erith Bight had been a magnet for the amateur sailor. It had had a sailing club too – the Erith Sailing Club, and they've had their men of the sea, men like bargeman Bob Roberts, and W. E. Sinclair who'd cruised extensively to the Baltic, Iceland and other places during the early 1920s in a four-tonner. Both of those men sailed together on a Brixham trawler, *Quartette*, yachting to South America and the West Indies. The Erith club became a 'yacht club' in around 1900 and until recently had been based on an old retired ferry, the *Folgefonn*, moored on the edge of a small patch of saltings tucked under Crayford Ness. It had moved into a spanking new building in 2010 that looked as grand as that of the area's earlier club, the Royal Corinthian's 1931 Burnham-on-Crouch clubhouse.

By 1899 the Corinthians had acquired a lease of some land and moved to a new clubhouse at Port Victoria, courtesy of the South Eastern Railway Company; however, a small group of men, more attracted to racing than cruising, had been ensconced on the River Crouch at Burnham since 1892. They had found that the river lent itself to racing. At first, the group had used a hired room at the White Hart, but by 1898 the 'Burnham faction' had opened a clubhouse at Prior's Wharf. The club then had two clubhouses. It could have caused a split, but Port Victoria remained the base and Burnham became a de facto branch. The status quo continued until the looming shadows of the 1914–18 conflict closed in over Europe's collective heads, when the land and buildings at Port Victoria were requisitioned by the Admiralty. The skipper was surprised to learn that the club were not sure if they have ever been paid by the Admiralty! Cowper's comment about Burnham's yachting growth from 1891 to 1901 was probably the Corinthians' doing.

Later, Burnham became the club's epicentre. When was unknown, but it was clear that the requisitioning of their headquarters for the duration of the war asserted the Burnham base as the dominating force. The club and the River Crouch had remained an important bastion of yacht racing of all forms, and many other yacht clubs sprang up to join the Corinthian on the banks of the lower Crouch. Of course, Burnham-on-Crouch had been connected to London by an efficient railway system too, and London men could escape on a Friday, 'arriving in droves', a contact of the skipper's later said, '… and change into seamen's clothing and board their yachts for a weekend of hard racing or frivolous jollity.' The contact, a gracious lady, and a past flag officer, had also said, 'A rumour that the rail company intended to axe Sunday afternoon trains returning to London was met with such uproar that there was a strategic change of mind.' That was in about 1900!

It also transpired that 'only a bunch of diehards' had wanted to remain on the River Medway before 1914. It was unknown, but it is probable that it was those men that had continued to remain 'in residence' after the conflict that ripped Europe apart, decimating her population, had fizzled out in the indecisive armistice that followed. An oil refinery loomed on the site of Port Victoria. It was soon built. The club building was, obviously, then obliterated and buried beneath cracking towers and many oil

The Corinthian Yacht Club (later Royal). Top right: The club's headquarters at Erith as depicted on an old postcard from *c*. 1890 – the extent of the buildings is clear. Top left: The Erith clubhouse, seen from the water during the 1890s. Bottom left: A rare Edwardian picture of the Royal Corinthian's clubhouse at Port Victoria on the Isle of Grain; it looked an imposing building. The vessel beyond, at the port jetty, appears to be a stern view of the HMY *Victoria and Albert III*: her two funnels were closely spaced and their lipped tops can be seen. Her mast configuration is correct. Bottom right: The building at Prior's Wharf that was used by the Burnham-on-Crouch branch from 1898 to 1911. Photograph courtesy of Royal Corinthian Yacht Club.

The RCYC's fourth base, an old boathouse a few metres upstream of their current headquarters on the Burnham River.

tanks. The refinery lasted a mere sixty years before it was itself dismantled, a blink of an eye in the world's history. A container port was built on the site.

The Admiralty ruled the roost on the river too and the river was busy with ships, let alone a huge number of spritsail barges. Now, in comparison, the river had returned to an almost pre-industrial-age quietness. Spritsail barges were now a rarity on this, their 'home' river, and the Admiralty had long departed after huge cuts in the country's defence spending during the 1980s. Ships, although fewer, are immense and their hulls loom large over the little river as they come and go.

'Ah,' the skipper said upon reading that piece of information, '... maybe the Port Victoria building was handed back to the Corinthian after the end of that century's first period of world conflict?' He'd grinned: the Corinthians had lost much of their archive material during many building moves. 'Maybe the truth has also been lost ...' Their fourth base from 1911 to 1931, just upriver from their present clubhouse, remains in use as a waterfront dwelling.

Interestingly, not long after the club had returned to having a single clubhouse, a southern branch sprang up, in much the same fashion as that at Burnham some fifty years previously. A past commodore set it up. The skipper's friend wrote:

> The Cowes branch happened by accident. Tiny Mitchell, Commodore 1931 to 1952, enjoyed sailing at Cowes but was not impressed by the Squadron's [The Royal Yacht Squadron] lack of recognition of the ladies, so bought the house immediately behind the Squadron and invited his friends and club members to join him there. The house gradually became an extension of the Burnham Club and the rest is history.

What an enlightened bunch!

However, the skipper was still on his cruise and getting back to Wigful's article about the River Crouch. There was another letter from an XYZ. 'A man? Or a woman? Who knows?' the skipper questioned himself caustically! The writer, obviously a local ditch-crawler of some sailing experience, had got hot under the collar ... XYZ said: 'Probably the best published description of the Crouch and Roach, Havengore Creek etc, with a chart of the district, occurs in "Yacht and Canoe Cruises," by H Fiennes

Further Reading

Ardley, Nick, *The May Flower: A Barging Childhood*, published by Tempus, 2007, and reprinted by The History Press, 2010.

Ardley, Nick, *Salt Marsh & Mud: A Year's Sailing on the Thames Estuary*, published by Amberley Publishing, 2009.

Ardley, Nick, *Mudlarking: Thames Estuary Cruising Yarns*, published by Amberley Publishing, 2010.

Baring-Gould, Sabine, *Mehalah*, originally published 1880 and republished by Braiswick, Suffolk [Author Publishing Ltd.], 2004. (A further edition has also been published by Seafarer, Suffolk.)

Bennett, A. S., *Tide Time*, published by George Allen & Unwin Ltd, 1949.

Betjeman, John, *Trains and Buttered Toast: Selected Radio Talks*, edited by Stephen Games, published by John Murray, paperback edition 2007.

Blake, John, *Sea Charts of the British Isles: A Voyage of Discovery Around Britain & Ireland's Coastline*, published by Conway, 2005 and reprinted 2008.

Carr, Frank, *The Yachtsman's England*, published by Seeley Service & Co., London, 1937.

Coote, Jack H., *East Coast Rivers*, published by *Yachting Monthly*, London, 1961.

Cowper, Frank, *Sailing Tours Part 1: The Coasts of Essex and Suffolk*, first published 1892 and republished by Ashford Press Publishing, 1985.

Durham, Dick, *On and Offshore*, published by Ashford Press Publishing, 1989.

Durham, Dick, *Maurice Griffiths: The Magician of the Swatchways*, published by *Yachting Monthly*, London, 1994.

Griffiths, Maurice, *The Magic of the Swatchways*, seventh edition, 1971, published by Conway Maritime Press, first published 1932.

Griffiths, Maurice, *First of the Tide*, published by Conway Maritime Press, 1979.

Griffiths, Maurice, *Sailing on a Modest Income*, published by Waterside Publications Ltd, 1996.

Griffiths, Maurice, *Little Ships & Shoalwaters*, third impression, published by Conway Maritime Press Ltd, 1985, first published by Peter Davies 1937, reprinted by Conway Maritime Press 1972.

Griffiths, Maurice, *60 Years a Yacht Designer*, published by Conway Maritime Press Ltd, 1988.

Hann, Andrew, *The Medway Valley: A Kent Landscape Transformed*, published by Phillimore & Co. Ltd, 2009.

Harber, Janet, *East Coast Rivers Cruising Companion*, published by Nautical Data Ltd, 2003.

Hardyment, Christina, *Arthur Ransome and Capt. Flint's Trunk*, published by Jonathan Cape, 1992, first published 1984.

Perks, Richard-Hugh, *George Bargebrick Esquire*, published by Meresborough Books, Rainham, Kent, 1981.

Irving, John, *The Yachtsman's Pilot Volume I: Rivers and Creeks of the Thames Estuary*, published by *The Saturday Review*, London, 1927.

Jones, H. Lewis, M.A., *Swin Swale and Swatchway*, published by Waterlow & Sons Ltd, London, 1892, and reprinted by The Press at Toad Hall, Philadelphia, 2005.

Leather, John, *Clinker Boatbuilding*, published by Granada Publishing (Adlard Coles), London, 1980.

Martin, E. G., *Sailorman*, published by Oxford University Press, 1933.

Messum, S. V. S. C., *East Coast Rivers*, published by J. D. Potter, London, 1903.

Morpurgo, Michael, *Singing for Mrs Pettigrew*, published by Walker Books, London, 2007, first published 2006.

Mulville, Frank, *Teschelling Sands*, published by Nautical Books (Imprint of Conway Maritime Press), 1987.

Ransome, Arthur, *We Didn't Mean to Go to Sea*, published by Puffin Books, 1969, originally published by Jonathan Cape, 1937.

Satin, Don, *Just off the Swale*, updated edition published by Chaffcutter Books, 2004, first published by Meresborough Books, 1978.

Smith, John, *Essex and the Sea*, published by Essex Record Office Publications, No. 30, second edition, 1970, Essex County Council, Chelmsford, Essex.

Thompkins, Herbert W., *Companion into Essex*, published by Methuen & Co., London, 1938, revised second edition, 1947.

Tripp, H. Alker, *Suffolk Sea-Borders*, published by Conway Maritime Press, 1972, first published 1926.

White, Archie, *Tideways & Byways in Essex & Suffolk*, edition published by Ian Henry Publications, 1977, reprinted 1979 and first published by Edward Arnold & Co., Ltd, 1948

ARCHIVES

Essex Records Office, Chelmsford.
National Archives, Kew, London.
United Kingdom Hydrographic Office, Taunton, Somerset.
Yachting World magazine, IPC Media, Blue Fin Building, London, SE1 0EU.

WEBSITES

www.canveyisland.org (Website for historical and present day Canvey Island)
www.gtgkm.org.uk (The BIG vision for Milton Creek)
www.kentarchaeology.org.uk (The Kent Archaeological Society)
www.KAFS.co.uk (The Kent Archaeological Field School)
www.pla.co.uk (The Port of London Authority)
www.royalcorinthian.co.uk
www.susantrust.btik.com (The Chelmer Canal barge trust)
www.upchurchmatters.co.uk (Website for the village of Upchurch, Kent)
www.wikipedia.org (Upchurch Pottery – Chelmer Navigation – Peggy's Cove, Nova Scotia)

Speed, published in 1883.' XYZ mentions a visit by Lewis, made before Cowper's, and then says, 'I first visited these rivers in 1885 on the advice of a yachting friend who knew them well ... I made many week-end visits every year, and nearly always met a yacht of some kind ...' and he goes on to say, 'Long before I first heard of them these rivers were a favourite objective of certain amateur cruising men during week-ends. So no one can be said to have "discovered" the Burnham River ...'

'Of course,' the skipper had chortled, 'it's remained a mecca for yachtsmen, in particular for the racing breed, ever since ...' Then, 'Now, where next?' he asked himself as his eyes had, once again, gone arovin'. A broad smile had smothered his face, puffing out his cheeks, as he'd said, 'But first let's look at what some others have said. 'Other early ditch-crawlers ...' the skipper had said chuckling, adding quickly, 'And there's been many since ...'

In his book *The First of the Tide*, Griffiths, when on a cruise titled 'By the Havengore Route', penned, when sitting back and waiting for the tide after a magic day sailing round the Roach creeks:

> This settling down to wait for the tide to run its course out into the North Sea, and then on the flood to come welling up into the creek again, was no hardship, for us no waste of time, but one of many quiet enjoyments of this ditch-crawling way of cruising.

The skipper had beamed broadly. It was as if it were himself and his mate awaiting the tide ... On a recent holiday with his mate, in their MG sports car touring around the Weald along the Kent and Sussex borders, the skipper had found an interesting period book by Frank Carr, *The Yachtsman's England*, published in 1937. He'd found a piece that tickled him, deep inland, under the crooked black beams of an ancient hotel's comfortable bedroom. Carr wrote, when talking about rivers:

> The man who does his sailing on the East Coast, and particularly in the waters bordering on the estuary of the Thames, finds a peculiar satisfaction in that form of the sport of yachting which is contemptuously called 'ditch-crawling'. He loves the banks of mud and sand ...

'Yes,' the skipper said. 'Both me and my mate love it. I'm a ditch-crawler. She's a ditch-crawler.' The mate had agreed when he'd shown her the passage too. The skipper added, 'Yes. Sure, I've done some deep-water coastal passages in this country and elsewhere [it was Nova Scotia, Canada], but ...' He'd paused; a wry look creased his face as he thought of some backhanded comments he'd had cruelly thrown his way before he'd added, firmly – he believed it utterly – 'I always say the best is on our doorstep ... the mystical Medway and the magical Swale!'

The skipper was away, on his passage down the outer Crouch, down the Swin and across the estuary. It took but a merest moment. He was soon sailing past the low, white, shell-covered spit at the eastern end of the Isle of Sheppey, romping along, as a rising sea breeze had come up during the afternoon, filling his sails. In his chair, his head was nodding vigorously up and down, faster than an oilfield's nodding donkey, until his hand had reached out, plucking his thoughts from the shelf. It was something written by W. Edward Wigful that he had remembered first: once again, in Griffiths'

Sailing on a Modest Income, there was a Wigful gem. He said, when writing about a cruise around the Swale:

> The Swale, as a cruising ground for 'ditch-crawlers' does not get the appreciation it deserves; it is used merely as a passage or refuge. But with a boat that will take the ground comfortably a week can be well spent there. The East Swale ... is almost equal to the famed Orwell River in picturesque beauty; there are the creeks to Milton and Faversham to be explored and a run out into the open to Whitstable ...

The skipper had had that book since it was published in 1996; he saw his comment, appended in pencil upon the first reading, 'How true! Even 80–90 years later.'

H. Lewis Jones, on one of his cruises round the Swale, said, 'It is a capital cruise round Sheppey.' Jones wrote about the area extensively in his book, *Swin, Swale and Swatchway*. He loved it, as he also did the skipper's beloved Medway.

The skipper was approaching home now. His energy had been sapped by the effort. He'd mentally sailed the traditional East Coast, wending his way in and out of rivers and creeks, supped in his imagination at a host of waterside hostelries and learnt, from a number of museums, about those places visited too ... Of the Medway he was going to say little: it, with the Swale, he had written about at length (in *Salt Marsh & Mud: A Year's Sailing on the Thames Estuary*).

There was one item, though, that had caught his attention earlier in his 'cruise' and he'd left it until the last moments. Jones, in *Swin, Swale and Swatchway*, had ruminated about Stangate Creek being utterly suitable as the base for a yacht club. He said:

Harty: the Ferry House Inn during the summer of 1950. The revellers returning downhill are the skipper's parents and grandfather. The picture was taken by an uncle, the other crew member. The skipper was assured that they'd only enjoyed 'a half of bitter'.

What is wanted is a combination of the London yacht clubs and owners of small craft into one large and wealthy association: they could then afford to create superb head-quarters in Stangate Creek … All that is wanted to make Stangate Creek accessible is a launch to ferry the men over from Port Victoria station. [It would seem that women at that point in time did not feature. He went on to discuss the use of an old hulk fitted out as a clubhouse afloat in the creek.] The Medway alone offers a field for a whole year of Saturdays to Mondays, and there is the Swale available as well, for the days when the Corinthian might not care to venture out into the vasty deep outside the mouth of the river: besides, what an advantageous starting-place it is for journeys to the Essex rivers and coast.

'Yes,' the skipper said, 'that argument remains as true now as it did then – a strong argument for a marina at Queenborough … For sure.'

Jones continued his argument thus, 'This scheme is really practicable, and would be worthy of a combination of London small craft men, if only somebody with enterprise and enthusiasm would take it fairly in hand, and now is the time to do it.'

'Phew …' the skipper exhaled, and musing aloud, said, 'Jones may have stirred people up, maybe people at the Corinthian Yacht Club … Maybe it's what the Corinthian's committee had in mind when deciding to leave Erith at the end of the 1890s.'

Continuing to flick through the pages of Jones' book, the skipper found himself in home waters. 'Goodness me …' the skipper suddenly said, shaking his head; it was late in the day too. 'I've reached my home shores.'

There was something that the skipper had remembered … it was something by Griffiths, a little something he'd written 'that was nice' about the skipper's home waters: Griffiths wasn't a fan, though the waters were in his time very industrial and the atmosphere would have been very different, clouded with the discharges from hundreds of chimneys … 'Ah,' the skipper had murmured and flicking through the pages, he'd added, 'Here it is …'

It was a chapter in *The Magic of the Swatchways* about sailing through the enchanting sands from the Crouch and Roach across the Thames and into the Medway … where Griffiths and his crew spent a night in the skipper's beloved Stangate Creek. Griffiths wrote:

> The still night in Stangate Creek, miles from civilisation it seemed, when a full moon arose and we rowed silently round the little black cutter, while from the gramophone in the well came the beautiful intricacies of Tschaikowsky's Romeo and Juliet overture and other lovely things, will live in my memory. It is for nights like this that a boat has the right setting. [Copyright: Maurice Griffiths, *The Magic of the Swatchways*, Adlard Coles Nautical, an imprint of A&C Black Publishers, Ltd]

The skipper had closed his book slowly, reached out and placed it carefully, reverentially almost, back onto the shelf. He'd felt quite exhausted. Getting up, he'd thought, 'Tea …' and wandered off to boil a kettle.

With his tray close by, he'd soon settled back down with his pot of tea and a hunk of cake (almost the last piece of his Christmas cake). Before him, his shelves had taken on a higgledy-piggledy look. They were no longer tidy – books were ranged awry.

Books, too, were scattered at his feet. He felt supremely happy. He was as elated as if he'd just got back into his mooring after a thumping thrash up Benfleet Creek ... Or a romp across to the Kent shore, for that matter. Sitting back, he'd grinned wryly. 'Ah, the lower Thames ... ah, yes ... such a superb sailing ground.'

For a short while the skipper had just sat, contemplating. Then, a thought had occurred to him. Looking up and thinking aloud, he'd murmured, 'What was it?' Rummaging his mind, questioning himself, he added, 'I read something about these waters ... surely it was just a moment ago ... wasn't it?' His eyes had suddenly alighted, 'Ah yes ... here it is ...' and pulling the book from the shelf, he'd sought it out again. 'Yes. Quite so!' he'd said. 'Just as I thought ... the Southend shore was Jones' base for many years too.' Pausing, he'd added, 'You should know ...' while looking up at a non-existent audience. After another pause, he'd continued, 'The great man was a member of the Alexandra Yacht Club. And incidentally ... it was named after Queen Alexandra ... once a regular visitor.' The skipper had felt pleased with that and added, 'The club was started in 1873 ... Not many clubs can claim to go back that far in time.' He'd chuckled, 'And, too, it was only the year after the famous Royal Corinthian ...' The skipper sat smiling, smirking even, thinking of something he'd seen written in some sailing magazine ... a comment about his estuary's sailors (a derogatory comment). Grinning, he'd said, 'So, dear reader, sneer not at sailors from these waters of the Thames estuary ... We've been around a jolly long time ...'

Then, a watcher would have seen the skipper gain an aura of supreme satisfaction as he leaned back and slowly sipped at his tea. He'd toyed with the last morsel of the season's heavily laced fruit cake, deftly dabbing at the succulent crumbs, while thinking of all the sailing to come ... He'd then laughed exuberantly, and exclaimed, 'Ah yes! That is so!'

At that, the skipper's cruise was done.

Outward Bound, by R. H. Penton. The Thames estuary in about 1930 – spritsail barges abound; smoke, from tall funnelled steam ships, smudges the horizon; and a gentleman's launch careers past them all ... It is thought to be a view up Sea Reach, in the vicinity of the Chapman Lighthouse.